Robert Barnwell Roosevelt

Florida and the Game Water-Birds

Of the Atlantic Coast and the Lakes of the United States

Robert Barnwell Roosevelt

Florida and the Game Water-Birds
Of the Atlantic Coast and the Lakes of the United States

ISBN/EAN: 9783337183479

Printed in Europe, USA, Canada, Australia, Japan

Cover: Foto ©ninafisch / pixelio.de

More available books at **www.hansebooks.com**

ROBERT BARNWELL ROOSEVELT.

FLORIDA

AND THE

GAME WATER-BIRDS

OF THE

ATLANTIC COAST AND THE LAKES OF THE UNITED STATES,

WITH

A FULL ACCOUNT OF THE SPORTING ALONG OUR SEA-SHORES AND INLAND WATERS, AND REMARKS ON BREECH-LOADERS AND HAMMERLESS GUNS.

BY

ROBERT BARNWELL ROOSEVELT,

AUTHOR OF "THE GAME-FISH OF NORTH AMERICA," "SUPERIOR FISHING," "FIVE ACRES TOO MUCH," "ISMS," "POLYANTHUS," ETC., ETC.

ILLUSTRATED.

NEW YORK:
ORANGE JUDD COMPANY,
751 BROADWAY.
1884.

Entered, according to Act of Congress, in the year 1881, by the
ORANGE JUDD COMPANY,
In the Office of the Librarian of Congress, at Washington.

PREFACE.

In preparing this work, after I had written the account of Florida, which, as a sporting country, had never been fully described, and was to occupy the principal part of my attention, and when I came to the second division, that relating to the game-birds of our waters and coasts generally, I found so much in a book on a kindred subject, which I had written years ago, that I concluded I could do no better than quote from it freely. The directions therein given are as correct now as then, the information as well founded, and I hope the reader will find the stories of sporting excursions as interesting.

My main purpose is to call the attention of my brother sportsmen to that paradise of the devotee of the rod and gun, the Southern Peninsula of our Atlantic States. Game is disappearing from our home country; woodcock and ruffed grouse have almost been exterminated; ducks are less plentiful; bay snipe now make many of their flights directly at sea without passing over the land; and if we are to obtain satisfactory shooting, we must go some distance for it. Many persons who are fond of outdoor life cannot stand exposure to cold weather, and still more, to keep up their interest, must have the chance of making a larger bag than they can count on at the North. Yachtsmen are in the habit of laying up their craft during the best season of the year for the enjoyment of sailing. They have looked upon the South either as an uninteresting or a dangerous country, a land merely of alligators or of hurricanes. They will be as surprised as pleased to learn that there is no better sailing ground, and that the Southern waters in winter are as safe as Northern waters in summer; so much so that small vessels and open boats have braved their terrors, while their sporting advantages are not to be surpassed, if they are to be equalled, by any in the world.

While not absolutely the pioneer in this exploration, I happen to be nearly so, for no completed work or continued record has been published which covers the ground described, or conveys the information contained in these pages. No more delightful excursion can be conceived than that to Florida during the winter, and no man can so thoroughly enjoy it as the yachtsman. Thousands of tourists have been going there for years, and their number is augmenting every season. But such persons merely rummage a country; they do not possess it; they rush along sight-seeing and curiosity-purchasing. Let the sportsman or the invalid go to remain during the inclement winter weather, and they will never regret the excursion.

THE AUTHOR.

PART I.

FLORIDA.

CONTENTS.

PART I.—FLORIDA.

	PAGE
CHAPTER I.—Florida.—The Inland Passage	9
CHAPTER II.—In Florida	59
CHAPTER III.—Currituck Marshes	116

PART II.—THE GAME WATER-BIRDS.

CHAPTER I.—Game of Ancient and Modern Days.—Its Protection and Importance.—The proper Shooting Seasons.—The Impolicy of Using Batteries and Pivot-Guns.... 139

CHAPTER II.—Guns and Gunnery.—Breech-loaders compared with Muzzle-loaders.—All the Late Improvements in Breech-loaders.—Hammerless Guns.... 159

CHAPTER III.—Bay-snipe Shooting.—The Birds, their Habits, Peculiarities, and places of Resort.—Stools and Whistles.—Dress and Implements appropriate to their pursuit.—Their Names and Mode of Capture.... 185

CHAPTER IV.—The New Jersey Coast.—Jersey Girls and their pleasant ways.—The peculiarities of Bay-snipe further elucidated.—Mosquitoes rampant.—Good Shooting and "Fancy" Sport.—Shipwrecks and Ghosts.... 219

CHAPTER V.—Bay-Birds. Particular Descriptions and Scientific Characteristics.—A Complete Account of each Variety.... 261

CHAPTER VI.—Montauk Point.—American Golden Plover or Frost-Bird.—A True Story of Three Thousand in a Flock. Lester's Tavern.—Good Eating, Fine Fishing, and Splendid Shooting.—The Nepeague Beach.... 301

CHAPTER VII.—Rail and Rail-Shooting.—Seasons, Localities, and Incidents of Sport.—Use of Breech-loader or Muzzle-loader.—Equipment.... 313

CHAPTER VIII.—Wild-Fowl Shooting.—General Directions, from Boats, Blinds, or Batteries.—Retrievers from Baltimore and Newfoundland.—Western Sport.—Equipment.... 328

CHAPTER IX.—Duck-Shooting on the Inland Lakes.—The Club House.—Practical Views of Practical Men.—Moral Tales.—A Day's Fishing.—The Closing Scenes.... 344

CHAPTER X.—Suggestions to Sportsmen.—A Definition of the Term.—Crack Shots.—The Art of Shooting.—The Art of not Shooting. 398

CHAPTER XI.—Directions for Building a Battery.... 415

FLORIDA.

CHAPTER I.

THE INLAND PASSAGE.

Florida—so named by its discoverers from the abundance, beauty and fragrance of its flowers. The Land of Flowers—what a beautiful sentiment. Alas, it was never called anything of the sort. Land happening to be first seen by the brave and sturdy warrior but not imaginative linguist, Juan Ponce de Leon, on Palm Sunday, his discovery was called, with due and Catholic reverence, after the day and not after any abundance of flowers, which were probably not abundant on the sand spit where he planted his intrusive feet. But no matter about the origin of the term, the epithet is more than justified, and the Peninsular State is not only glorious in the endless beauty and variety of its flowers —till in good old English it might be termed one huge nosegay—but it is magnificent in the grandeur and originality of its foliage. The jessamine climbs above the deep swamps and lights up their darkness with its yellow stars; the magnolia towers in the open upland a pyramid of vestal splendor; the cabbage palmetto waves its huge fan-shaped leaves, seven feet long, like great green hands, and the moss hangs and sways and covers the bare limbs with its ragged clothing.

To the rough, practical Northern mind, Florida

is a land of dreams, a strange country full of surprises, an intangible sort of a place, where at first nothing is believed to be real and where finally everything is considered to be possible. When the visitor first arrives he cannot be convinced that the cows feed under water; before he leaves he is willing to concede that alligators may live on chestnuts. The animals and birds are as queer and unnatural as the herbage, or as a climate which furnishes strawberries, green peas, shad, and roses at Christmas. There is the Limpkin, the pursuit of which reminds one of hunting the Snark. You are in continual terror of catching the Boojum. It is a bird about the size of a fish-hawk, but it roars like a lion and screeches like a wild-cat, although it occasionally whistles like a canary. It has a bill like that of a curlew, adapted to probing in the sand, and yet it sits on trees as though it were a woodpecker. It is conversational and talks to you in a friendly way during daytime, but at night it harrows up your soul and makes your blood run cold with the fearful noises it utters. If you hear any charming note or awful sound, any pretty song or terrifying scream, and ask a native Floridian, with pleased or trembling tongue, "What is that?" he will calmly answer, "That? that is a Limpkin." There are no dangerous animals in Florida, only a few of Eve's old enemies, and the sportsman is safer in the woods at night under the moss-covered trees and on his moss-constructed mattress than in his bed in the family mansion on Fifth avenue. If he hears any unearthly noises, any soul-curdling shrieks, he can turn to sleep again with the comfortable assurance "that it is only a Limpkin."

To the sportsman it is needless to say that Florida, when properly investigated, is a Paradise. Birds and fish and game are only too plentiful, till it has become a land of shameful slaughter. The brute with a gun slays the less brutish animal for the mere pleasure of murder when he cannot get, much less use, what he kills, till on most of the pleasure steamers shooting has been prohibited; while the idiot with the rod fills his boat with splendid fish that rot in the hot sun and have to be thrown back, putrefying, into the water from which his undisciplined passion hauled them. Sportsman should not come to this land of promise and performance unless they can control their instincts, for fear that they should degenerate into mere killers. In truth, the excess of abundance takes away the keener zest of sport, which is largely due to the difficulties that surround success. But for the ordinary inhabitant of the rugged North, the quaintness of this border land of the equator has an immense charm, while to the invalid the pure, dry, warm air of both winter and summer brings balm and health. The feeble and sickly, especially the consumptive, should seek Florida, for to them it offers the fabled springs of perennial youth, which Ponce de Leon sought more coarsely in vain. To the seeker after amusement, to the man and woman of leisure, who wish to improve as well as enjoy themselves, it is a very wonderland of delight. It has a store of novelties which are absolutely exhaustless, and tracts of interesting country which, while perfectly accessible, have never even been explored.

To enjoy Florida, however, one must seek it aright. If the visitor follows the beaten track, he will see the beaten things—well beaten by many vulgar footsteps. If he takes the steamers and lives at the hotels, he will make quick trips and have good accommodations. If he wants originality he must pursue original methods. There are many ways of reaching this floral El Dorado—the ocean steamer will carry you to Savannah, whence the steamboat will transport you through byways and inside cuts to Jacksonville, or the railroad will drag and hurl you through dust and dirt by day and night at headlong pace from the St. Lawrence to the Gulf. But if you want to enjoy Florida, if you want to go where no man has gone, and see what no eye has seen, and handle what no hand has touched, then go there in a yacht—in a small yacht, just as small and of as light draft of water as will accommodate comfortably the party, that must be composed of individuals sufficiently accustomed to one another to be sure they can live together for three months without quarrelling. Then, indeed, will you learn what Florida is, will possess its charms in close embrace and have experiences and pleasures never to be forgotten and not otherwise to be obtained. How is this to be done, you may ask, and the purpose of this chapter is to tell you exactly how.

A wealthy magnate may go in a big yacht to Florida, give good dinners aboard and live in grandeur and luxury, and he will see about as much—not quite—as if he had left his yacht at home; or the hasty-plate-of-soup man may take a little steam launch and stave her in on the first snag or oyster rock he runs her against. But if the traveller and his friends hire or buy a light-draught sailing vessel, they will require more time, but they can go almost everywhere and see absolutely everything. It was just such a vessel that I had built for use in the shoal Great South Bay of Long Island—a sharpie, to give its nautical appellation—of sixty feet length and fifteen beam, with two state-rooms, a cabin having four comfortable berths and over six feet head-room, and a cuddy for the men and for cooking, although we had an auxiliary cook stove in the cabin. This vessel was intended to carry six passengers and two men; but boats of seventeen feet length and a catamaran have safely made the passage to the St. John's River and are there now, so that a much smaller craft would do. The advantage of the sharpie style of construction was that the yacht only drew two feet of water, and as I proposed to run entirely by chart, and not to use the services of a pilot, this was an inestimable advantage. We could have braved the battle and the breeze of the Atlantic and gone outside all the way, but those who know most of the ocean care least to have to do with it unless equipped on the most thorough basis to encounter its buffets. As an old sea captain said to me:—"When I go to sea I want to go in a steamer, and the biggest and strongest steamer at that." Moreover, the inside route is much the more interesting; there is nothing very novel about the sea but the danger of it, whereas the bays, creeks, canals and rivers furnish a fresh and continually changing panorama. There is a frequent encounter with strange people, with vessels of queer rigs and builds, an alternation of scenery, the arrival at and departure from cities, the chance to occasionally kill a bird or catch a mess of fish—something new happening every day. At sea there is the ocean—a great deal of ocean—and nothing else.

There exists a complete inside route from New York to the St. John's River, with the exception of about a hundred miles south of Beaufort, North Carolina, and on this stretch there are many accessible inlets only a few miles apart, so that no vessel need be caught out overnight or can fail to make a safe harbor in case of necessity. The charts are nearly complete and enable a person of ordinary intelligence, in a vessel drawing not over four feet of water, to be entirely independent of pilots. The lighter the draught, however, the better, and I should not advise the use of any boat which requires more than three feet to float in, two feet being greatly preferable.

Do not start for the South before the first day of November unless you wish to encounter a multiplicity, variety and intensity of fever that would be the delight of the medical profession. Until frost comes, there is waiting for you a choice between fever and ague, intermittent, remittent, typhoid, putrid, break-bone, yellow, and *d'engue* fevers, each of which, when you have it, seems a little worse than all the others until you have one of them also, an event which is very likely to happen, when you discover that your first conclusions were erroneous. Then before you start get good and ready. Look over your fishing tackle; be sure you have cartridges enough, and load them all with powder, but not shot, so as to avoid unpleasant explosions. Use your five hundred pounds of shot for ballast.

Lay in a tub of Northern butter and some white potatoes, but do not imagine you are going to a land of barbarism. You can get better hams, better hard-tack, and as good and cheap canned goods in Norfolk as you can in New York. Fresh eggs are to be had everywhere, turkeys and chickens are fair, and are sold in market cleaned, and if Southern beef is tough it has a peculiar game flavor which is very agreeable. Take in a good supply of coal; use it for ballast if there is no other place to stow it, for you may get frozen in during a cold spell, and will surely want plenty of extraneous warmth before you reach the " Sunny South." Then when you are ready, sail up Raritan Bay, get a tow through the Raritan and Delaware Bay Canal, and even across to Delaware City if you please, and so across to the Chesapeake Bay, where your journey may be said really to commence, for thenceforth you will have to rely on your sails and your brains, your motive power and your charts. There are very thorough and complete charts of the Chesapeake, six in number, carrying you the entire way to Norfolk and insuring you a good and safe harbor whenever you need it. Do not forget that this is a big sheet of water, and that you are on a pleasure trip, and will be much more comfortable if at anchor during the night. Besides, there is time enough; you have all winter before you, as you cannot get back until spring if you wanted to, now that Jack Frost is about shutting the gates. From Norfolk you can take a tow through the Albemarle and Chesapeake Canal or not, as you please; much better not if you happen to have a good northerly wind, as there is only one lock, and you can make the distance more pleasantly and safely under sail. If your vessel draws less than three feet, you leave the canal when you reach North Landing River, of which there is a chart, and you go down through Currituck Sound by Van Slyck's Landing, and thence through the Narrows. Beyond that for some distance, as the chart says, you "can only carry three feet of water, and that with difficulty." If your vessel is of greater draught, you must take the extension of the canal which carries you to North River, from which point there is plenty of water all the way. You can get a condensed chart from the Albemarle and Chesapeake Canal Company, which will give you a general idea of the route from Norfolk to Smithville, and which will be found very useful. But the Government charts of Pamlico Sound, which were completed in the fall of 1883, should by all means be taken also, as they are simply invaluable in case of storm and the necessity of seeking harbor unexpectedly. Government chart No. 40 or 140 (both numbers are used) will give you Currituck Sound from just above Van Slyck's, and also North River from the mouth of the canal, all that is necessary of Albemarle Sound, Croatan and Roanoke Sounds, either of which you may take, and the magnetic courses and distances to steer by as far south as Roanoke Marshes Light. The post office at Van Slyck's Landing is called Poplar Branch Post Office, Currituck County, N. C., and you can get your letters and coarse supplies there, but no bread. The next good harbor is Kitty Hawk, where there is also a store and post office. If you go through Roanoke Sound, remember that below Shallowbag Bay the channel runs close along shore, closer than it seems on the chart. You will have to feel your way carefully across below Broad Creek. There is plenty of water if you find it, but it is not easy to find. From the southerly end of Roanoke Island to Long Shoal Light the course is south by west; from Roanoke Marshes Light it is south, one half west. You can go a mile inside of this light, but not further, as the shoal beyond has not a foot of water on it. Just north of this light is Stumpy Point Bay, where you can make a good harbor, carrying clear inside four feet of water. From Long Shoal Light the course is south-west to a buoy on Bluff

Shoal; but as there is seven feet of water on the shoal, accuracy is not necessary, and the same course continued will take you near Royal Shoal, which is easily made out, as there are two lights on it. From this the course is south by west to Harbor Island light, at the entrance of Core Sound. This light is abandoned and is falling down, but during the day the building is visible a long distance. If you can get a free wind, you can make the run from Long Shoal to Harbor Island in a day, provided you get under way early, which every sensible yachtsman is careful to do. If not, you must hug the main shore and look out, as there are many shoals and no tide to help you off if you get aground. The waters are salt and only moved by the wind; and as Pamlico Sound is a miniature ocean and gets up a big sea, it is well to be careful. If you are caught near Royal Shoal, unless you are acquainted with the channels, steer for the beach, where you can get holding ground if not much of a harbor. The charts of Pamlico Sound are Nos. 42, 43, and 44.

There is a good chart of Core Sound, which is shallow but well staked out, the stakes having hands on them to show on which side is the best water. You can carry two feet of water close along the shore from the buoy off the middle marshes, just west of Harker's Island into Beaufort, but the main channel is more to the southward and runs to the point of Shackleford Banks. Then you go up Bulkhead Channel, keep along the north shore of Town

Marsh a hundred rods, and then northeast and keep the lead going to Beaufort, N. C. From here you can either sail through Bogue Sound, of which there is no chart, or go directly to sea. As the land trends westward, it makes a lee even from a northeaster and is as safe as any outside sailing can be.

There is a chart of Beaufort, N. C., which takes you a few miles into Bogue Sound, but that is all. South of Bogue Inlet, New Topsail Inlet is one of the best, then Masonboro, and from either of these a good wind will carry you past Cape Fear, the only spot you have to dread and where you must manage not to get caught. There is a good chart of Cape Fear, but the rule of the local pilots is to follow the eighteen-foot shoal down till you open Fort Caswell by the main Light on Bald Head, and then steer straight for the Fort, which will give you six feet of water up to the beach. But remember, there is shoal water outside of you, and you must look out for breakers. The next harbor is Little River Inlet, and then comes Winyah Bay, of which there is a chart, and then Bull's Bay, of which also you can get a chart.

From Bull's Bay it is inside work and a shoal, but not a difficult passage, to Charleston Harbor. Of this there is no chart yet printed, and it ought to be run, if possible, in a tide which will help at both ends by running up from Bull's Bay and down into Charleston Harbor. You come out at the cove near Fort Moultrie where it is well to stop, as Charleston Harbor is a large place in rough weather for small boats. Here you begin on Coast Chart No. 54 (or 154). Go up the Ashley River till St. Michael's Church (which has the whitest spire) opens to the north of the rice mills, and steer into Wappoo Cut, which lies just south of some prominent buildings on a point on the left shore. It will carry you without trouble into the Stono River. Here the chart fails you, you ascend the Stono, keeping a westerly course past the first branch to the north which heads toward a railroad in full view. When a large mill on the north side is reached a lead branches to the south. This must be avoided, and a mill with a tower will soon be reached. This is on Wadmelaw River, where the chart resumes its proper vocation. Thence across the North Edisto, the Dawho River, thence into the South Edisto, around Jehossee, but not through Wall's Cut, which the natives assured me was not open. Just at the south point of Jehossee Island, Mosquito Creek enters the South Edisto; take the westerly lead where they branch just inside the mouth, and then through Bull's Cut into the Ashepoo; down the Ashepoo and across St. Helena Sound and either up the Coosaw and past Beaufort, S. C. The name of the town being pronounced Bufort, which is about as short as any route, or across the Sound to Harbor River and through it and Story and Station Creeks into Port Royal Sound. This is a big place again and uncomfortable at night in a storm with a heavy tide and sea.

You now take Coast Chart No. 55 (or 155). There is a special chart of the route from St. Helena to

Port Royal, but it is not necessary. You steer nearly west from the buoys off the mouth of Station Creek to Bobee's Island at the mouth of Skull Creek. There is an oyster rock in the middle of Skull Creek where it makes its first bend to the southeast, and this is the only danger before reaching Calibogue Sound. In crossing Tybee roads, keep well out to Red Buoy No. 2, whether you go directly south or turn north to visit Savannah. If the latter, go by the Light Beacon and to the westward of it, if the former, take Lazaretto Creek into Tybee River and Warsaw Sound. Keep well out by the buoys again and head for Romerly Marsh Creek.

If you have gone to Savannah, continue your journey by the way of Wilmington River to the same place, unless your boat is small enough to pole easily, in which case you can go through Skiddaway Narrows. Romerly Marsh and Adams Creeks will bring you into Vernon River, when you steer for Hell Gate, between Little Don Island and Raccoon Key. If you have come through Skiddaway and down the Burnside and Vernon Rivers, you can go inside of Little Don Island. Here you use chart No. 56 (or 156). Cross the Ogeechee River, and follow up the west bank to Florida Passage, through it and Bear River to St. Catharine's Sound, across it and up Newport River to Johnson's Creek; thence down the South Newport to Sapelo Sound.

There is good fishing in Barbour's River, just above where the words "Barbour's Island" are on the chart. Continue across Sapelo Sound and into

Mud River ; take the middle of this to New Teakettle Creek, which will bring you into Doboy Sound. Keep to the north of Doboy town, which is a prominent object on the flat meadows. Here chart No. 57 (or 157) begins, and you go from Duboy straight through Little Mud River and the same course across Altamaha Sound; then follow the channel northwesterly into Buttermilk Sound; then either through Mackay's or Frederica Rivers, as the wind best serves, into St. Simon's Sound. Here the water is deeper and you can go directly across from the black buoy No. 7 to the black buoy at the mouth of Jekyls Creek. There are two mouths to this creek. Take the easterly one and run straight from the ranges on the point. Follow across Jekyls and St. Andrew's Sounds up Cumberland River. At its head waters there are some islands; the channel is from a stake on shore to the west of the eastermost island, then by ranges on the point, which carry you past a little island with ranges which give you the course south. Use the lead here. Thence down Cumberland Sound by Dungeness, formerly the property of Gen. Nathaniel Green, and which is much visited by tourist parties, across the St. Mary's River and up the Amelia to Fernandina.

Here chart No. 58 (or 158) begins. From the Amelia River you go to Kingley's Creek past two drawbridges. The railroad bridge is out of order and will not open square with the bulkhead. Be careful here, as several accidents have happened and the tide runs strong. Continue across Nassau Sound to Sawpit Creek, at the mouth of which there is a black buoy not laid down on the chart. Keep to the southward of this buoy and run on through Gunnison's Cut, which you will recognize by two palmetto trees that look like gate-posts at a distance. Down Fort George River to the Sisters Creek and thence to the St. John's River where you will find a dock—a watermark not to be forgotten on your return trip. There are three charts of the St. John's, which give it in full from its mouth to Lake Harney; the points to remember are to cross from Hannah Mills Creek to St. John's Bluff, and thence back again to Clapboard Creek, whence you follow up the north shore, keeping it as far as Dame Point close aboard. Beyond this you can have no trouble, as the St. John's has but one or two shoals where there is less than six feet of water, and it is well marked out with buoys and beacons.

If this description sounds a little tedious to the reader, he will not think it so when he makes the trip. If you want a pilot for any part of the route, one can be had by applying to Captain Coste, of the Lighthouse Service at Charleston; but there are few persons who know what I have herein recorded, and none of those will tell. We have had a long trip—for long as it has been on paper, it has been longer in reality. Two weeks from New York to Beaufort, N. C.; ten days thence to Charleston, and ten more to Jacksonville may be required, unless the traveller is one of those lucky fellows who always have a free wind through life. So he may want to rest, have his clothes washed, dress up in "a boiled shirt" for a change, and revive the fact that he is one of the aristocracy, not an ordinary seaman. He will soon tire of civilization, however, and long for the pleasures of the chase. Then let him ascend any of the tributaries of the St. John's from San Pablo at its mouth to Juniper Creek, which empties into the southerly end of Lake George. It was on the latter stream that I nearly killed a Limpkin.

The man does not live who has actually caught or shot a Limpkin. There are no Limpkins for sale in the curiosity shops, where almost every other production of Florida is to be had. It is admitted that the Limpkin, like the recognized ghost, is proof against powder and ball. But the writer never misses—that is, on paper and when he is recording his shots. All writers do the same. So when the Limpkin sat on a limb and whistled and chuckled and bobbed and bowed and finally flew away just before we were near enough, and I fired as he disappeared with horrible screams through the forest, one leg dropped! I had not killed him, but even a Limpkin was not quite proof against my aim. Mr. Seth Green, who was with me at the time and can vouch for the truth of this statement, remarked in a melancholy tone of voice that he wished he had had his rifle. As he had not succeeded in hitting anything with his rifle thus far since we started, although he had fired away half his cartridges, there is a chance that he might have succeeded this time by way of a change, and so I agreed with him heartily.

Alligators will not appear till warm weather—that is, till the middle of January—by which time the tourists will think he has got into the dog days, but fish are abundant in all the fresh-water streams. In that very Juniper Creek we caught so many big-mouthed bass with fly and spoon that we not only gave up fishing, but had to salt down dozens. And, by the way, these fish are much more of game fish than they are at the North; the smallest fight well, take the fly freely and jump out of water as frequently and fiercely as the small-mouthed variety in our waters.

Before leaving the instructive branch of my subject I wish to advise the yachtsman against giving too much weight to the appearance of the Southern sky. This will often cloud up toward evening in the most threatening way. Such a heavenly monitor at the North would warn us to make everything snug and get the best bower over, but in the South these appearances signify nothing. After a most frightful-looking evening the morning will break clear and warm and quiet. There are few storms in Florida during the winter, a "norther" occasionally and possible a thunder storm, but no fierce northeasters and no hurricanes. As to the comparative advantages of working through the tortuous creeks with changing tides, or running outside for short stretches, a preference might be given to the latter were it not that the shoals off the mouths of the inlets extend so far to sea. Many of the rivers have carried down so much sediment that they have made shoals ten or fifteen miles off shore. So that apart from questions of safety and comfort, the distance by the inside passage is the shortest.

In going South the yachtsman will pass large and numerous flocks of bay snipe on all the marshes south of Charleston. These marshes are muddy islands and of a peculiar nature. On the surface when dry they are firm enough for walking, but their shores are unfathomable ooze beneath which a man would sink at once out of sight and into which an oar can be run for its entire length without an effort. Curlew, willet, marlin, all varieties down to the tiny ox-eye, and in immense flocks, frequent these islands, where they seem to find food without stint. To stool them you can set out your decoys in the thin grass and make a stand near by from reeds or bushes. They are quite wary, however, and seem to have learned the evil significance of a gun. These marshy islands are honeycombed with the burrows of the fiddler crab, and mussels grow on their surface in soft mounds of earth. They are covered by very high tides and are always more or less damp. The bay snipe, however, do not seem to winter here. They leave a small proportion of their numbers, but the main body goes further South, possibly beyond the equator. There are no such myriads as the Northern flight would require, and they grow fewer and fewer as the season advances, till in March they are almost scarce. Let the sportsman take his toll from them while he can; stopping amidst the lonesomeness of these islands where it is certain death to pass a summer, and few of which are inhabited, and where he may sail tens of miles without seeing a man, white or black. Let him try the deep holes alongside of bluffs or where two creeks meet for sheepshead, using for bait the Southern prawn, that gigantic shrimp, with its body six inches long and its feelers ten; and if he can catch no fish and misses the birds, let him rejoice in knowing that there are millions of both in Florida.

In describing my trip to Florida, I do not intend to pursue any consecutive plan, or follow the positive order of events. It is not important to know that we turned out—to use the proper nautical term—at a certain hour in the morning of a certain day, and that we turned in again at night at some other division of mean sidereal or solar time, nor that we went a certain course or made so many miles one day and so many more or less the next. That is, the reader does not want to have too much of this, although a little now and then may tend to give a general idea of the trials, difficulties, and enjoyments of a yachtman's life. But whether we arrived at a place at five P. M. or five A. M., important as it may have been to us at the time, cannot, so far as I can judge, interest the reader as deeply as I hope to interest him. For all such information I will refer him to the ordinary books of travel. That we did occasionally make fast time in our little half scow, half yacht, that I built on the scheme of putting a sail in a canal boat, will be proved by this single event; when running across St. Simon's sound in a fog, we passed a large steamer yacht, called the "Gleam," one of the largest and finest of Herreschoff's productions. We found her again in Jacksonville when we reached there. She had left Savannah on the second of January, we had left Charleston on the tenth; she had arrived two days ahead of us, so that by being able to keep inside out of the storms and fogs of the Atlantic, we had actually gone nearly double the distance in six days less time.

The personnel of our party was made up of a sporting medical man, Mr. Seth Green, the famous fish-culturist, the ladies of the families and myself. We went without any restriction as to time, which is a most essential point in a yachting trip, and we stopped where we pleased, and as long as we pleased, we shot where there were birds to shoot, we fished where there were fish to catch, and where there were neither, we lay in the shade of the awning, if the weather was warm, and smoked, or ate those globes of concentrated lusciousness, the grape fruit when we felt too energetic to loaf, and not energetic enough to fish or shoot. Our trip was something of an exploring expedition, and we had possible dangers and inevitable inconveniences to encounter. Other parties had gone to Florida in the same way, but they had left no record of their adventures, no guide-posts for those who should come after them. So far as we were concerned, the country from North Carolina to the Land of Flowers was a *terra incognita.* We knew that there were birds, and beasts, and fish, in that equatorial region, but where to find them, how to reach them, and by what methods to catch and kill them, were wholly unknown to us. No one, after reading this record, will have the same complaint to make. Several of the Government charts were not completed, notably those of Pamlico Sound, and the corrections of that from Charleston south, so as to show the inside route had not been made in the year 1882, which was the one I had selected for the expedition.

We had sent the "Heartsease" to Norfolk, and were to meet her there, as by so doing we would save time that could be better utilized than by going over ground with which we were pretty well familiar—that of New Jersey, Pennsylvania, and Virginia. At Norfolk, after we had purchased what hard-bread, cake, pies, and other stores and luxuries we needed, and had been through the fish market, and selected an abundance of the largest "spot," which is regarded as the most delicious native fish, although it is nothing more than what we call the Lafayette fish at the North, we engaged a tow and started on our journey. We had to go through the Albemarle and Chesapeake canal, and made our first mistake in supposing that a tow was a necessity for the operation. The puffy, dirty, fussy, little steamboat ran us against everything that she came near, and were it not that she was unable to attain any considerable rate of speed, our journey might have terminated before it fairly began. She jammed us against the dock when we were starting, banged us into the first vessel we met on our way, bumped us into the banks of the canal when we had entered it, dashed us into the only lock there was to get foul of, and then rammed us against a dredging scow so fiercely, that there was a momentary doubt whether we should not be dredged out as an impediment to travel.

However, in spite of all these misadventures, we made Currituck before night. We determined to stay there some days for duck shooting, but I shall not stop to describe the sport we had. It is enough, that we loaded down our vessel with provisions, which, as the weather came out cold, kept till they were all consumed, and saved us from recourse to those last resources of the way-farer, the insipid canned meats, which, somehow, the manufacturers manage to make taste so nearly alike, that one will answer for the other, whether it is called mutton, beef, or fowl. Then we sped away south, running into Kittyhawk Bay for a harbor and a turkey, for no one must imagine that it is necessary to starve in the South, even amid the desolation of the desolate Eastern Shore. Not only does the proverbial hospitality of the Southern people still exist as far as the effect of a desolating war has left it a possibility, but there are certain kinds of food to be got there more readily than even at the North. It has heretofore been a reproach to our Southern colored brother, that the attractions of a hen-roost and lusciousness of a fat turkey gobbler were too much for his virtue. But this state of facts and morals is changing, the darkey is turning poultry fancier, he is getting to raise chickens and sell eggs, he is fast becoming a bloated fowl holder, and regular goose and turkey wing clipper; in his eyes the chicken is assuming a different status, and hen-roost marauding is fast becoming a heinous crime, than which there is none more unpardonable. He will soon be the fowl monopolist, and when that day comes I predict that the chicken will be regarded as a sacred bird, and placed in the same catagory as the ibis of Egypt. As it is, eggs can be obtained almost anywhere, and wherever there is a darkey's hut, there the voice of the cackling hen ascends in welcome and suggestive music to high heaven, resonant of omelettes plain, omelettes *aux fines herbes*, with ham or with onion, of scrambled eggs, boiled, roasted eggs, of pan cakes and sweet cakes, of custards, egg-nog, and all the thousands delicacies towards which the hen contributes with enthusiastic zeal, and greatly to the happiness of man.

The course of the contraband can be exemplified by that of the milk farmer, if the story which I once heard from an eminent retired politician is true, as I think it may be. Many of the farmers living in the neighborhood of Utica were in the habit of supplying that city with milk from the herds of cows that the magnificent meadows of the vicinity easily supported. Those careful and conscientious gentlemen, aware of the heating properties of milk in its strong and crude state, felt it was but a duty they owed their fellow beings, and especially their customers, to make sure that they did not incur the evils which were certain to arise from the unguarded use of so deleterious a beverage. They mixed the dangerous fluid with a sufficient proportion of water to kill the germs of disease, and lest their motives should be misunderstood, they did not mention their thoughtfulness to the consumers. Hence it was that Utica enjoyed unexampled health, and it would no doubt have continued in the same enjoyment except for a change in the methods of milk culture. Milk, instead of being converted into butter or sold in its natural state, came in time to be manufactured into cheese. Great cheese dairies were established, to which the farmers sent their milk, in place of disposing of it by local trade. Now it was essential that the milk so delivered should be absolutely pure, for the excellence of the product not only depended on this, but also in order that the amount might be fairly credited to each of the persons furnishing a share of the supply. Then the bucolic view that had heretofore obtained in that neighborhood was modified, and of all the sins in the decalogue, none was quite so henious as the adulteration of milk. I do not vouch for this story, although a long course of lactic experience in the city of New York gives it an air of possibility. Certain it is that since the introduction of cheese factories, the health of Utica has declined, but then no one can positively say that this change is due entirely to the purity of the milk.

On our way to Kitty Hawk, we had passed a number of nets which the local fishermen were hauling, and Mr. Green, who had a mania for interviewing every one he met, had promptly boarded the first of the boats, obtained all the statistics, and even helped make one haul. He found out that they caught what they called chub, the big-mouthed bass (*Grystes salmoides*), as large as eight pounds; white perch; the robin, which is our sunfish; red fin, our yellow perch; bull sucker, our black sucker; sucker-mullet, our mullet, which were taken in the creeks and up in the swamps, and nanny shad, which seemed to be our gizzard shad, known in Baltimore as bream. As they did not have all these varieties in the boat at the time, we were not quite sure as to the last. The fishermen knew nothing of the spawning season, but we found roe three inches long in a seven-pound big-mouthed black bass.

There is a club house at Kitty Hawk Bay, belonging to the Kitty Hawk Ducking Club, but it was deserted when we were there by the club, and given over to the possession of Captain Cain, who runs the principal fishery in that part of the country. He told us that the bass spawned in March, and that the same kinds of fish were caught near there which I have described. While we were ashore enjoying his hospitality, a sudden squall came up and blew most of the water out of the bay, so that the small boat in which we had come ashore was left a hundred feet from the edge of the water.

The next day, which was December 8th, we

passed Nag's-head Hotel, and came to anchor in a perfect little harbor in the lower part of Roanoke Island, where Captain Cain once had a terrapin farm. It was a charming, though deserted, spot, a bay just large enough for the yacht to swing in, and completely land-locked, the buildings tumbling to pieces, the terrapin ponds still there, but with not only their occupants departed, but the very fences falling down or being used for firewood. The speculation had failed, because even there, in the very home and abiding place of the terrapin, he had grown so scarce that a sufficient business could not be done to make it profitable. Terrapins are taken, as Mr. Green soon found out, in bag or trawl nets, that are drawn along the bottom, as we at the North use a dredge for oysters. On the front of the net, which hangs loosely behind, is an iron bar, of sufficient weight to lie close to the bottom as it is being dragged; this slips under the terrapins, which are thus carried into the net. We readily understood that they were not plenty, when we were informed that "count" terrapins, that is, those over six inches in length, bring on the ground one dollar apiece.

The weather had become very cold for yachting. The thermometer fell to eighteen degrees during the night, and we found that all the resources of our vessel were hardly equal to keeping us warm in our berths. Early next morning we obtained our first oysters. We had brought oyster tongs with us; in fact, if there was any kind

of rod, reel, line, net, hook, sinker, swivel, or
fishing device whatever that we had not brought
I should like to be informed of it. When Mr.
Green joined the yacht and produced from the bowels of an immense trunk, a luxury that in itself I
never knew him to allow himself before, and which
was in our way the entire journey till we got rid of
it at Jacksonville, much to its owner's chagrin—first
two breech-loaders, then a rifle and a hundred weight
of ammunition, then an immense bundle of sporting
rods, next a box of lines and reels, and finally an overgrown scrapbook filled with all manner of gangs of
hooks, the doctor and myself felt that the sporting
interest would not suffer. As I had sent him word
that he need bring neither guns, fishing tackle, nor
ammunition, it was evident that he intended we
should not fall short. But now when our men began tonging up the delicious bivalves which we had
not seen for so many days, on account of the freshness of the water, we felt thankful for one of our
precautions. Here let me warn the reader that he be
sure to bring oyster tongs with him. He will find
it difficult to get them in the South at all, and if he can
they will be much heavier and more awkward than
those in use with us. Just south of the opening into our night's harbor, and in the main channel, we
found a man at work oystering and we joined him
promptly, confident that where there was enough for
one there was in this matter enough for two. Either
the oysters off the lower end of Roanoke Island are
very delicious, or else our appetites were sharp from

abstinence. For as fast as our man Charley brought them to the surface and deposited them on the deck, we opened them with a skill founded on some experience and more desire, and devoured them with hearty gusto.

We loaded up with oysters and then started once more on our course, but the wind fell off and we anchored in Stumpy Point Bay, some thirty miles to the southward and on the main shore. At our last stopping place a sick man had come aboard for advice, and here we not only found two others, but were also informed that their mother was at the point of death. There seemed to be a sublime faith in these people that all Northerners must know something of medicine, as none of them had a suspicion of our having a physician in the party. Indeed they came for "a drawing of tea" as they called it, rather than for any special medicine, for they appeared to consider sickness the natural condition of man, as among those terribly unhealthy swamps and low lands it probably is. After that almost everywhere we went we were asked for "a drawing of tea" for some sick person.

Their ailments were evidently only too well founded, and as the people were clearly not a complaining set, we were sorry that we had not brought more of the coveted article with us. The whites of this coast looked weazened, thin, yellow, and cadaverous, as if they had a perpetual conflict with fever in which they invariably got the worst of it. They had the shadow of death in their faces. In their motions they exhibited a langour which strangers are apt to attribute to laziness, but which I believe due to disease. Let a man once take the southern fever, and it will be many months if not years before he feels like himself again. Our latest patients were fishermen, and to Mr. Green's insatiable inquiries they explained that they caught in their seasons shad; rock, our striped bass; trout, our weakfish; hickory shad, white perch, mullet, spot, round-nosed shad and flat backs, though what these latter were was more than we could guess. They said that the fishing had fallen off greatly of late years, but that the prices had increased and that now they were paid seventy five cents for a roe shad, and thirty for bucks.

Next day was clear and cold, with a strong and favorable wind from the north-west, so much so that even the imperturbable doctor was impatient to be off, but Mr. Green had an idea, and when he has anything of that sort he is the last man to part with it without full fruition. To our proposal to get under weigh early he replied.

"Beyond this you tell me that we have a great stretch of open water?"

"Yes," I answered, "the entire Pamlico Sound, which must be a hundred and fifty miles long and fifty broad, so the more advantage we take of this favorable wind the better."

"Well, you expect to find ducks, don't you, on the route?" he inquired by way of response.

"I hardly know what we shall find," I answered, "but I should like to find ducks, and have heard that there are innumerable brant on the ocean side."

"That is just as I supposed," was Mr. Green's reply, as he took up the axe that lay on the deck, "and as you have no battery, how do you expect to kill them?"

The doctor and I had nothing to reply, and Mr. Green, carrying the axe, called one of the men and rowed away to the shore in triumph. During his absence the doctor, who is a *cordon bleu*, prepared the turkey that we had purchased at Kitty Hawk for cooking, by stuffing it with the oysters that we had tonged at Roanoke Island. By the time this culinary feat was accomplished, our master of fish culture had returned. He had cut a dozen stakes about eight feet long, which were to be used to improvise a blind, by thrusting them into the bottom and tying strings around from one to the other, and hanging reeds or grass tied in bunches over the strings.

These precautionary measures being taken, we got under-way. The wind had increased to almost a gale, and our brave little vessel fairly leaped before it towards the South like a race horse. Quite a sea had made in the broad expanse of Pamlico Sound, which can be stormy enough when in the humor, and the waves rolled after us in vain and vindictive fury. There were two large steamers going South, and we held them for some time, and had hopes of keeping up with them, but they slowly drew ahead, and left us alone in the waste of tumultuous waves.

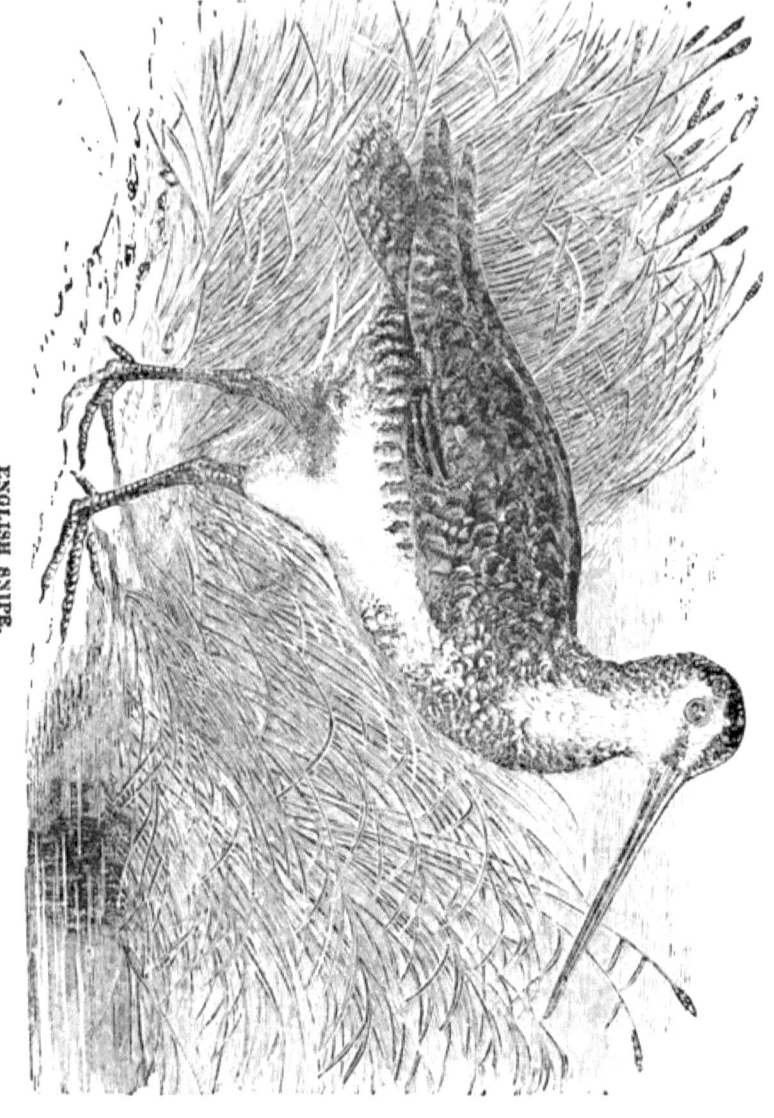

ENGLISH SNIPE.

We made one of our best runs that day. The weather was too perfect for us to stop for fish or birds, although we saw clouds of the latter rising up in the distance from the disturbed surface of the Sound. We ought to have gone to Hatteras, or Roanoke Inlet, where we had been assured by the residents the brant shooting was magnificent, but we could not lose such unusually favorable weather, and sped on and on through the seething waves, hour after hour, till when the sun was still quite well above the horizon, we ran through the narrow channel into the peaceful waters of Core Sound.

What a change came over the spirit of our sailing, from the boisterous violence and rough seas that beat our vessel's sides turbulently, or followed us fiercely to the scarcely ruffled bosom of the small and shallow bay, only a few miles wide, and shut in on all sides by the land. We managed to reach Lewis's Creek before sunset, where we saw a number of working boats going to find security for the night. When we had anchored among them, the fishermen told us that there were the usual kinds of salt water fish, although there was no tide in Core Sound other than that made by the wind. They said there was good oystering off the point of Lewis's Creek, and next day proved their words. It was a wild spot. The only mark of human habitation being an old wind-mill, which stood on the point. The weird effect was further heightened during the darkness by the lighting of fires by the fishermen, who had no sleeping accommodations on their boats, and who went ashore for the purpose.

"Would you like to kill an English snipe?" called out Seth Green to me next morning from the shore, whither he had already gone with our boatman, Charley. I had been busy, or perhaps, if the truth must be confessed, sleepy, and had just come on deck.

"Of course," was my instantaneous reply, the idea of any one not wanting to kill an English snipe being too ridiculous to entertain for a moment.

"Then get your gun, and Charley will come for you in the boat."

In five minutes the doctor and I were both ashore, and in less than as many more we had put up and bagged our first bird. It seemed that Charley, who, as I have already stated, was an old gunner, had heard the bird as he flew over, and had seen him alight. He did not know that there were more than one, but we found quite a flight of them. The spot was not large, but it was evidently a favorite one. We had no dogs and went floundering about through the mud, but at every few steps a bird was flushed, and his appearance commemorated by the report of a gun or the cheery cry of, "mark!" It was a delicious episode in our trip, for no sport is more appreciated by the true sportsman than the killing of our gamest of all game birds, the stylish English snipe. In two hours we had bagged thirty-one. In fact we had killed them all, for if we did not get them at the first rise, it was easy to follow them up, as they seemed so fond of the place that they would not leave it. After we had gone on board with our trophies, and while we were getting under way, we saw new whisps arriving to take the place of those which we had killed, as if they were informed of the event, and were anxious to profit by the disasters of their friends, even at the peril of their own lives.

Core Sound was full of wild fowl, of which many were red-heads and canvas-backs, and had we had a battery, we could have killed unlimited numbers. We had to do as well as we could with Mr. Green's substitute, which, although better than nothing, was not at all equal to the proper machine. Neither had we time to wait. Florida was a long way off, and well we knew that, once there, we should have all the game we wanted; so as we struck another favorable wind, we did not stop at Harker's Island, where the best shooting is to be had, but ran on to Beaufort. We had actually dawdled not more than three or four unnecessary days in Core Sound, before going into the narrow, shallow and difficult harbor of what was once the watering place as well as business mart of that section of the Southern country. The port dues are heavy, and I would advise the yachtsman to avoid it altogether and go. if he needs must go into any port, directly to Morehead City, which is rapidly appropriating the trade and fashion of its older rival.

There is a large business in oysters at Beaufort, and the civilization of moss-bunker factories has been introduced from the North. Fish were scarce, but we purchased some very fair beef at very moderate prices, eighteen pounds of porterhouse being sold to us for eight cents a pound. The town is a pretty one, and the next day being Sunday, we went to the colored Methodist Church, a thing that no visitor must fail to do, and heard some very charming singing. This was our first experience of the quaint, wild, and slightly barbaric harmony of the voices of the negroes, of which we were to hear a great deal before our return to the North.

Beaufort was the first thoroughly Southern town, with its fig trees in the open air, the Yupawn, or native Tea tree, the red-berried evergreen bushes, whose name we could not ascertain, and its genial air of Southern indolent happiness, which we had visited. We were sorry to leave it, and had Florida been only placed where it ought to have been, five hundred miles nearer New York, we should have stayed days if not weeks longer. But the time was flitting by, and still we were a thousand miles from our destination. So without more ado we put to sea. From Beaufort to Cape Fear there is such a bend in the coast that it is laid down on the charts as a bay. Being shielded from the terrible northeasters of the Atlantic, which reach no farther than Cape Hatteras, it is as safe for a small vessel as any part of the boisterous ocean ever can be. But I was glad when Heartsease got through the voyage. With care there is no danger, and the trip is not half as perilous a one as we are accustomed to take at the North, where we are at home, without a thought of fear. There are numerous and very practicable inlets, and the yachtsman should make sure of getting into one of them at night. The same may be said of the stretch beyond Cape Fear. Treat the mighty ocean with the respect it deserves, and it will never illtreat you. On the charts the northern or old inlet of Cape Fear is laid down as closed by a bulkhead. This it is no doubt intended to be, to the discomfort of small sailing craft, but at the time I speak of it was open. Possibly it was only opened temporarily by a storm, and may be shut again now.

There were some birds in Bull's Bay, but not enough to induce us to pause, as we were anxious to get the yacht to Charleston as quickly as we could. So we made the most of the wind and the tide, and anchored over against Fort Moultrie early in January. Does any of my readers care to hear how we enjoyed Christmas Day! If so, I will in that connection, and with the happy sacredness of that day in my mind, make a confession. In one of the opening paragraphs of this history I mentioned the fact that we had a stove, a cooking as well as heating stove, in the main saloon. I did not, however, acknowledge what I am now about to make public, that every one of the party, from the state-rooms to the forecastle, was a cook, and in the opinion of him or herself a most sweet and dainty *chef de cuisine*. Aware of this divine afflatus, they were none of them entirely content unless they were exhibiting their skill, so both stoves were run to their utmost capacity, and as the appetites of the party were good and daily growing better, a vast consumption of provisions was continually taking place. While each was at heart assured that their own productions were a little the best, and tempted the others to admission of the fact by the offering of special delicacies where delicacies were not needed, there was no one mean enough to repudiate the work of a brother or sister artist, even if it were ruined in the preparation or burned to tastleseness in the cooking. Christmas was by common consent set apart as the day on which each and every member of our briny household should cook whatever they found best in their own eyes. The store-room was thrown open and free liberty of selection was given to all.

To the male kitchen genius the most difficult article to prepare, is the most necessary one, bread. Within the realms of civilization the staff of life seems, as it were, to grow of itself. It can be found on every corner; stares in fat complacency at you from the shop windows on every block; there is never any dearth of bread so long as there is a penny to purchase it; delicate-minded tramps scorn it, and in every well-regulated household enough of it is thrown into the waste pail to feed another household of equal numbers. But at sea this is different, and when man, though he pride himself on the brilliant hue of his blue ribbon, is required to make good the deficiency, he is apt to come to grief. So the queen of our marine family announced that she would make a big batch of bread for that special festivity.

While no one could or would dare to dispute the ability of that lady to do well whatever she undertook, yet in the matter of bread making her methods were peculiar. In the first place she had to have the cabin to herself, and as bread has to be set over night, we were all turned out on Christmas eve and left to shiver on the deck. Then she has a way of strewing flour about in the operation till she covers the tables, the chairs, the floor, even the sides of the saloon and sometimes the cabin roof with dough or its ingredients. It was not five minutes after we were allowed to return, the "rising" having been made an accomplished fact and set away in a corner, before our hands, our clothes, our faces, and our very hair were covered with incipient bread. But worse even than that was the injunction that was solemnly laid on us under no circumstances to presume to touch the "rising" which had been deposited directly over the stove, and without moving which it would be impossible to get breakfast. As our lady was a late riser herself, and would never stir till she was assured through the state-room door that her breakfast was ready and on the table, the question of having that important meal was as complicated as getting the fox, the goose, and the corn over the stream.

One of the associate lady patronesses devoted herself to making biscuits, as the bread would not be cooked till dinner time. I evolved pancakes, the doctor compounded a hash, and altogether we began Christmas with such a breakfast as is rarely met with on the desert surface of the inland water communication between the North and the South. Seth Green had reserved himself till, as he politely remarked, "the rest of you should be through your mussing," then he began. But his efforts did not last long unmolested, he had split open a duck, a fat one had been especially selected for so unusual an occasion. This he had laid between the wires of an oyster broiler, then he opened the entire top of the stove and proceeded to broil it upon the hot coals. It is unnecessary to remark that such a proceeding evolved an amount of smoke that filled the cabin full in a moment. The rest of the party were busy at their breakfeast enjoying the delicacies which had already been prepared, when they were fairly suffocated by this torrent of smoke and began to realize as never before the sad fate of the inhabitants of Pompeii.

"Seth" I exclaimed, "can't you keep part of the stove covered so as to let some of the smoke go up the chimney?"

"Mr. Green, Mr. Green," came from the ladies all at once, "please don't smother us."

"Smoke and the gas of cooking" gasped the doctor, his philosophy almost dissipated in it "are injurious at meal times, there is such a thing as being asphyxiated."

"For heaven's sake," I implored, for by this time the condition of the atmosphere was unbearable, "do throw that duck out of the companion way."

"Oh Mr. Green do stop cooking that horrid

duck," exclaimed our princess, "if you do not I shall have to leave the table."

That last threat was too much, Seth could not bear to be ranked as an obstructive when he was accomplishing a culinary triumph which was to delight our gustatory nerves and establish forever his reputation as a cookist. He turned a reproachful face towards the party without showing the slightest sign of discontinuing his fell work, and with an air of bitter rebuke retorted upon us.

"This is the first time that I have done any cooking. All the rest of you have cooked as much as you liked. I have stood to one side and got out of the way and never had a chance, and now the very instant I cook a little duck you all make a fuss. I don't think it's fair. I did want a piece of duck for my breakfast and I picked out the smallest one for fear somebody would think I was greedy, and now you ask me to throw it overboard; it is almost done, and if you will only have patience for a few moments I will be through."

His manner was more impressive than even his words, and no one had the heart to reply. We tearfully held our napkins to our noses to keep out the smoke and smell as well as we could, we coughed and choked, but we allowed him to finish. Unfortunately Seth believes in cooking a duck to a chip, and hence he was occupied longer than he had promised, but he was through at last, and then not only was he happy in the vindication of his culinary knowledge, but he had the satisfaction of bringing our ingratitude home to us, by pressing on us choice morsels, which he offered in a delicate and forgiving way upon his own fork, and which we were fain to accept and swallow in the same fashion under pain of again offending him.

Nevertheless the duck was good, the biscuits were good, the pancakes were excellent, the hash was superb, every article of diet all day long, from the gorgeous breakfast to the gorging at supper, when appetite had been more than sated, were unsurpassable and we had a Christmas long to be remembered.

We remained in Charleston for two weeks. If the reader asks what we were doing all that time, let him go to the old time Queen City of the South, now apparently being displaced by her enterprising rival, Savannah; let him roam about her quaint streets and mingle with her hospitable people, and he will find out. There is much of physical and human interest in and around Charleston, from the live oaks on her Battery or White Point Park, and the moss covered trees of her famous Magnolia cemetery, to the oysters growing in thousands around her sea-wall, and which would furnish unlimited sustenance to her citizens were they not oyster surfeited. We stood and gawked at the tropical plants in full foliage, and at the orange trees in full bearing, in the house door gardens till the residents, unacquainted though they were personally with us, took pity and gave us the names of the plants and told us that the oranges were sour, none of the sweet varieties being able to grow so far north. We loafed around the market which was an ever renewing delight to Mr. Green, who, before we left, had established a personal bond of admiration and friendship from every darkey fisherman who brought his cargo there. We fed the turkey buzzards, we ascertained that the fish about Charleston were, in their various seasons, mostly sheepshead, bass, the drum of North Carolina and channel bass of Florida, *Corvina Ocellata;* sea-bass, here called black fish, which are mostly caught by the negroes outside the bar in their open boats; sea trout, our weak fish; mullet, which they told us were becoming scarce; blue fish which are never caught in winter, and which also were diminishing in numbers; black drum; big porgees of four or five pounds; both the salt and fresh water varieties of cat fish, which were very abundant; whiting, our king fish, and their finest table delicacy; angel fish, crevalle; fresh water trout, our black bass, and shad, which begin their run in January.

All around Charleston the negroes seem to be in possession of the country. They are pleasant, polite, and lazy, are content to do the old slave tasks even when working for themselves, and will never consent to do more when working for others at any price of remuneration, as though if they worked too hard the work would be exhausted and there would soon be nothing more to do. They are paid fifty cents a cord, for instance, to cut wood, and they stop when they have cut one cord, although they are through at one o'clock. They look more healthy and happy than the whites throughout the entire

South, which is a probably a climacteric result, but pregnant of many possibilities for the future. It is they who supply Charleston market, it is they who do the fishing and the work, and more important still, it is they who make all the Sea-island cotton and bring it to the city in their boats from the shores where inevitable death lurks for the superior race. That most valuable of Southern products, the old time king of the world, arrives in driblets, here a pound and there a pound. It is badly baled, but it comes and in good order too. To day the negro controls the whilom king, which is indeed putting the bottom rail on top.

The Charleston "Eagles," as he called the buzzards, were a source of infinite complacency to the philosophical soul of the doctor. He would watch them by the hour, sympathizing with their metaphysically thoughtful ways. He would study their awkward and ungainly motions on the ground, and wonder that anything so ungraceful on foot could be so exquisitely elegant and graceful in the air when on the wing. These queer creatures stay around the market, and although the law forbids their being fed, as it is found with them as with human buzzards that necessity is the mother of scavengering, your butcher is always ready to throw them a surreptitious piece of meat for your amusement. They are the only street cleaners, and if they got their dinners gratuituosly they might cease their useful public labors.

On January tenth we tore ourselves away from

Charleston, bidding good bye to its pretty streets, its tall spires, its beautiful gardens, and its pleasant inhabitants, among whom we must especially mention Commander Merril Miller of the Light-house service, who was very kind in furnishing us charts and assisting us in many ways. We bid a last farewell to Forts Sumter and Moultrie, and all the historic memories which are entwined with those names; to Sullivan's Island, the Coney Island of Charleston, to the Three Sisters, three palmettos which guard the gate where once the confederate soldier stood sentry, and to the tomb of Oceola close by, to the buzzards and the beauties of the city, catching a last glimpse of White Point Park to which we waived a tender adieu. We headed our course towards the creek which has received the euphuistic appellation of "Wappoo Cut." We carried away from Charleston this one valuable piece of information: to make "Hop-in-John," boil one quart of cow peas (a sort of small bean), and one pound of bacon till thoroughly cooked, then put in two quarts of rice, boil for about half an hour longer and until well done, then add salt and pepper. This recipe came from the colored *chef* of the Charleston hotel and must be correct. Hence hereafter no man or woman can claim to be so ignorant that they cannot cook "Hop-in-John."

Beyond Charleston we had our first disagreeable adventure; it occurred when we were running through Wappoo Cut. We had been offered a volunteer tow by a small steam tug that we met there, but had hardly hitched fast to her, before a passenger steamer came in sight going the same way. This vessel gradually gained on us, and when she was close at hand, finding there was no room to pass, as the cut is extremely narrow near its outlet where we were, ran deliberately between our yacht and the tug, cutting our stern line away and nearly sinking us. This was an occasion, in which we should have been justified in shooting the pilot at his post, but we were in a foreign country, so to speak, and all we did was to cast loose our lines and get clear the best we could. The whole performance was the less excusable, because the wheelman saw there were ladies on board our boat, and that we were strangers. As this was the only piece of discourtesy shown us on our entire trip, I give the name of the vessel which was guilty of it, and warn all passengers to shun the "Pilot Boy." It was by good luck alone that we escaped, for hardly had we got clear, than the two steamers jammed together, filling the cut from side to side, so that both were aground, and we heard the crashing of timbers and saw them fast there for nearly an hour. Had the "Heartsease" been between them, she would have been crushed. If any of our readers go South by the inland passage from Charleston, and it is a pleasant way of travel, we hope they will in a measure revenge our wrongs, and give a brutal captain a lesson in decent behavior, by refusing to patronize the "Pilot Boy."

One of the most interesting features of the country we were now passing was the rice fields. These were separated by dykes, and being nearly rectangular, gave a novel appearance to the low, marshy land. Had we known where to go, we could probably have had good English snipe shooting. But we did not stop to give Mr. Green a chance to interview any one to find out. We, however, saw numberless flocks of bay snipe on the lower part of the South Edisto, where the wind left us one night, and where Mr. Green killed a couple of dozen. On the following day, that gentleman was so pleased with the performance of the yacht in crossing St. Helena Sound in a squall, that he insisted on our putting to sea, upon the ground that he was tired of such tame sailing. The rest of the party were nothing loth, and the good little ship was soon across the bar and on the broad bosom of old Mother Ocean, a very step-mother as she can at times prove herself to be. Unfortunately, the wind died out, and we were becalmed or nearly so, and crawled slowly past Fripp's Inlet. When we were just outside Port Royal breakers, which we reached at sundown, there was a dead calm, and we drifted backwards till we came to anchor in some four fathoms of water.

Our luck did not desert us, and before dark a nice breeze sprang up, which carried us into the harbor and up to the mouth of Skull Creek, where we passed the night in perfect comfort. Next morning the wind came out strong from the northeast, blowing what sailors would call half a gale of wind. We got under way as soon as we could, and were soon slashing along at a good nine miles an hour. To be sure of our speed, I proposed to make a log line. Now there is one point about Seth Green, which is if possible more decidedly developed than another; while he is perfectly satisfied that anything he does is better done than it ever was, ever will, or ever can be, by any one else, he is equally well convinced that no one else can do anything that he cannot, so when I made this proposition he simply smiled an incredulous smile. Under the force of that implication, a log line had to be made, and made to work, if all hands had to swear that she was making ten miles an hour when she was only making two.

It was an original species of a log. I knew the proper divisions for a fourteen second glass, which was the one we had on board, but the "chip" had to be manufactured out of the side of an old cigar box. I never shall forget Seth's air of triumph, when having driven in the pin too hard, it did not slip out at the scientific jerk I gave when "time" was called on the first trial, the result being that the line parted when I was drawing it in. This merely encouraged me, as there was no difficulty in curing that defect, the only danger having been that my improvised "chip" would not hold well enough. So the log was soon in working order, and informed us that we were running nine miles an hour, and repeated the figure so often, that the skeptic was convinced, and asked me to join him while he apologized.

More bay snipe of all sorts, little and big, but no

time to shoot them. They were flying about by twos, by threes, by dozens, by hundreds, but the wind was too fair and too fresh for us to lose it. We might be punished by being reduced to living on canned food, which, with the exception of corned beef, vegetables, and preserves, was an abomination to the entire party, and we did not stop voluntarily, till we reached Jekyl's Creek. In reference to Jekyl's Creek, there is an entry in my log, that is interesting to show how history repeats itself; "Oysters Excellent." Half a century before, Professor Bache, who made the very charts by which we were sailing, had appreciated the excellence of the Jekyl Creek oysters, and had them barrelled and sent to him every year. I doubt, however, whether he knew how to cook them, at least in the quantity necessary for a hungry yachting party, and with the limited cooking appliances of a yacht.

They are called " Raccoon Oysters," for the reason that the raccoons exhibited so much human nature in first appreciating their excellence, and in getting at their contents. They exist in immense mounds and piles, and to the Northern eye seem inexhaustible in numbers, covering hundreds, if not thousands of square miles, and averaging three feet thick. They line the shores of the creeks and water courses like two walls, and cling to branches of bushes, till it can be truly said of them that they grow on trees. Their natural position is with their edges upward, and these are nearly as sharp as razors, and will cut one's fingers or a raccoon's paw terribly, unless care is taken in handling them. The 'coon's plan is to slyly watch at low tide, when the beds are bare, till the unsuspicious bivalve, longing for a breath of the pure air of heaven as a change from the insipid diet of salt water, opens his mouth, when he quietly creeps forward and drops a piece of shell into the opening. Master oyster endeavors to resume his natural closeness of mouth, but in vain; the early closing movement has no reference to him.

My plan of treatment was different, although the final consequence to the oyster was about the same. To open such sharp-edged creatures in the ordinary way would soon have put our crew, experienced in oyster opening though they were, *hors du combat*, or to state it in English, useless for rope-hauling. Even to separate them from one another was a perilous job, so I hit upon the simple plan of putting them in bunches just as they grew into the ovens of the two stoves. There I let them roast till they opened their mouths of their own accord, precisely as they had done for the raccoon, but under a little more compulsion. Cooked in this way they were so delicious as to be worth a trip to Jekyl's Creek merely to get. We almost lived on Jekyl Creek oysters, and if any one of the party got out of spirits, if Mr. Green or the Doctor wanted to propitiate one of the queens of the yacht, and the Doctor especially was continually engaged in that way, he never failed with a roasted raccoon oyster.

CHAPTER II.

IN FLORIDA.

And now we are at Fernandina, in Florida at last. It has been a long but a delightful trip. Of all the yachting we ever did, and all of us have been more or less followers of the sea, that is, the inland sea, since childhood, we agreed unanimously this sail from New York to the South by the inland navigation, was the most delightful. It was an unbroken charm from the beginning to the end, with no more of real danger about it than would have been encountered on Broadway under falling bricks and over caving vaults. The variety of scenery was charming, the oddity of the trees and plants most interesting, and had we had the time to devote to it, the fishing and shooting would have been superb.

We had passed old Fernandina, and came to anchor opposite the new town of the same name, which had been selected on account of its having a better harbor in a norther, that terror of southern latitudes in winter, and which must have raked the old town pretty thoroughly. We had to go ashore at once. The tides have a great rise and fall, and we were glad to avail ourselves of the boat club landing which was kindly placed at our disposal. We found Fernandina a quaint old town, with a mixture of newness and age about it. Northern men coming for their health had brought Northern ways and extravagances; there were modern villas and trim gardens, but the old mansions were still to be seen, and a few of the ancient houses built of coquina, a combination of lime and shell. No innovations could do away with the Southern foliage, which here was in rank growth and profusion. We saw orange trees in full bearing; palmetto trees in abundance, from the scrub saw-palmetto to the lordly cabbage palm, and cactuses six feet high, together with all the other trees and plants of the warm latitudes.

There is a fine shell road to the sea beach that is so hard that the wheels of a wagon scarcely make a mark upon it. This beach is the favorite promenade drive of natives and visitors in the season which had not come quite yet, although near at hand. Boys in the streets were selling sugar-canes at five cents a stick, and banana bushes, which are herbacious plants, were growing in many of the gardens. Mr. Green proceeded first to indulge in the entire luxuries of a barber's establishment that he found, and then to interview the whole population. He came to the yacht in time for supper, laden with information and two fine Southern weakfish, which are much better to eat than our Northern variety, and which are locally known as trout.

The fishing around Fernandina is exceedingly good, and we found the colored population, which takes to fishing as naturally as the bee is nautically supposed to take to a tar bucket, everywhere, pursuing the finny tribes through the numerous creeks and arms of the sea. Here we saw for the first time the circular cast net. It was used for catching the enormous shrimp or prawn, which, while shaped like the common shrimp, has a body six inches long, and feelers still longer. This curious creature is mostly used for bait, though it is excellent eating when boiled. There is good sheepsheading in the creek opposite the last house before reaching the cut, and as it was impossible to keep Mr. Green quiet longer without a day's fishing, we had to let him go while the rest of us enjoyed the mere pleasure of existence in the delicious climate. We ate oranges and sucked sugar-cane in true childhood style, and wandered through the village while he was pursuing science. We were not a little ashamed of ourselves when he returned with a magnificent string of sheepshead, both the large and small kinds, sea trout, and a dozen other varieties, victualling the ship for several days. Then our sails were once more set and we were off for the further South, for there always is a higher height and a deeper depth; so there is a further south, a further west, and a more inaccessible north. We did not go far, however, before we had to stop. Not that there was any dire necessity, not that any member of our party was sick, nor that the wind or the bread had given out; not that we had lost our course or were actually impeded in any wise, but still we had to stop—in order to catch crabs. I take it for granted that there is none of my readers so unfortunate as never to have eaten that most delicious of table luxuries, the hard-shell —for I have never given my allegiance to the soft-crab. If that is so, then I will have no occasion to make further explanation, when I say that the finest crabs which we got in the Southern waters, we caught at Fernandina, or rather between that place and Jacksonville, for the crabbing was good all the way. Mr. Seth Green is especially fond of these strange animals, who insist on wearing their bones outside of their skins, and no inducement except satiety will persuade him away from good crabbing ground. The Doctor is also found of crabs, and so were all the rest of those on board, and hence there was not the slightest objection when Mr. Green made the following sensible remark :

" Well now that we have got to Florida, don't you think it 'most time to begin to enjoy ourselves? You have kept us all hard at work as if our lives depended on it, driving away through good weather and bad, through rain and shine in order to get here, and now that we are here don't you think that you might let up for a few days at least till we could have a little of the pleasure we came after?"

The wild ducks which we had killed in Currituck were gone long ago, the snipe we had found on the way down, had lasted only a short time, but Mr. Green had supplied us with all the fish we could eat, oysters lay around us begging to be picked up and roasted, and now we had an unlimited supply of crabs, which merely requested us to offer them a piece of refuse meat in exchange for their luscious bodies.

If a man wants to live well and cheaply let him go to Florida, there certainly never was such a place for a yachting expedition. When we had boiled a reserve of nearly a hundred crabs, and we had all eaten as many as we could, we ceased crabbing and went to sailing once more.

Instead of going through the Sisters Creek, which is the shorter course, we stood out to sea from Fort George Inlet and ran into the St. John's, a thing which I would advise no man to do unless he was well acquainted with the bars, or had like myself a very light draft vessel, for both the channels are narrow and shoal. When we were once inside the St. John's we got out our nets in order to ascertain just what the waters contained. Although net fishing is not so stimulating as that with the hook and line, it is more certain even if both are in skilful hands.

We were rewarded by some small yearling mossbunkers and bluefish, which, while the Doctor looked on them as a disappointment, were valuable as settling the question that both of these fish spawn in the Southern waters. A further result of our efforts was, that we hurried on to Jacksonville as fast as we could. On the way we ran over a shad net. It was early in the morning, and there was a sort of haze on the water, so that we did not see the log that the fishermen tie to the end of their nets, to point out where it is. The owners of it were taking it in from the other side of their boat, and even so old a fisherman as Mr. Green was deceived as to the direction in which it was stretched. We carried a piece of it away with us, and had to cut it off from our rudder. For this we were sorry, but were miles off before we had even got an idea of the extent of apology we would have to make, or of the damage for which we would gladly have paid.

At Jacksonville we felt almost as much at home as if we were in New York. We found friends there, we made others, and enjoyed ourselves so thoroughly that it was only the imperative demands of sport that compelled us to move on. Just in the neighborhood of so large a city there is naturally not much to shoot or to catch. There are innumerable cat-fish which Mr. Green was never tired of taking, and which weighed as much as ten pounds each. He insisted they were excellent eating, a matter in which we allowed him to have his opinion without contesting the question. The water on the surface is fresh, and some black-bass can always be caught in the vicinity. The condition of the water in the St. John's is different from that of any other stream with which I am familiar. Even as high up as Pilatka, eighty miles above, the surface water is absolutely fresh, while near the bottom there is a current so salt that crabs are caught in the shad nets. The salter fluid seems to be denser and heavier than the other, and will not mingle with it, so that we have the anomaly of both fresh and salt-water fish being caught at the same time and place.

Into the St. John's there empty at every few miles tributary streams that are rarely ascended by the visiting sportsman, and where the birds and fish exist in their primeval abundance and fearlessness. It is unnecessary to specify these by name, or to particularize any as better than others, for they are essentially alike. We could not explore them all, but those which we did, we found filled with fish and with a fair amount of game. It was too early in the year for alligators, if they can be called game, to show themselves, but birds were to be had plentifully, and fish were simply innumerable. Of these we killed so many that we had to salt them down. There is an additional interest, the interest of new explorations, in ascending the secluded rivers, and I advise every tourist who visits this portion of Florida in his own conveyance, not to omit going up one or more of them.

This was a late season, shad were running, and we had them continually on our table, but roses were not in full bloom in the open air, and as for strawberries, which are usually abundant by New Year's, they had not come in at all yet. We had bought up all the curiosities that we could distribute among our Northern friends; we had played with the baby alligators in the jewelry stores; we had listened to the first installment of the wonderful Florida stories; we had dined at all the excellent Jacksonville hotels, and were ready to withdraw once more from civilization. So the Heartsease spread her sails again, and started up the river. I say "up," because by the current our course was up stream; but it was down by the map. We were going south, the St.

John's being one of the few of the North American rivers which seem to run the wrong way, that is, from the south to the north. In our short stay in Jacksonville we had learned that alligator-tooth jewelry is occasionally made of celluloid; that one of the best drinks in the world of bar-keeping is a punch compounded from the native sour orange; that Florida stories are always reliable, even when they assert that mosquitoes are so abundant that hogs make meals of them, or inform us that the favorite game fish of Florida, the tarpon, jumps six feet out of water when he is hooked, or that sharks will seize a man if they have to leap as high as the deck of the yacht to do so. In leaving Jacksonville, we supposed we were leaving all this behind us, not knowing that Florida is full of quaint jewelry made, as the jewelry of no other part of the world, out of fish scales, saurian teeth, sea beans, shells, orange tree woods, and sharks' molars; that everywhere there are wonderful stories which only differ from one another in size; that palmetto hats were to be bought in every village store, and that sour oranges hang from innumerable trees, valueless for traffic, and only begging to be made into nectar fit for gods.

By the time the Doctor had made these philosophical reflections, Heartsease was tearing along before a favoring breeze past Mandarin, past the Magnolia Hotel and Green Cove Spring; past Tocoi, the terminus of the St. Augustine Railroad, till she made anchorage by nightfall off Pilatka. On the way we had put up many ducks, had seen the cows up to their backs in water feeding off the cabbage at the bottom, and thrusting their heads clear under to get it, and we began to realize that in the end we might come to believe anything of the wonders of this wonderful land. On the last day of our stay in Jacksonville, we had given a little lunch on board, and to show what dinners can be got up there, and how easily, I will reproduce the bill of fare. Everything had been prepared on board, and although our cabin could only seat twelve, we placed before the guests cold turkey, beef and tongue, chicken salad, prepared by the Doctor in most artistic style, stewed oysters, roast potatoes, radishes, and for dessert banana salad—an invention of the better part of the party,—Dummit Grove oranges, sapidillas, and grape fruit, with *pièces montées* of palmetto leaves and sour oranges *en branches*. There was a little *paté de fuies gras* also, but that need not be counted, because it came from the North.

We found that when we had reached Pilatka the stories, instead of diminishing, developed yet more astonishing proportions. The mosquitoes, that the hogs fed on at Jacksonville, put out the head light of the locomotive at Pilatka, extinguished a bonfire, and made nothing of the negroes "light wood torches;" the tarpon of Jacksonville could only jump six feet high when hooked, while the tarpon of Pilatka, without being hooked, bounded clear over the rail of the steamboat Seth Low, which was ten feet from the water, struck the captain in the stomach, and knocked him down. We had not been at Pilatka two days, before we were ready to swallow any mental hallucination, so rapidly does faith grow in the glorious, and balmy air of Florida.

If Jacksonville had been attractive, Pilatka was equally so. Opposite to it is the famous orange grove of Mr. Hart, which we had to visit, and where we ate our first oranges, plucked by ourselves from the trees, beside tasting mandarins and tangerins, lemons, limes, guava and bananas, and that best of all oranges, the grape fruit. There were great plantations of bananas, which grow by suckers from the roots, and increase like weeds. They have to be three years old before they bear, and the development of the flower and fruit, which was going on while we were there, was a pretty sight. The top of the stalk turns over and produces a huge purple flower of a single leaf, as large as the hand of a giant. From under this large leaf starts a circle of small sprouts like fingers. The big leaf falls off, but from the ends of the fingers burst other, much smaller purple flowers. Then below the row of fingers grows another large flower like the first, and it also uncovers another row of fingers, so on till the entire bunch of bananas, as we know it in the market, is formed. Even then the flower point does not cease growing, but exhibits flower after flower, which are merely ornamental and do not result in fruit. Sprouts start so freely from the roots, that the young bushes have to be cut away every year with scythes, or they would become crowded, and the fruit degenerate. Every day, that was spent studying the wonderful productions of Florida, every new tree or bush, which attracted our attention by its beauty, or its oddity, every new species of fruit, which charmed our palate with its originality of flavor, made us more in love with this interesting country, and wish that it and its accompaniments could only exist in a colder climate. There was but one feeling in the minds of the party on leaving Mr. Hart's plantation, which was that each of us could own an orange grove, and have it close at home.

One evening as we were returning after a sailing excursion to visit the neighborhood, we heard cries which sounded like cries of distress. The negroes were so in the habit of laughing at, and jibing one another, that we at first took no notice of these. It was nearly night, so dark, that objects could not be distinguished at any considerable distance; but the cries continuing, we determined to see whether they meant merely fun or something more serious, and kept away in the direction from which they came. That moment's delay cost at least one man his life, and brought sorrow to one household. After sailing a few minutes, we were able to distinguish an object in the water, which looked like a boat capsized. Such it turned out to be, and as we approached, we could make out a number of men clinging to its sides. It was a launch belonging to the crew of a steam ferry boat, and was used by the men after their day's work was over to take them across the river, as they left the steamer on the other side. It was abundantly able to carry the number that started in it, and more, but some of them had been pouring out libations to Bacchus, or had been carried away by foolish animal spirits, we could not exactly determine which, and the result was, that the party of merry-makers was suddenly turned into one of mourners.

We luffed up alongside, and lay to, while our men lowered the boats, and picked up all the poor fellows who were left. Two were unaccounted for, one of whom had been seen to let go his hold and sink. Several of the others would have soon followed his example, except for our timely arrival, for the water happened to be cool that evening, and quickly benumbed their warm southern blood, although they were whites, and not blacks, as we at first supposed. After they were all on board, and it was apparent that there was no use in looking for their lost comrades, we hitched a line to their boat, and towed it behind us towards the shore. As the men crowded on our deck, they seemed so miserable, and did so tremble with the cold, that the hearts of the ladies were touched, and nothing would do but they must be brought into the cabin, and warmed at the stove, there being not room enough for so many in the forecastle. Their clothes dripped and drained over our pretty carpet, and left stains, which never were to come out, but we felt only too glad that we had been able to be of some use to any of our fellow "toilers of the sea." We finally warmed their blood, and put fresh life into them with liberal rations of rum, which was fifty years old. Amid their sufferings what caused them the most pain, was, that they would have to tell the wife of the engineer, who was lost, of his death. This they dreaded as much as they would have dreaded another struggle in the water.

There is often danger from the heavy fogs, which roll up dense, and dark on the St. John's in the night time, and we saw several accidents from that cause. We took the precaution of always anchoring, when not in port, on some flat, and making sure of a well filled anchor light. The steamers invariably follow the channel, for their own protection, and the pilots run at full speed, as in that way alone can they be sure of their position, a knowledge which comes to them by habit. There was, however, one annoyance, which no lights would prevent, no mosquito nets keep out, and no preparation mitigate, the plague of gnats; they come, when they make up their minds to come, in myriads, pour down the companion way, preferring the inside of the cabin to the outside, make themselves at home, push into the state-rooms, and do not care in the least how many millions of their number you immolate. I had been advised that insect powder, if burned in the cabin, would drive them out. On their first visitation I tried the remedy. It is to be feared that the heartless person who gave me that recipe was a practical joker. There is nothing in the nature of gnats to specially provoke merriment so far as I could ever see, or feel, but there are persons who extract pleasure from a funeral. I placed a small quantity of the powder on a piece of paper, which I lighted. The paper was soon consumed, but the powder remained intact, in fact it preserved that part of the paper, which was directly under it. Then I added some chips, and laying the whole on an old plate, tried it again; failure number two, the powder was still unconsumed, and the gnats, who had not neglected these opportunities, while I was busy, to pay their respects to me, were as happy and lively as ever. Determined not be foiled, I then built a fire in the stove, and leaving the stove holes open, poured the powder on the flame. In vain, it only put out the fire. After that I lost faith in the virtues of insect powder, and had to endure as well as I could, lamentations coming faintly through the doors of the state-rooms "Oh what are these strange things that are biting us so." Patience seems to be the only cure for gnat bites, and we did not carry that article with us.

"Doctor," said Mr. Green one morning, after we had spent a couple of weeks in the delightful laziness of sight seeing and curiosity buying, "how much longer do you think the skipper intends to keep us idling here?" He had devoted his attention lately to dragging the Doctor with him on his interviewing expeditions, and they had just returned from their tenth call upon the northern shad fishermen, who, having brought their nets from their homes to try and catch the earliest run of shad, were camping in the woods beyond the town.

"I am afraid," replied our medical associate with base dishonesty, for he was fully as fond of the *dolce far niente* as myself, "that he intends to remain here for the rest of his natural life."

"What, going to stay here for ever!" came from the pretty mouth, which belonged to a pretty head, that just then appeared above the companion way, "I do like to go fishing, and get away from people."

"Yes," came faintly from another in the bowels of the cabin, "I am always fond of a change."

"We havn't caught a fish since day before yesterday," continued Seth in a most injured tone of voice. "I should like to catch something beside cat-fish once more."

This is the sort of thing that the yachtsman has to bear from his mutinous crew, and there is but one way of dealing with it. I went forward without a word, called my men, and we were underway so soon, that the breath was nearly taken from the party, and I heard low grumblings about provisions, which ought to have been laid in, and curiosities, which were to have been bought, and which never could be got again, for an hour afterwards, as we were rapidly running up the river.

The weather had become hot, the thermometer marking eighty-nine in the shade, and mosquitoes made their appearance in the evenings; for those we were prepared, as the yacht was especially fitted with mosquito screens. But the heat was too much for us, and it was unanimously determined that we must take a bath. We had brought our bathing dresses more by good luck than good management, for we had no expectation of quite so summery a time in the midst of winter. We had been assured that snakes never enter the waters of a sulphur spring, and that there was a sulphur spring at Welaka on our way. So we stopped where we thought it must be according to the chart, and in that instance, as in all others, the chart was right. In fact from the beginning of our trip to the end we found ourselves, by the aid of the charts, masters of the situation, and generally much better informed than the natives.

We anchored the yacht at the bend of the river just below Welaka, and taking the small boats rowed into the spring, which was only a hundred yards away. What a glorious sight it was, no puling little affair, such as is called a spring at the North, but a basin two hundred feet across, the water boiling up in the centre in a jet as large round as a hogshead, and rising a foot above the surface, clear as crystal, and gleaming like gems, the irridescent waves spreading away from the central source in lines of glistening transparency, the sunlight reflected from every ripple, as from a thousand prisms. Such a perfect bathing spot we had never seen before, it was a bath-room fit for Diana and her nymphs. We had put on our bathing clothes before leaving the yacht, and it took us but a few moments to fasten our boats and plunge overboard.

Snakes are one of the drawbacks of this warm tropical State. On some of the keys on the Gulf side, they are so numerous that no man is safe in landing. The most deadly is the rattlesnake, but the most disagreeable is the mocassin, which, although not so fatal, sometimes attacks a man in the water without provocation. The latter's bite produces paralysis more frequently than death, but as his attacks cannot be guarded against, he is really a more unpleasant enemy. The traveller's safety in bathing consists in seeking one of these wonderful sulphur springs, into which snakes do not enter, although fish abound in them, looking like moving motes in liquid amber. The temperature of these springs is not cold, being the same as that of the rivers, but there is something exceedingly exhilarating in bathing in them. The feeling of the water is different from that of any other bath. There is a peculiar sense of cleanliness, and a lightness of spirits, which may account for the fancy of Ponce de Leon, that he had at last found the source of eternal youth. Many of these springs are brought within the destructive dominion of man, and are open to every passing tourist, but the one where we were was sacred to him, who has his own conveyance, and was not to be defiled or polluted by the common wayfarer.

We had a delightful bath. There is a common delusion that the water of the sulphur springs is so thin and light, that it will not support the best swimmer. We soon ascertained that this was a totally unfounded fancy, so far as the Welaka spring was concerned. We not only swam to and fro without difficulty, but enjoyed an additional pleasure in getting directly over the boiling spout itself, and being buoyed up by it, where the water was ten feet deep. All of us were sorry, when evening and hunger compelled us to return to the yacht.

The stories concerning the dangerous nature of the snakes of Florida are probably exaggerated, as we saw no more of them, than we would have seen in the same amount of country life at the North. The negro children bathe off the docks of Pilatka and Jacksonville as a common thing, and later in the year, when the peril from snakes is greater. There are spots, where, as I have said, they are to be dreaded, and we heard well authenticated stories of men being snake bitten, but on the other hand old hunters, who were in the woods most of their time, told us they were never troubled by their attacks, and the camping out parties, which we encountered all over, seemed not disturbed by them. Still, while on the subject, I will give the prescription which was kindly furnished us by Dr. Kenworthy of Jacksonville, and which will doubtless prove a better cure than the common one of getting drunk on whiskey; mix two tablespoonfuls of the carbonate of ammonia with enough spirits of camphor to make a paste. Apply this on a rag to the bite, changing the rag as often as it gets discolored. Our medical associate gave his approval to the remedy, and if those two authorities could not cure a snake bite, no one can.

As our little yacht shot out from the St. John's River, nearly two hundred miles above the place where we had entered it, and came into full view of that beautiful sheet of water, Lake George, thousands of wild ducks rose three gunshots off, and flew away. The sight rejoiced our eyes, for we had passed several days on the river without seeing any large birds except the strange water-turkeys, or snake-birds. Unfortunately we had no battery with us, and had to trust to finding a point of land that the ducks would approach. This was no easy thing to do, and we sailed half the length of the north shore, before reaching a promising spot, a narrow point running out between two bays, and at the outer end of which the birds were crowded together in flocks of thousands. There was nothing to be done till the next morning, and seeing a farm house on the neck of land, Mr. Seth Green went ashore to get what information he could from the owner. This gentleman was at the moment working in his garden, and although the thermometer stood at eighty in the shade, he wore the encumbrance of a pair of long India rubber boots. As these seemed rather out of accord with the torrid temperature, he was delicately asked his reasons for wearing them; "well," he replied philosophically, "they cannot strike over those." This sounded ominously, for although, as I have said, we had heard a good deal about snakes, we had seen nothing of them yet. Our doubts were removed when the gentleman pointed out an immense dead rattlesnake hanging on the limb of a bush, and added, "I killed him yesterday." We returned promptly to the yacht, contented to make our explorations by water thereafter, till we should get over the effect of so sudden an introduction to a new acquaintance.

Next day we devoted to the ducks, but we were not properly rigged for them, and soon learned that without a battery we could not expect to kill many in the wide waters of Lake George, they were mostly broad-bills, but did not seem to be as healthy as our Northern ducks. One of my men, who was an old gunner, said that their feathers appeared to be burnt, as though they had been scorched by the sun. They are continually chased by all the visitors to Florida, silly shooters, who fire at them from every passing steamboat, or who pursue them in the small steam yachts, which are becoming a feature of Southern travel. The day following, we sailed across the lake to the south-west corner, intending to ascend the Juniper Creek, which empties into it there. Mr. Green and myself were all of the party who cared to make the exploration; we took one of the small boats, and struck into the outlet, which we had found without difficulty and commenced the ascent. It was a strange, desolate river, quite unlike our Northern streams, slow and sluggish most of the way, half grown up with grasses, weeds, and cabbage plants, lined on either side by a rank, tall mass of reeds, that were yellow with age, and approaching decay, overhung here and there by some Southern plants or bushes, and once in a while winding between groves of palmettos. There was a sombre, savage, and deadly appearance in the water itself. We proceeded quietly for a time, but Mr. Green, who is more alive to the contents of a stream than to its air of gloom or brightness, broke the silence.

"Now," he said, as he began setting up his rod. "I will show you my favorite rig for catching big-mouthed bass. Look at that trolling spoon, it is something of my own invention, although the tackle shops are getting them lately."

He had a special arrangement of feathers and tin, not be described on paper, but long experience has made me skeptical about new all-killing inventions, and possibly my countenance betrayed my thoughts, for he went on, as he saw me getting out a cast of bass flies.

"I know" he observed, throwing his lure overboard, "that other rigs will take some, but you see now, I shall have one within a minute."

I had no choice, as I was seated in the bow of the boat, and could not have used a trolling spoon if I had wished, as our lines would have fouled. I had to put on flies and fish by casting.

"That is all very well," I replied, "at certain times, and in a stream like this, but if we had a large, deep river, I would rather use a number of flies on a long leader."

"There," said Mr. Green at that moment as he struck a fish, "what did I tell you. If you want to take black-bass, particularly this kind—"

He never finished his observation, for at that moment a four-pound fish seized my fly, and it took our joint skill and attention to keep from fouling. He managed, however, to get his fish in quickly, as

it was a small one, and give me an opportunity to
play mine with the light tackle that I was using.
We saved them both, but they were only the fore-
runners of an unlimited number. The spoon did
undoubtedly kill the most, but there were all that
we both wanted, ten times over, and we had to stop
fishing, to avoid destroying more than we could use.
I had the satisfaction of catching the largest, however, with the fly.

We had brought a gun, as well as our fishing
tackle. Suddenly from out the bushes there rose
with much noise and flurry a large bird. I had
hardly time to grab my gun, before he was out of
range, and although I fired, it was ineffectually.

"Oh, I am sorry you missed him," said Mr.
Green sadly, for he always takes a dejected view of
other people's failures, " that was a Limpkin, and I
should like to have got him."

"I thought it was a water turkey," I replied, referring to the queer creature that we had seen on
ever stick and stump in the St. John's. " But whatever it was, it was out of range when I fired."

" I think he was a Limpkin," persisted my companion, "don't you, Charley?"

The stream was becoming rapidly narrower, and
as that made the fishing more difficult, and we had
all the fish we wanted, we took in our lines. Soon
Charley had to cease rowing and resort to poling.
We finally came to where it was so narrow that
there was scarcely room for the boat, and the over-
hanging branches and bushes swept against our

faces. We were just about to give up any idea of further advance, when suddenly we shot out from the small brook into a broad river. Instead of having ascended to the head waters of the Juniper, we had hardly been in it at all, having mistaken one of its mouths for the stream proper. The hour was growing late, but this new river seemed so attractive, we were so sure that it was the one we had been looking for, and that it must lead into the lake not far from where we had left our yacht, that we determined to descend it instead of retracing our course by the way we had come. Here it was that I fired at and wounded a real Limpkin, as I have already related. We went down with the current, having in the broad stream a good chance to use the oars. The sun dropped behind the trees, which were more numerous on the banks of this stream than they had been on those of the other. On and on, and still we did not come to the outlet. It began to look as though we had made a mistake, and this river was a different one from what we had supposed. The prospect of spending the night in the woods now forced itself upon us. My coat was thin, and already the evening air felt chill; we could make a fire, for we were too old stagers to be caught without matches, but the thought of snakes was not pleasant, in spite of the assurances of their rarity, and the excellence of our antidote.

Charley had been rowing a long time and was getting tired, so I offered to "spell" him. This I did till the sun had gone entirely and darkness was closing in upon us fast. Still no signs of the lake, or of an end to this apparently endless river. Strange noises rang through the forest, cries like those of wild beasts, but such as we had never heard before, often as we had passed the night in the woods. I recalled what I had read of the puma, the dreaded Southern tiger, and realized the fact that against him number four duck shot would be a feeble defence. The noises grew louder and louder, the forests fairly reverberated with the unearthly screams till, when one more than usually horrible burst upon our ears, Mr. Green inquired with a composure, which seemed slightly assumed :

" What sort of an animal do you think it is that makes a noise like that ?"

I had never heard anything so appalling in my life before, but was not to be outdone by my associate in coolness, and replied in a hollow mockery of jest :

" That ? Oh, that is a Limpkin. There can be no doubt of that."

To this reply Mr. Green made no direct response, though his face intimated that jokes on some occasions were out of place. The unnatural stillness of the country made these noises perhaps more ominous and unearthly. There was not a breath of air to stir the trees, no ripple or current to the stream which might have diverted our thoughts by its musical babble, and deathlike silence hung over the land, except when broken by the ringing screams. The night was getting darker and darker, and at last we came reluctantly to the conclusion that we had better stop, in order to prepare our camp and make sure that there were no rattlesnakes while there was light enough to do so.

"Let us go to the next turn," said Seth, who had even a greater dislike than the rest of us to spending the night in the woods. "If we do not see any signs of an outlet there we may as well give it up."

"Agreed," I replied, as I bent once more to the oars, "let us keep up hope."

We proceeded, but with little expectation of any good results. What was our surprise and joy then, on reaching the point, to behold the broad waters of the lake spread out before us, and the Heartsease lying in full view with her light up. The sight gave me such vigor that I rowed the rest of the way, although Charley announced that he was rested and wanted to take the oars.

In spite of the beauty of the country, there is a sense of desolation about the wilder parts of Florida. The great trees, covered with moss, and many of them going to decay; the dull, sluggish rivers with slow discolored current, the low lands never rising above a shell-mound of twenty feet height, combine to produce a feeling of dreary solitude. This was particularly noticeable on the journey to and from Florida, through the endless swamps, marshes, and reedy islands, which border the narrow inland passages, and was only occasionally broken by passing a town, or one of the few country seats that are to be found on the unhealthy shores. Nor do there seem to be many water fowl on the Southern Atlantic Coast, until you pass to the south of St. Augustine and reach the neighborhood of Indian River. In making the trip to and from the St. John's, we only saw, beside the ducks and English snipe the bay-birds, of which I have spoken, and a number of the handsome and imposing white herons. These stood in solemn grandeur on the shore of some creek, and seemed too glorious to shoot. Occasionally, however, we could not resist, and had to murder them for their loveliness. Then one of us would hide himself among the reeds on the shore, while the other would go to the extreme end of the line of stately creatures, and put them up. They fly slowly along the edge of the water, and if the sportsman is well hid, there is no difficulty in getting a shot at them. They should never be killed, unless it is to set them up and preserve them, as was done for us by the Doctor.

In Lake George there were millions of mullets jumping continually out of water, like dancing silver arrows, they would not take the fly, or trolling spoon, and as we had all the fish we could use, we did not try the net. We visited a splendid spring, called by a name which seems to be given by common consent to most of the sulphur springs of Florida, that of "silver." It empties into the lake on the western side, about half way down. A bank of snail shells, which must have been cast up by the waves, marks the outlet. Many of them are in good

WILD TURKEY TRAP

preservation, and quite pretty. Several sorts of fish were swimming hither and thither in the spring, and the stream from it was filled with a thin green moss, which the ladies converted into a becoming head covering, and dubbed the "mermaid's wig." We saw some big turtles and alligators and enjoyed a bath.

It was not safe to take the yacht through the narrow and crooked river above Lake George, if we were to limit ourselves in the remotest degree to time, for none but free winds would move us either one way or the other, so we had to leave our pleasant aquatic mansion and descend to the humdrum of the little stern wheel steamers, which were continually passing us, and throwing up fountains of water from their latter ends. By the same means we explored the Ocklawaha, which falls into the St. John's further north. The vessels are adapted to winding round through the circuitous bends of the streams, where the trees nearly meet overhead. In order to see their way, the pilots have to build fires of pine knots at night on the top of the pilot house, which gives a peculiarly romantic and interesting appearance to the scene. On the way we saw no end of alligators and forest birds, especially the famous Limpkin, which laughed, yelled and jeered at us in the security of a regulation which forbids the discharge of fire arms on board the boats.

But we had to be getting back, if we were to complete our explorations of the rest of Florida, so as soon as we could finish our steamboat travel, we hurried down stream once more to Jacksonville. The run outside to St. Augustine is not a long one, but this coast is more dangerous than that further north. An easterly wind strikes it more heavily, and the inlets are shoal. Especially is this the case in the long run below Matanzas and Mosquito Inlets. In fact I cannot do better than quote the words of a report on the inland navigation of that section, kindly furnished me by Mr. J. E. Hilgard, the efficient Superintendent of the United States Coast Survey, to whom I am under many obligations for information and advice:

"There is no inland passage from the St. John's to St. Augustine. You must cross St. John's bar (with eight feet mean low water), but must take a pilot, as the channel is constantly shifting and changing in depth. On the whole, I would advise taking a smooth time at St. Mary's and going outside all the way to St. Augustine. There is excellent anchorage off Old Fernandina (but a short distance from the bar); and the whole run is but about fifty miles, and can be made in a few hours.

"When off St. Augustine, a pilot will take you up to the town. There is nine feet on the bar, but it constantly shifts. The famous 'fresh water springs' in the ocean are situated eight miles S. by E half E. from the 'entering buoy' of this inlet.

"Bound to the southward, Matanzas River carries you from St. Augustine through a distance of nearly thirteen miles to Matanzas Inlet. The channel is winding, but has deep water for a little over seven miles, where there is a seven-feet bar. Below this, for nearly two miles, five feet is the least water, in a crooked channel close under the eastern bank. Thence are depths varying from nine to twenty feet until Matanzas Inlet is reached. The route to the southward leads across this inlet with seven feet at mean low water; and on entering the river again, on the south side of the inlet, you will have but six feet. Matanzas River heads in the midst of extensive marshes between five and six miles to the southward of the inlet; and but two feet can be carried through.

"Beyond this there is no navigation. Wishing to proceed still farther southward, you must retrace your course to Matanzas Inlet, cross the bar and skirt the Florida coast for about fifty miles to Mosquito Inlet. Your pilot (for you must have obtained one at St. Augustine or you cannot enter at all) will take you over the bar with about six feet at mean low water—the mean rise and fall being two feet. Once in the inlet you may go to the northward, through Halifax River to its head, twenty miles above. While in the narrow passage, which extends from Mosquito Inlet for over five miles to the northward, you will carry not less than ten feet; but when the river expands you will find shoal water—the depths varying from three to nine feet, except in occasional deep holes. The channel is very narrow, and can only be followed by the stakes. The small settlements of Port Orange and Daytona are situated on the western bank of this river. Three feet at mean low water can be taken to its head, but there is no lunar tide after you get above the influence of the inlet—the rise and fall being governed solely by the winds.

"Going southward from Mosquito Inlet you enter Hillsborough River; which, through a winding course between fifteen and sixteen miles long, brings you into Mosquito Lagoon, twelve miles to the southward of the inlet. Two miles and a half up Hillsborough River is New Smyrna, a pretty little settlement on the western bank among orange, fig and banana trees. Nine feet may be taken to abreast of the village; not less than five feet is found for five miles beyond New Smyrna; but above that point no more than three feet can be carried through to Mosquito Lagoon;—although there are deep holes with as much as three and a half fathoms. The channel is narrow and very crooked.

"Mosquito Lagoon is wide and shallow—its width ranging from one to two and a half miles. It has a general course about S. E. by S., and is between fifteen and sixteen miles long. A bar of three and a half feet obstructs the entrance from Hillsborough River; but, that once crossed, a good channel, with from five to ten feet takes you to within two miles of its head. This terminates the inland navigation, unless the vessel be able to pass through 'Haul-over Canal.' There is but a foot and a half water in this canal.

"Indian River may be entered from seaward by Indian River Inlet, which cuts through the sandy strip of coast-line about one hundred miles to the southward of Mosquito Inlet and sixty miles below Cape Canaveral. I would not advise a small vessel to attempt to navigate this coast; as it is very dangerous should the wind come to the eastward (which it often does in this vicinity), and there is no shelter except the precarious anchorage under Canaveral. The bar at Indian River inlet has seven feet over it at low water, but shifts constantly in both depth and position, and can only be crossed in the smoothest weather. Besides the bar there is an 'Inner Bulkhead'—so called, over which there is but four feet. It is said by the natives, however, that by taking what is called the Blue Hole Passage, five feet to five and a half may be taken safely into the river."

The fishing at St. Augustine, which is a quaint old town, said to be the oldest in America, and well worth a visit in itself, is better during the winter months than any to be had north of it. Plenty of boatmen can be hired who will pilot the stranger to the best spots. Around here the foliage becomes still more tropical. The frost will occasionally penetrate, and the most famous oranges are to be grown only still further South, on the shell hammacks of the Indian and Banana Rivers, where single trees bear as many as six thousand of these golden fruit each. But we were actually tired of fishing, and looked on complacently with the pitying superiority of accomplished success at the patient anglers, trying their best to kill a few inoffensive finny creatures off the bridge, across the St. Sebastian River, or bringing triumphantly home in the native's "dug out," the proceeds of a day's hard work on the bay. The Doctor was especially indifferent, and excited universal envy when he told of the wondrous sport we had had during our two months of recreation. While I do not for a moment intend to impugn his absolute veracity, some of the adventures which he related had passed from my memory or had grown since I heard them last. He would make no more violent sporting effort than repeating these tales, and preferred to sit on a chair upon the plaza, retailing them, with the encouragement of a sour orange punch, or wander through the coquina built Fort Marion, visit the old Cathedral, or roam the narrow streets. We laid in a supply of native preserves, sketched the graceful date palm, and never ceased wondering at the odd and extravagant beauty of the semi-equatorial foliage and plants. There is interesting, although not very extensive sailing in the harbor, and many varieties of bay snipe to be killed. A yachting club, which will show every courtesy to brethren from the North, has a boat house on the shore.

The further one goes South the better the shooting and fishing become, and I would advise any one, who feels as if it were impossible ever to get enough of either, not to stop in the St. John's, or short of St. Augustine. There he can spend several weeks profitably, and should thence go on South to Halifax River and New Smyrna, where he will think nothing of catching a hundred sheepshead in a day.

no tiny fellows either, but weighing from six to ten pounds a piece, or half as many channel bass of fifteen to twenty pounds each, together with as many sharks thrown in as he has stomach or tackle for. By the way, I forgot to mention that among our outfit was a couple of shark hooks and a line of a hundred fathoms, as thick as the little finger, all of which did good but rather brutal service. Back of New Smyrna, the woods are full of venison and bear meat, turkeys, and other feathered game. The best duck shooting is in the southern part of the lagoon or river, but the bars and beaches everywhere are alive with bay snipe, herons, cranes, pelicans, and a thousand smaller birds.

But a truce to this everlasting repetition of sport, which was growing monotonous even to Mr. Green's insatiable sporting appetite, and turn to something pleasanter. The royal lady of the house had resolved to give us such a feast as we had not had before. The supplies laid in at St. Augustine enabled her to carry out her idea, but the selection of the day and date for the event was a mystery. I supposed it must have been to celebrate my birthday, which, it is true, had come and gone six months before; but as it had not yet been kept, needed commemoration as badly as though it had never taken place at all. No matter what was the moving inducement, the banquet was worthy of it. We men had been smuggled out of the way while the preparations were being made, so that, while we had a general idea of the drift of things, we had no conception

of the gorgeousness of the result. It was not a
feast fit for a king merely, but a sufficient banquet
had all the gods been invited. There were raw
oysters, two kinds of fish, sheepshead boiled, and
channel bass baked, chicken soup, and turtle soup,
from turtle caught on the spot, roast wild turkey,
and boiled mutton, scalloped oysters, venison, and
wild ducks, bay snipe, potato salad, peas, tomatoes,
beans, and baked sweet potatoes, while for dessert
there was such an array of goodies, that the room
in my log book was in danger of running short, and
I could only record a few, such as fresh cake, strawberries, spiced figs, and all the preserves and spiced
fruits that the table would hold, closing with cheese
and coffee. The only wonder was, that after such
a dinner to which our appetites and our loyalty both
pressed us to do more than ample justice, any of
the party survived. If you have doubts of our
state of minds and bodies, go on a three months'
cruise and wind up with such a dinner, and "you
will know how it is yourself."

Of all places on the eastern shore of Florida,
the Indian and Banana Rivers are the most delightful and interesting. Here, when you are once inside the bar, which, as I have said, is a little perilous, there is room and occupation for a winter.
The salt water fishing is mainly near the inlet, but
in the tributary streams is an unlimited supply of
the fresh water varieties. The sailing is splendid,
and the climate, except for its warmth, delicious.
By the time the reader peruses these pages, it is

probable that inland communication will have been opened with the Indian River, either by the "Haulover," which in the year 1882 was only twelve feet wide and one foot and a half deep, or from the St. John's, by the way of Lake Washington; and that there will be finished another canal from Indian River to Lake Worth and Biscayne Bay, making a safe and easy passage round the keys to the Gulf side. This was to have been done when we were there, and if not yet finished, soon will be.

Then if the sportsman is not yet satiated, or if he is suffering from consumption, and wishes to regain his health, he can make the grandest trip in the world, by either sending his yacht to Jacksonville, or to Cedar Keys, or buying one there, and spending the entire winter in the exploration of the southern part of Florida. As it is, the voyage from the Indian River is not difficult or dangerous. Numerous keys or islands make a shelter from the seas, and once on the Gulf side, the climate, the country, the water, everything is delightful. Storms are rare, the Gulf is generally smooth, harbors are numerous, and the shooting is unsurpassed by any in the world. If the sportsman does not take his own vessel, he can go by railroad directly to Cedar Keys, and thence take what conveyance he prefers farther south. At Cedar Keys small sail boats, suitable to those shallow waters, can be hired, as well as guides, if they are needed. To enjoy a visit to Florida in its full scope and meaning, and to make it an expedition never to be forgotten, make up a pleasant party, hire a sailing vessel, and her master as pilot, and coast along from Cedar Keys in water mostly not more than two feet deep, between forests of primeval wildness, in company with countless water-fowl and over unnumbered fish, taking toll from turkey, bear, and alligator, as you go. Sail around the Gulf shore and Cape Sable, and finally up the eastern shore of Florida, into the Indian River. Remain there till your heart is glutted with sport, and your palate with fruit, and thence return to the North by rail or boat. Such a trip makes a date of delight in one's life.

On the Gulf side the most interesting spots are the rivers which flow into the sea, the Caloosahatchee, Crystal and Hamosassa, all of them full of fish and game. Alligators, the sport of killing which is indeed more to be honored in the breach than in the observance, are so abundant as to be almost troublesome. The only difficulty with Florida is that the sport is excessive, and that any one except sporting gourmands will get tired of it. Even Mr. Green, who, as I have said, is almost insatiable, became surfeited, the Doctor and myself being long before content. The voyager, whether by sea or land, must bring certain books with him, such as will not so much help him pass the time, as assist him in his researches. He will find a thousand things to amuse and occupy his hours, but will need information which he can not obtain on the ground. The vast and quaint variety of shells which he will pick up, the new and curious birds and fish he will kill, but above all, the strange mass of tropical flowers, plants, and trees, which he will meet at every foot of the route, require to appreciate them not only all the books which have been written specially on this portion of our country, but a well selected assortment of popular botanical and conchological works, and ichthyological also, if he is not up in that subject.

There is no shooting and little fishing directly around Cedar Keys, where the wayfarer doth very much abound, but some twenty miles south Colonel Wingate keeps a sportsman's hotel, and he can ensure the land traveller a good time, without separation from his family for an extended period. His place is at Gulf Hammock, and to reach it, the sportsman leaves the cars at the station just short of Cedar Keys. From his house parties are made up to explore the waters further south with the aid of boats and guides. I mention his place because he is well known to many of my Northern readers.

I have spoken mostly of the coast shooting, because it was what we mainly had in view in our trip, but it must not be imagined that it is the only kind of sport to be had. We took no dogs, but meeting a party of Northern sportsmen at Gainesville, we tried the quail. The sport was magnificent, with a single drawback. There was no trouble in killing seventy-five birds to three guns, and several times the bag exceeded a hundred, once reaching a hundred and six; but the weather was so hot that it did not seem like quail shooting, and the true exhilaration of the sport, as we Northerners know it, was lost. Deer are plenty everywhere, but to hunt them to any advantage, you must put yourself under the guidance of the native hunters. We only tried it once, and then could use but a small part of our venison on account of the heat of the weather. Bears are occasionally shot; we did not see any, probably because we were not looking for them, and if any one has the patience, he can kill wild turkeys. Good water-fowl shooting is also to be had on the uplands in any of the innumerable lakes which dot Florida from one end to the other, if they are not too near civilization. A very capital house was kept by a former employee of Delmonico, at a town called Waldo, where inland sport of all kinds could be had in reasonable amounts. It seems almost invidious to specify particular places, as so far as I could judge, there was shooting and fishing everywhere off the regular beaten track of tourists.

"Doctor," remarked Mr. Green with a quiet subdued intonation which long practice enabled me to recognize as malice aforethought, "Do you know what bird I prefer to eat?"

"I should presume from your past actions," replied the learned gentleman thus addressed, "that of all the birds, which swim, fly, or have feathers, you give a decided preference to broiled duck."

"Especially," I interposed, in order to head off the coming attack if possible, "provided that the duck is cooked over an open fire in the cabin when the rest of the party are at breakfast."

'Broiled duck is good," Mr. Green responded, uncrushed, "if unreasonable people do not deprive it of its natural flavor by complaining of the manner in which it is cooked. But there is a better bird than even a wild duck."

"Yes," said the doctor, "there's the woodcock, but what is the use of exciting our minds, and aggravating our palates by referring to abstractions, which cannot be realized as there are no woodcock in Florida?"

"There is a good bird in Florida, the very one I refer to, and which could be killed, if a person was allowed to stop on hour or two and not be kept forever on the move like the wandering Jew," persisted Mr Green, cocking back his chair on its hind legs, a favorite position of his, although he had already reduced two of them to kindling wood by the operation.

"You don't mean bay snipe!" exclaimed the doctor in a disgusted tone, "we have had enough of them."

"He probably alludes to water-turkey," I observed quietly, "he has tasted every thing else."

"I don't mean water-turkey either, although for all you can tell it may be a good bird to eat. I mean turkey without the water." With that he brought the front legs of his chair to their natural position with a thud that shook the deck.

"Turkey," shouted the doctor with enthusiasm, "just talk turkey to me, tell me where and when and how. I would swim ashore, if there was a chicken much more a turkey in sight, or the hut of a darkey, who might have either to sell."

"Well then suppose we go ashore and kill one," remarked Seth with quiet complacency, as though such a feat were the simplest everyday occurrence of life.

That settled it. "Oh dear, I should so like a piece of turkey" came from the cabin. "Yes, I am so tired of fish," was was the chorussed approval, and although I felt assured that, strangers as we were to the country, and without a guide accustomed to the work, there would be no chance of success, I had to give in and come to anchor.

Mr. Green got out his rifle, and the doctor his breech-loader, taking a dozen cartridges loaded with buck-shot. Our head man Charley was to accompany them, while I remained in charge of the yacht. None of us knew by experience much of the habits of turkeys, and as it was still early in the day it was determined to start at once, and return again on the following morning if it should be deemed advisable.

"Now," said the doctor, "if we only had a turkey call, we would be sure to succeed."

"Can you use the call?" I inquired.

"Oh no," he answerd promptly, "but I dare say Mr. Green can."

Seth said nothing when I looked at him for a response, leaving me to imply what I pleased as to his accomplishments. I had suddenly remembered that I had one aboard among some old shooting traps which had been thrown in together as a sort of refuse addition. Being perfectly confident that neither of the turkey hunters could use the "strange device," it was with a malicious pleasure that I went below, and after a short search found it. An odd-looking affair it was, which I had once been able to use, but time had utterly obliterated the recollection of the way to manage it. At one end was a piece of bone about four inches long with a hole through it, and a larger mouthpiece of wood at the other. Blowing through it had no effect whatever, as I had previously found out, and the memory of the proper labial pucker had passed from my mind and my lips. I handed it calmly to the doctor without a word. He held it in his hand regarding it with puzzled uncertainty, evidently to make up his mind, which end was to go in his mouth, till noticing the knob on the smaller, he correctly concluded that that was the part to blow through, and applied it to his lips. Then he blew, at first mildly, producing no result other than a gentle hissing of air; he increased the force, the hissing was louder, but that was all, no sound which by the most vigorous imagination could be construed into the cluck of a gobbler issued. He next tried to pucker up his lips like the trumpeter breathing into his trumpet, but with worse effect if possible than before. Dismayed at his futile efforts, he gazed critically into the end as though some of the machinery must have been lost, but finding nothing to encourage such a supposition, gave up the attempt and held it out to Mr. Green, who had been watching the operation with interest. The latter gentleman was not to be caught, and waving it indifferently aside said with admirable assurance:

"We won't need that, turkeys are too plenty, all we shall have to do will be to keep our eyes open to kill as many as we want."

In that happy state of confidence they departed. We were anchored some little distance from the shore on account of the shallowness of the water, but I thought I heard several shots and wondered what they had found to fire at, as the probability of their killing a turkey was too slight to be worth considering. Early in the afternoon they returned with an air of curious self gratulation in their behavior, the manner of persons who had done an act on which they plumed themselves, but which would bear a good deal of concealment. This was noticeable even before they had reached the yacht, and prepared me in a measure for what followed—the production of a fine fat gobbler from the stern of the boat. Charley handed it up to me with an air of deprecation quite in contrast to the truculence with which Seth climbed on deck and exclaimed:

"There, what did I tell you, are you satisfied now? Where would the supplies come from to keep us alive, except for me. You would have had us down to hard tack and salt junk long ago, if it hadn't been for the fish and birds I have had to kill. Have you anything to say against that?"

I was examining the turkey critically. I had heard of turkey pens, and suspected that this came from one of them, but did not see how to prove the fact. Its head had been shot nearly off.

"That is where the ball hit him, and I call it a

pretty good shot at twenty rods," continued Mr. Green, referring to the wounded spot.

"Was he as far off as that?" I inquired, as I handed him over to be picked. I was not familiar enough with a trapped turkey to detect the deceit if there was any, and Seth, seeing my inability, made the most of it.

"What is to be our reward for the hard work we have been doing? I tell you it is no easy thing to stalk a turkey, and if any other of the party had done as much, I wouldn't grudge them the nicest sour orange punch that could be made."

Turkeys are caught in parts of the country by a curious trap or pen, and I had heard that such a pen was used in Florida. It is built of logs on the four sides and over the top, a hole being left at one side just large enough to allow the bird to enter in a stooping posture. Corn is strewed on the ground leading to this hole, and scattered about so as to attract attention, and the way the trap works is this: the turkey finds the food and follows it, picking up grain after grain, keeping his head bent down, and in that posture enters the pen without trouble. There he remains without a suspicion of wrong till he has consumed all the corn. After the food so kindly supplied is gone, he begins to think of moving on, when to his surprise he discovers that man rarely does any favor without expecting a return, no less in this case than the toothsome body of the recipient. The turkey never stoops, even to save his life, he looks upward and not downward, he will not bow his royal head to escape by the road through which he entered. Becoming alarmed he springs up, dashing himself against the logs, he thrusts his head between the crevices and tries to fly through the roof by main force, but in vain, the pen is too strong, and the only method of escape which is open he will not condescend to take.

The owner of such a pen does not visit it regularly, and the turkeys are often shut up in it for days, frequently falling a prey to wild cats that find them before their lawful proprietor comes to claim them. My unholy suspicions were that the doctor, the Superintendent of the New York Fishery Commission, and the captain of the yacht Heartsease had accidentally found such a pen, and acted the part of the wild cat. For although I could see nothing suspicious about the bird, it was strange that persons who had stalked a wild turkey through a dense Southern forest hardly seemed to be tired, and wished to sit up half the night to smoke and talk. Still the bird proved to be delicious, and the entire party were grateful for him whether honestly obtained or not, so little does hunger weigh questions of morality.

Two days after the turkey adventure, when we were sailing along before a mild breeze, Mr. Green steering, the doctor smoking, and the rest of us reading, Charley suddenly called out from forward where he was standing:

"Look at that large bird flying over the woods to the west."

We all looked in the direction indicated, and saw

an immense bird moving grandly and steadily, with slowly beating wings and extended neck and legs.

"What an enormous creature," exclaimed one of the ladies.

"It must be a rock," chimed in the other.

"Here take the stick, while I get the glass," saying which, Mr. Green let go of the tiller, and plunged into the cabin to reappear with the binocular, which he fixed on the wondrous bird.

"What do you make out of him?" inquired the doctor, who had forgotten his pipe in the excitement till it had gone out.

"It is a crane," replied Seth, "but the largest one ever I saw. Charley," he asked our captain, "did you ever see such a crane as that before?"

"No, I never did," was the answer. "It must be something of the sort however, from the way it flies and holds its legs."

"I wonder whether it can be the whooping crane?" I inquired, "I have heard that they are occasionally seen on the coast, although supposed to be more numerous in the interior."

"Oh can't you shoot it, what feathers it must have for hats." The origin of this remark was obvious.

"If you want feathers a yard long! Why it is nearly as large as an ostrich."

"Well, don't we use ostrich feathers? Oh do shoot it, I want some long white feathers."

"It is a little too far off," I replied.

"How far?" was the persistent inquiry.

"I should say about a mile."

"That is the way always," was the disgusted response, "you pretend to be great sportsmen, but you say every bird we meet is too far off. If I knew how to shoot, I wouldn't be making excuses all the time. If we ever come to Florida again, I hope we will have somebody with us who can hit his mark, and not pretend that every bird is too far off."

At this the fair speaker retired below just as the crane disappeared over the distant trees.

It was several days after this occurrence that we saw what we took to be another whooping crane standing at the edge of the water, not far from some bushes. He was quite white, and towered up against a back ground of grass and sand-bar till his head seemed to come in line with the trees beyond, and his body to be as tall as that of a man. The yacht was slowly approaching him by the aid of a light breeze, and Mr. Green was growing more excited the nearer we came. The crane stood motionless, not alarmed at the bigger bird, which was gradually swooping down upon him, and apparently quite tame.

Mr. Green had redeemed his reputation with the rifle of late, my sarcasm about the Limpkin, and some ironical allusions from the doctor had improved his aim, so that we no longer smiled incredulously when he brought out his rifle. In fact he was a splendid shot, as his innumerable prizes taken at tournaments abundantly proved, but the motion of the yacht had at first unsettled his aim. There was not more than half a mile between us and the bird,

GREEN TURTLE.

which seemed to loom up higher and higher as we approached.

"Hadn't we better make sure of him," asked Seth anxiously," we may never have such another chance. You tell me these cranes are very scarce!"

"Perhaps we had," I answered," what do you think we had better do?"

"By all means," interrupted the doctor, who was roused out of his usual equanimity, "let us make every effort to kill him as a specimen. They are exceedingly rare."

"If you lay to," replied Seth, "and let Charley row me ashore, I will get behind those bushes, and think I can crawl within range of him."

"If you are willing to take the trouble on the chances," I answered. "Do, Mr. Green," begged the ladies both together, their hopes of such feathers as had never yet graced bonnet quite carrying them into enthusiasm.

Seth did not consider the labor of crawling through the matted dense undergrowth in the hot sun, nor the danger of snakes in the long grass, all that he saw was the immense bird and all that he wanted was to kill it. In a moment he and Charley were off in the boat, and pulling for the shore. Heartsease was luffed up into the wind, and lay motionless on the scarcely ruffled water, contrasting by its apparent indifference with the eager excitement of the party on board. We watched the small boat till it reached the bank, and was hastily concealed by Charley, while Mr. Green disappeared immediately in the bushes. Then we could see nothing further except the big bird, which had not been alarmed by the preliminaries, and which there was now every probability would become our prize. The ladies were in their hearts already priding themselves on the loves of bonnets to which his gorgeous attire was to contribute, the doctor had already dissected and stuffed him in imagination, and I was wondering whether he was good to eat. We waited till our patience was more than exhausted. Crawling through the tangled mass of a Southern swamp is no easy matter, and we could do nothing but watch the imposing bird standing there, unterrified, and as still as though he were a graven image, instead of being a thing of beauty and vitality.

Suddenly he gave a great leap into the air, and then fell upon the sand in death throes which had almost ceased before the report of the discharged rifle came booming over the water. In a moment the deceitful calm of the previous moment passed away, we hauled aft our sheets, and swinging round her head, got Heartsease under way. Charley shoved out the dinkey which he had concealed in the bushes, and in another minute Mr. Green pushed his way through the underbrush to the side of his magnificent victim. When our boatman joined him, the two stood for some time gazing at and handling the crane, while we waited impatiently for their return.

At last they threw the game, it seemed to us irreverently, into the bottom of the dinkey, and pushed off. We awaited their approach with eagerness, arising from the fact that none of us had ever seen the American whooping crane, and were proud of being the participants in the capture of one. The two fortunate sportsmen did not hurry themselves to gratify our desires, but appeared exceedingly at their ease, and it was not till they had nearly arrived that we discovered the cause of their indifference by perceiving in the boat not a whooping crane at all, but an ordinary white heron. The clearness of the atmosphere, the bright rays of the sun, or the nature of the background had tended to mislead us and had added immensely to the stature of the bird. The ladies retired to the cabin hatless, so to speak, the doctor was for throwing the deceiver overboard instead of skinning him, and to this day I am uncertain as to the taste of the great American whooping crane.

The Indian River is so shallow in places, that the direction on the chart of Currituck Sound could be applied to it: " Only three feet of water can be carried, and that with difficulty." In other parts it is deeper; it varies in width from one mile to three, and as a general rule where it is narrow, it is deep, and where it is wide, it is shallow. Although it approaches nearly to Mosquito Lagoon, it does not join the latter unfortunately, and a canal has been cut called the Haul-over, of which I have already spoken. In the Haul-over, which is only fourteen feet wide, there is but one foot and a half of water, and for some distance below not much more than two. There are many rivers emptying into the Indian River on the west or shore side; these are generally deep and full of fish, and well repay the explorer. The only inlets are in the southern end, Jupiter Inlet at the lowest extremity, and Indian River Inlet a short distance above.

Banana River, which is rather a branch of Indian River than a distinct stream, is in places broader and deeper; it connects with the main river at its southern extremity, and by Banana Creek at the northerly end. The creek of the name is both narrow and shallow, and can only be used by small craft. There is most interesting yachting in the Halifax and Hillsborough, north and south of New Smyrna, which is situated on the Hillsborough, about three miles from Mosquito Inlet, as well as in Mosquito Lagoon, which is reached through a narrow and tortuous channel among innumerable islands from the Hillsborough. So also do the Indian and Banana rivers furnish safe and delightful cruising grounds, with plenty of harbors or shelter for even small open vessels, the only danger being that of running on oyster shoals.

A narrow strip of sand separates Indian River from the ocean, and the yachtsman can occasionally, by climbing into the rigging, see the blue waves of the Atlantic. On this bar the bay-birds often collect in large flocks, and may be killed in numbers more than needed. They are of the same kinds which have already been described, and are found in the summer at the North. Bear are occasionally met with, and now and then a wild-cat; deer are more plenty, but the sportsman will be fortunate if he finds any of these unless he goes especially after them.

A yacht-club has been established at New Smyrna, with headquarters in Indian River, where the members expect to do a large part of their yachting. An excellent choice was made at the first election of officers, and its prospects for introducing the sport into the waters of Florida are promising. The president is Mr. Herman Oelrichs, and the vice president Mr. Girard Stuyvesant, both of New York.

In extended yachting trips there is often trouble in getting fresh water, a difficulty which is increased at the South, where the land is low, and there are none of what at the North would be called springs; the ice-cold jets of water bubbling from the ground. It is not generally known that sand is so effectual a filter, that drinkable water can be obtained by digging down into it almost anywhere. To take advantage of this, and for many other purposes, it is advisable to carry a spade on board. Water so obtained may be a little brackish, but by boiling it will be made, if not quite palatable, at least healthy. Rain falling on the deck is apt to take up portions of the paint, infinitesimally small, perhaps, but sufficient to give an unpleasant and unhealthy taste. On the western keys a bush with a peculiar rich leaf, easily distinguishable by those who have once seen it, often grows where water is to be found.

It would be easy to go on recounting the attractions of Florida indefinitely; there is always something more to say, a fresh point of interest to speak of, additional beauties to describe, other and still other reasons for visiting this strange and delightful country. There is but one way in which even a slight appreciation of the charms of Florida can be obtained; and that is, to go there as often and stay there as long as possible. For health, for recreation, for sport, no place in the world can be compared with it. A vast portion, that of the Everglades, the "Grassy Water" of the native Seminoles, has never been explored, and there are thousands of rivers, lakes, and ponds which have rarely been disturbed by the presence of a white man, and which would amply reward the adventurous spirit who would explore them.

When we first arrived in Florida, the flowers, which its name promised us, were not to be seen. Deceived by the temperature and a thermometer that recorded rarely less than eighty degrees, we failed to recognize the season of the year, or recall the truism that, as all nature must have its spring, it must also have its winter. The climate and the foliage were as summer-like as we had ever seen them. The grand orange trees, with their brilliant shining green, flecked with spots of golden yellow, were the most gorgeous sight that our eyes had ever beheld in field or forest. The moss-covered forest evergreens, although turned slightly brown, were still magnificent in their richness of foliage. There were bare limbs here and there of deciduous trees, but their nakedness was nearly covered by the unfading leaves of their neighbors. The shrubs and undergrowth were as bright in hue, seemingly, to our uneducated eyes as possible. But by the time we were leaving, even we could notice a decided change. The green had put on a deeper verdancy, the brown had disappeared, and suddenly there sprang into life a myriad of flowers. The yellow jessamine covered the swamps and filled them with a mass of perfume as well as an array of loveliness. Scarlet lobelias thrust their bright heads boldly from the water-side, along with white lilies and arrow-heads, and on the higher grounds hundreds of wild flowers, many of which we could not name, charmed us with their beauty. The magnificent magnolia was bursting into bud. As the orange trees were being denuded of their ripe fruit, the tiny sweet smelling blossoms made their appearance, till the branches bore at one and the same time, buds, flowers, and green and ripe fruit. The inland lakes and ponds were covered with pond lilies, which are called "bonnets" by the natives, and made a delicious picture with the broad green leaves and the bright yellow flowers. Language fails in describing the exquisite beauty of the verdure of the country. We found Florida laden with fruit; we left it covered with flowers.

CHAPTER III.

CURRITUCK MARSHES.

Duck shooting has held its own better than any other kind of sport in the States east of the Mississippi. Ruffed grouse have almost disappeared, woodcock have grown scarcer and scarcer, English-snipe visit us less abundantly, while the bay-birds have nearly ceased to be in sections where they were once overwhelmingly abundant, but it is possible still, on Lake Erie, along the coast, and at many inland places to make a fair, if not, as often happens, an excellent bag, of ducks. But the best place, one where the birds seem to exist in their original abundance, and where magnificent shooting is still to be had, is on the eastern shore of North-Carolina. Of this favored locality Currituck is the most famous. So celebrated is this county that the entire marshes, the duck-haunted lowlands, have been purchased, and to-day there is absolutely no free shooting to be had. A stranger is as thoroughly debarred as if he were in the most barren portion of our land. No one is allowed to shoot from a battery unless he is a native, and to get a chance to go out at all after the innumerable flocks of wild-fowl that temptingly cover the water, the visitor must belong to one of the numerous sporting clubs which have so wisely and assiduously secured all the shooting grounds, and most of which are so particular that they exclude invited guests.

But if you are one of the favored shareholders you can have a glorious time. Fifty ducks a day to each gun is no unusual average, and while a hundred is a large bag, a hundred and fifty is nothing uncommon, and as many as two hundred and fifty have been killed by a sportsman and his gunner in a single day. Moreover the birds are of the best possible kind ; there are canvas-backs in the open water, redheads in still greater abundance, and broad-bills or blue-bills so plenty that they are rarely shot at, while in the pond holes black-ducks, mallards, and widgeons abound. These are all well-fed and fat, and such a thing as a poor duck is unknown. The law wisely forbids shooting before sunrise or after sunset, and the club members are wise enough to keep the law, knowing as they do that one gun fired after sunset is more injurious than a dozen during the day, so that the ducks do not seem to diminish but rather to increase and multiply, and as fine a day's sport has been had by the members of the club during the past few years as at any time in the history of the country. A result partly due to breech-loaders perhaps, while from a battery it is nothing unusual to kill a hundred brace of red-heads or canvasbacks, and some times twice as many.

This favored spot is, as it ought to be, of no easy access. The sportsmen must first go to Norfolk and thence take either the little steamboat Cygnet, endeared to so many of us by the memory of pleasant excursions in the past, or travel by a new railroad just finished which passes twenty miles from the traveller's destination, a place known from the name of the enterprising widow lady who formerly owned it, as Van Slyck's Landing. By boat the entire day is spent in the journey, and by rail it is not much shorter, but the boat arrives so late that it is not always possible to make the trip across from the landing to the club house the same night. Opposite Van Slyck's are the two most famous and successful sporting clubs in that section of the United States, the Currituck and the Palmer's Island clubs. They own or control immense tracts of land, and below them to the southward the bay widens out so that there is no chance to kill ducks to advantage. There are a few good stands at Kitty Hawk Bay, thirty miles further south, and at the lower end of Roanoke Island Raft ducks can be shot from batteries. Then again along the eastern shore of Pamlico Sound, at Hatteras and Ocracoke inlets and in the western part of Core Sound, to the south of Harker's Island, there is good duck, and in its season brant shooting, but these places can only be reached by the fortunate sportsman who has his own private conveyance. Therefore it may practically be said that the Palmer Island marshes are the *ultima thule* of duck shooting.

As a general thing, there is attached to every sporting club some old experienced gunner full of wild-fowl lore and quaint and curious phrases, who is a mine of interesting information to him who will explore the vein. Such a one belonged to the Palmer Island club, in the person of William S. Foster, a resident of Long Island, who had followed Shinnecock Bay for many years, knew the ways and habits of the birds as well as if he were one of them, and was as fond of shooting as the most inveterate sportsman. Honest to a farthing, faithful, anxious to give the person he was with the best sport he could, he was ready to take any amount of trouble, endure any labor for a good day among the ducks, the members of the club looked on him, rather as a friend than a paid employee. Many is the hour I have spent with him on the Currituck marshes, many a day of splendid shooting have I had, many the big bag have I made with his aid. One of his peculiarities was that he never was in a hurry. No matter how thick the birds were, how easy it seemed to choose a point, he would stand quietly in the bow of the boat with the sea-glass in his hand scanning the movements of the flocks and deliberately selecting the best place. I would often grow impatient and fear he was losing valuable time, but the result rarely failed to justify his judgment and vindicate his deliberation.

The first and most important object, as he explained it under such circumstances, was to so arrange the stools that the ducks would "come right," that is would approach without fear and would offer the sportsman a fair shot. This is a matter of the greatest moment and is not understood by men who consider themselves expert wild-fowlers. First, there is the question of the wind to take note of, then the position of the sun, next the cover, and last, but by no means least, the nature of the species of ducks that are flying. It will not do to string out the decoys dead to lee-ward of a point as is so often seen, except perhaps when canvas-backs and red-heads are alone expected, mallards, sprigtails, and especially the wary black-duck will never or rarely approach a point. If a point, with the wind blowing directly off from it has to be chosen, it is better to stretch the decoys around to one side of it so that the wind "will catch the birds under the wing" as he expressed it and swing them in farther than they expected. Points projecting far out into the open water are the favorites of tyro gunners, but they are especially unsuited for any of the marsh ducks, the black-ducks, mallards, sprigtails, and even the widgeons, all of which give a wide berth to such spots, especially after they have been shot at a few times, and most of which prefer to alight close under the lee of a bank, in the "slick" as it is called.

There are two great divisions of ducks, the deep water, diving or raft ducks, and the shoal water or marsh ducks, which reach down for their food and can never feed in water more than two feet deep. The habits of these two varieties are remarkably dissimilar. The open-water birds, fearless of ambush, are less timid than their pond-loving brethren, who dread an enemy in every tuft of grass or bunch of reeds, when canvas-backs once make up their minds to come to the stools, they come straight on regardless of deficiencies in the gunner's blind, and very frequently pass completely over the stools. On the other hand, a black-duck in approaching the stand is a model of caution, he is all eyes and ears, the slightest movement by the sportsman, the least evidence of danger will arouse his suspicions, and he will veer suddenly off. Black-ducks and mallards rarely cross the stools to alight at the head of them, but if they reach them at all, drop in at the lower end, or more often stop short and alight at a distance just tantalizingly out of shot, where they remain to lure off every fresh arrival unless they are driven away. Their noses are especially keen, and care must be taken to so arrange the stand that the wind will not carry the scent of the gunner across the water to the lee-ward of the decoys, and the birds get it before they reach them. If they come in contact with such a warning they jump into the air as if they had been shot at, and flee with all the speed that terror can lend to their usually vigorous wings. It is desirable to set the stools under the lee of a bank of reeds or rushes, for none of this class of ducks likes the open water, and the most convenient plan is to place the stools to one side of the stand, quartering as it were across the wind, so that even if the birds alight before actually reaching them, they may be within gun-shot.

The location of the stand is most important. I remember once when I was shooting from what is known in the club as "Kidder's Point," that I was particularly impressed with this fact. The day had been dull and rather quiet, with but a few birds stirring all through the morning ; a haze lay upon the marshes, not dense enough to prevent the ducks flying if they had been so minded, which they did not seem to be, the wind scarcely stirred the reeds or rippled the surface of the bay, which was spread out before me. I was making a poor bag and hardly expected to do better, when about midday there came a change over the spirit of the earth and air, the clouds began to condense, the wind commenced to blow, the air became rapidly colder, a thin steak of gray faintly marked the sky in the nothwest, while in the south the clouds grew blacker and denser. Then the rain fell in spits and flurries viciously. The atmosphere intimated a decided change in the weather, which the ducks were the first to recognize and regulate their proceedings by. Evidently a vast mass of widgeons were bedded to the lee-ward of us. They commenced to fly not in their individual capacity, but as the part of a great movement, as if suddenly they had made up their minds all to go. In whisps of threes, fours, tens, twenties, in large flocks, or solitary and alone, they came heading towards me directly across the marsh and visible for miles. Then it was that I learned that I was not in exactly the right place, that the birds for some reason best known to themselves did not care to cross that spot in their migration. Most of them, especially the largest flocks, passed outside of me and just beyond the range of my gun. I was in the wrong place, I knew it, but I had no time to move, the ducks

FLORIDA "CRACKER."

were flying too fast and too many of them came within range as it was for me to lose the time necessary for a change. The rain that was falling, although not heavy, interfered, and would have wet our guns and clothes which were pretty well protected so long as we remained still. So we stayed where we were, and as it was the sport was splendid. The entire mass of widgeons had determined to change their feeding grounds, and that at once, there was no moment when some of them were not visible in the air, they came from one quarter and flew in one direction. I had learned to whistle for widgeon as well as a professional, and did my best with the aid of William Foster to inveigle them within range. Very often we were sucesssful, and it was an afternoon of excitement. Not a minute passed that we did not have the prospect of a shot, and although the larger flocks mostly kept on their course outside of us, the smaller whisps and the single ones came in freely.

"Why is it that the birds seem to be all moving at once?" I asked of William during the first moment of partial leisure that we had, "and why are they all going in the same direction?"

"It is a question of food with them," he replied, "as is the case with most other animals. Widgeon can only get their food by reaching down for it, so they must keep where the water is not over their heads; that is so that they can touch bottom with their bills by tipping up, as you have often seen tame ducks do. Now in these shallow marshes a change of wind means a change of depth of water, it is shallower to windward, the water being piled up to leeward and the ducks, knowing this, fly against the wind, all the shoal feeding birds do so. The canvas-backs, red-heads, and broad-bills make little account of the wind."

"But," I answered, "this wind cannot as yet have affected the depth of water."

"No, but the birds know that it soon will, and they are getting ready for to-morrow. There will probably be a greater change than we expect, wild animals know much more about the weather than man can ever learn, they have a sort of instinct that is given to them for their protection. I have always observed that the ducks sought the windward side of the marshes. If the wind is blowing from the south, I make it a rule to go to the southward to choose a stand, if from the west I look through the western marshes and so on. Of course I am not always right."

"No," I interrupted him to remark, "but we have observed that the member who goes out with you generally brings in the most birds, so the results tend to demonstrate the theory."

"Well, I have studied these marshes as thoroughly as I could; there is not a tree that I have not climbed, nor an island that I have not explored."

"Can you see much from the trees when you do climb them?" I asked.

"Yes. A little elevation will enable you to see over the entire marsh, and many a pond hole have I found in that way that is not known to most of the gunners, and not always to the natives."

"Keep still," I remarked at this point of our conversation, "there comes a magnificent flock of ducks, if they would only turn this way what a shot they would give us."

We were silent except for whistling, which we did with the finest touches and the utmost skill. The flock, spread out against the distant sky in an angle-pointed line, was headed directly for our hiding place. We had crouched down on their first appearance, and grasping our guns and watched them, waiting with increasing impatience and anxiety. Nearer and nearer they came, over the distant marsh undisturbed by any other gunner, and unattracted by other decoys until they were directly in front of us and not more than three hundred yards distant. It was a moment of intense excitement, for if we could once get our four barrels into those serried ranks, there was no telling how many we might not kill.

On they came still nearer, we whistled more softly and they answered with undiminished confidence. Now they were over the meadow just beyond our stools, a few minutes more of the same course and they would be in our power. But alas, just as they struck the open water they deflected their course a little, not much, but enough to carry them beyond fair reach of our guns, so that when we fired we were only rewarded with three birds that plunged from the flock headlong into the water. As they were being retrieved by our four legged companion, William sagely remarked:

"I have observed that generally there is some misfortune connected with what would make the finest shots, and that at such times something is sure to go wrong ; either the birds do not come in right, or a twig or reed gets in front of you, the gun misses fire, or something else happens, so that the best chances usually prove the worst."

"There is an awful deal in luck," I replied, "after all is said, Napoleon's star was not an imaginary planet by any means. I never was a lucky sportsman, and have had to earn my game by the sweat of my brow."

"Did you ever know a sportsman who would admit that he was lucky?" inquired William, calmly.

"I can't say that I ever did ; but if you will keep still and not fluster me with unnecessary generalizations, I will kill that pair of widgeons that are coming over the marsh, luck or no luck."

After uttering that boast, I had to make my words good, and though I detected a twinkle in my companion's eye, as if he would not mind should I happen to miss just that once, I took care to aim straight, not the sort of excessive care that invariably results in a miss, but the rapid and confident deliberation that first holds the gun right and then pulls it off when it is right, without waiting until it gets wrong.

"Good," said William, *sotto voce*, in his quiet way, as the two ducks, doubled up by the full charge of shot came down splash into the mud, close to our stand, "I have seen a good many misses when a man was most sure of hitting : I hardly expected that you would kill them both so neatly."

The sport kept up. It is useless to describe each individual shot that we made. There is endless variety in every one that is fired, for no two birds come to the decoys precisely alike. There are never the same conditions of wind, sun, position, readiness, and what not, so that each is more or less of a surprise. These the sportsman enjoys at the time, they constitute the great charm of shooting; but they would tire in the repetition in the cold blood of white paper and black ink. It is enough that we had a magnificent day's sport ; "magnificent" is not hyperbolical; we had sport that will be a memory through life, and until the age-weakened arms can no longer wield the faithful fowling piece, nor the time-dimmed eyes note the birds approach. Our store of game lay in a pile uncounted : we knew there was a goodly number, and when at last the tired sun had performed his allotted task and gone to bed, we were not surprised to add up nearly a hundred of what is one of the finest of all the ducks, the handsome little widgeon. Few of our gunners, even the oldest of them, know that there was a time when the widgeon was valued more highly than the canvasback, when in fact in firing a sitting shot the market gunner would "shew" the latter out of the way, in order that he might have a better chance at the former. Had we been in exactly the right spot, there is no doubt that I would then have reached the bag of two hundred, which it has been the ambition of my life to attain.

On another occasion I had the same misfortune, although from a different cause. I was with Jesse that time, Jesse who, or Jesse what, I cannot tell. So faithful and trustworthy a fellow must have another name, a full name; but often as I have availed myself of his care in the marshes of Currituck, I am ashamed to confess that I have forgotten it. Every one calls him simply "Jesse," out of kindly feeling no doubt, for a better fellow never set out a stand of decoys; so as simply Jesse he must go down to the immortality that this book will give him. He is devoted to the pleasure of his employer, and never more delighted than when the latter brings home a fine bag of birds; but he is not quite so skillful as his older associate, William Foster. He had observed, when out the day previous, that the birds had a favorite feeding place in a little bay near what in club nomenclature is designated as "the horse-shoe." To this place we wended our way as soon as we could cross the intervening three miles of distance. The bay was not large, and at its mouth was contracted into two narrow points which were hardly a hundred yards apart. I had never shot at this particular point, and Jesse did not think of the effect of the sun when he made his selection. One point was probably as favorable as the other, with that exception, but the one he selected brought the birds directly between me and that luminary when he shot his burning and blinding rays from mid-heaven. The result was, that before the day was over, reeds and ducks and spots swam before my eyes in prismatic hues. The heavens become alive with them, mixed up with grasses and flowers, the gorgeous colors of condensed sunlight. Scarlet ducks, golden ducks, fiery ducks floated before my bewildered vision, interwoven with such flaming reeds and rushes as were never seen by mortal eye before. To say that under the circumstances I could not shoot with my accustomed skill, is unnecessary; I could not help occasionally mistaking the flaming bird for the natural one, and no doubt would have killed him, had he only been real enough to kill. This was the second occasion when I might have reached my stint of two hundred, if I had only been so fortunate as to locate properly in the first place, or even had had the courage to change when I found out that I was wrong.

There are myriads of wild geese and swans in Currituck Sound and its adjoining waters. The swans are hard to kill, and it rarely falls to the fortune of any sportsman to bag more than two or three of these beautiful birds in a season, but the geese are shot in immense numbers on favorable days—"goosing days," as they are called. Such days are made by a southwesterly wind blowing hard enough to constitute a gale, and the harder the better, which causes the water to rise and enables the geese to reach the beaches where they go to sand. For this shooting a "stand," as it is called, of tamed wild geese are required. The sportsman hides himself in a large, water-tight box, which has been sunk in the sand at the spot which the birds frequent, and the "stand" of living decoys are tethered in front by stout strings fastened to their legs and pinned to the ground. The geese come to the stools in flocks, and the slaughter at times is enormous, as many as two hundred being no unusual bag, and that is often rounded out with forty or fifty ducks. It is customary on such occasions to put a live swan or two with the geese decoys, if the sportsman happens to be so fortunate as to possess them, and I never shall forget seeing four swans come to a stand which was located some distance from my own, but in full view from it. I have always believed that birds could converse and had a language of their own, and on this occasion my theory received confirmation strong as holy writ. When I have sat listening hour after hour to the unceasing conversational cacklings of geese, who appear to be the most talkative of birds, I fancied that I could almost make out the words they uttered, and which were certainly understood by the fowls themselves, as the dullest observer would be convinced by their actions. Their expressions of comfort, their mild observations about the weather may not have been quite comprehensible, but their cries of alarm, their notes of warning, no one could mistake. Ignorant hearers not versed in goose language, and a very pretty tongue I have no doubt it is, may call it contemptuously "gabble," but so is the language of any foreigner "gabble" to those who do not understand it.

In the instance that I am about to mention with

the swans, there could be no difficulty in understanding every word. There were four of them, the wise father, the inquisitive mother, and two pretty, innocent, dove-colored cygnets. They were sailing along far up in the heavens, away out of danger, when the attention of the young ones was attracted to a nice, gentle old swan seated happily among a body of geese that were evidently having a good time and abundant food. In all the innocence of their uncorrupted hearts they uttered a shout of joy and started to join him, the mother who was curious to understand the meaning of so happy a combination, following eagerly behind them. In vain the cautious father warned them to " go slow." They would not stop to listen or to heed. On they flew or swam after alighting on the water, giving free expression to their feelings of pleasure. Louder and louder grew the warning notes of the head of the house, who hung back and tried to keep the others back, but his efforts were useless, the young were guileless, and the foolish wife inquisitive. He was too devoted to leave his family, although the danger into which they were running was apparent to him. Soon his worst fears were realized. He was out of gunshot, but his wife and children were within the fatal reach of the deadly gun. Several loud reports followed one another, and all was over. In an instant he was childless and wifeless. The two cygnets were killed dead, but the mother was able to fly a hundred yards, and it was pitiful to see him go to her, braving all danger, and to hear his cries of lamentation. He could not save her, however, and when the boat approached with a gunner to complete the deadly work, the poor old swan had to leave her. Still he kept circling round for some time and filling the air with his bitter lamentations.

In wild fowl shooting it is essential to learn the various calls of the different species of ducks and of the geese and swans. These it is impossible to reproduce on paper, and about all that can be said is that the raft ducks make various modifications of the word "pritt," if it can be called a word; that the widgeons whistle, the geese honk, and the mallards and black-ducks quack. Jesse had a curious way of calling the shoal-water ducks by uttering in rapid succession the word "Kek-kekkek, kek-kek-kek-kek;" and he seemed to attract them as well as the patent duck-call which I had purchased in the gun store for a dollar. For black-ducks, however, I prefer the manufactured duck-call, and in going out for them, I cannot too strongly impress upon the reader the necessity for the utmost caution and the most careful hiding. When shooting at some small pond hole in the middle of the marshes, it is better to only use one or two decoys and to be covered entirely, except for a single opening in front, just large enough to fire through, overlooking the stools. A single tamed wild duck for this kind of sport is worth all the wooden decoys in the world, and his quack is better than Jesse's "kek" or my "squawk." Some gunners can set up the birds they have killed so as to be almost as natural as the living bird, and to deceive even the elect, but it is not an easy knack to acquire. Usually such imitation stools look so fearfully and abnormally dead, that they would drive any duck, with the fear of ghosts before his mind, out of the country. It is only the most experienced gunner that can take such liberties with the dead.

At the North, where the winters are colder than they are at Currituck, it is customary to shoot in the ice. No waters that ducks frequent are ever entirely frozen over; there are always what are called "breathing holes," where the gunner can place his stools, and which the ducks frequent for food. He dresses himself in white linen over his other clothes, so as to be as near the color of the ice as possible, and he uses a light skiff provided with iron runners underneath. This he shoves rapidly over the ice without much labor, carrying his dozen or so of stools aboard, and using an iron-pointed pole to propel himself with. He has his oars stowed under the narrow deck, so that he can row across open water, and is safe in case his skiff should break through the ice. When he has reached the open hole that he has selected, he throws out his stools and cuts a place in the ice at the edge of the hole, to hide himself and his boat, piling the cakes that he takes out alongside of him, to further assist in hiding him. The decoys he uses are black-ducks and whistlers, which will stool to one another indiscriminately. He must then lie down on his back in the skiff, and no matter how cold he may be, he must not move or stir. Though his blood chills and the marrow of his bones freezes, he must bear it, for there is no telling at what instant the birds may dart down upon him from the heavens, as they have a way of doing without giving the sportsman the least warning. Shooting in the ice has sent many a healthy man to a consumptive's grave.

In closing this article, let me give a final bit of wisdom in the words of William Foster. It is well known to every wild-fowler, but his way of putting it covers in a few words the whole ground: "Remember, that as a general rule, the shoal-water ducks go with the shoal-water ducks, and the diving ducks go with the diving ducks, so they will pretty well stool in the same way. Each prefers his own kind a little the best, I think, but not enough to make a decided difference, provided the stools are of the same class. Widgeon like widgeon, and canvas-backs will only stool to canvas-backs or red-heads, but broad-bills will come to canvas-back stools almost as well as they will come to broad-bill stools. Black-ducks prefer black-duck stools, but sprigtails and mallards will come to black-duck stools nearly as readily as they will to their own. Don't, however, use canvas-back stools for black-ducks, nor, above all, black-duck stools for canvas-backs."

PART II.

GAME WATER BIRDS.

CHAPTER I.

GAME AND ITS PROTECTION.

By the ancient law of 1 and 2 William IV., chap. 32, under the designation of game, were included "hares, pheasants, partridges, grouse, heath or moor game, black game, and bustards."

Hunting and hawking date back to the earliest days of knight-errantry, when parties of cavaliers and ladies fair, mounted on their mettlesome steeds caparisoned with all the skill of the cunning artificers of those days, pursued certain birds of the air with the falcon, and followed the royal stag through the well preserved and extensive forests with packs of hounds. The term game, therefore, had an early significance and positive application, but was confined to the creatures pursued in one or the other of these two modes.

The gun was first used for the shooting of feathered game in the early part of the eighteenth century; it soon became the favorite implement of the sportsman, and was brought into use, not only against the birds, but the beasts, of game. The huntsman no longer depends upon his brave dog and cloth-yard shaft, but upon his own powers of endurance and of marksmanship. Instead of watching the savage falcon strike his prey far up in the heavens, he follows his high-bred setters, till their wonderful natural instinct betrays to him the presence of the game.

Where he once rode after the yelping pack, sounding the merry notes of his bugle horn, he now climbs and crawls laboriously, until he brings the wary stag within range of the deadly rifle. No more brilliant parties of lovely dames and gallant men, chatting merrily on the incidents of the day, ride gaily decked steeds; no more the luxury of the beautiful faces and pleasant companionship of the gentler sex is to be enjoyed; the ladies of modern times— except in England, where they occasionally follow foxes, which are rather vermin than game – preferring the excitement of ball-room flirtations to outdoor sports and pleasures, take no part in the pursuits of the chase.

Together with the change in the mode of capturing game, comes a necessity for a change in its former restricted meaning. Who would think of not including among game birds, the gamest of them all—the magnificent woodcock; nor the stylish English snipe, nor even possibly the brave little quail —unless he can be scientifically proved to be a partridge—which is at least doubtful! Migratory birds were not included in the sacred list, and the quail in England, as the woodcock and snipe of both

England and America, are migratory, although the mere temporary character of their residence does not, in our view, at all alter the nature of their claims. The larger European woodcock is by no means so delicious or highly flavored a bird as our yellow-breasted, round-eyed beauty, and is much scarcer; while the foreign quail, on the other hand, is smaller than ours, and in southern Europe is found in vast flocks; but both are entitled to high rank among modern sportsmen.

The term Game Birds, therefore, should be, and has been by general consent, greatly extended in its application, and applied to all the numerous species which, whether migratory or not, are killed not alone for the market, but for sport; and which are followed on the stubble fields, in brown November, with the strong-limbed and keen-nosed setter, or shot from blind in scorching August; slain from battery in freezing December, or chased in a boat, or misled by decoys. All wild birds that furnish sport as well as profit are therefore game; and the gentle dowitchers along our sea-coast, lured to the deceitful stools, are as much entitled to the name as the stately ruffed grouse of our wild woods, or the royal turkey of the far west.

To constitute a legitimate object of true sport, the bird must be habitually shot on the wing, and the greater the skill required in its capture, the higher its rank. The turkey, therefore, although frequently killed on the wing, is more a game bird by sufferance than by right, and partly from his gastronomic as well as from his other qualities. Under this classification, then, we must include, not merely the ruffed and pinnated grouse, which, although the only species in our country coming within the ancient definition, furnish far less sport than many other varieties, but woodcock, snipe, quail, geese, ducks, bay birds, plover, and rail; without regard to the fact that all, except the quail, are migratory, and most were unknown to our British ancestry. It has been even supposed that the quail, in parts of our country free from deep rivers and impassable barriers, are also in a measure migratory; but this has no other foundation than their habit of wandering from place to place in search of food, and collecting late in the season, as they will do where they are numerous and undisturbed in large packs.

To the protection of this vast variety of game it is the sportsman's duty to address himself, in spite of the opposition of the market-man and restaurateur, the mean-spirited poaching of the pot-hunter, and the lukewarmness of the farmer. The latter can be enlisted in the cause; he has indirectly the objects of the sportsman at heart; and with proper enlightenment will assist, not merely to preserve his fields from ruthless injury, but to save from destruction his friends the song-birds.

As the true sportsman turns his attention only to legitimate sport, destroying those birds that are but little if at all useful to the farmer; and as at the same time, out of gratitude for the kindness with which the latter generally receives him, he is careful never to invade the high grass or the ripening grain—so also, from his innate love of nature, and of everything that makes nature more beautiful, he spares and defends the warblers of the woods and the innocent worm-devourers that stand guardian over the trees and crops. The smaller birds destroy immense numbers of worms; cedar-birds have been known to eat hundreds of caterpillars, and in this city have cleared the public squares in a morning's visit of the disgusting measuring-worms, that were hanging by thousands pendent from the branches. And who has not heard the "woodpecker tapping" all day long in pursuit of his prey?

With the barbarous and senseless destruction of our small birds, the ravages of the worms have augmented, until we hear from all the densely-settled portions of the country loud complaints of their attacks. Peach-trees perish; cherries are no longer the beautiful fruit they once were; apples are disfigured, and plums have almost ceased to exist. Worms appear upon every vegetable thing; the borers dig their way beneath the bark of the trunk and cut long alleys through the wood; weevils pierce the grain and eat out its pith; the leaf-eaters of various sorts punch out the delicate membrane by individual effort; or collecting in bodies, throw their nets, like a spider-web, over the branches, and by combined attacks deliberately devour every leaf. While these species are at work openly and in full sight, others are at the roots digging and destroying and multiplying; until the tree that at first gave evidence of hardiness and promise of long utility to man, pauses in its growth, becomes delicate, fades, and finally dies.

The destruction of these vermicular pests is a question of life or death to the farmer. He may attempt it either with his own labor, by tarring his trees, fastening obstructions on the trunks, or by killing individuals; or he may have it done for him, free of expense, by innumerable flocks of the denizens of the air. The increase of worms must be stopped; the means of doing so is a question of serious public concern, and none have yet been invented so effectual as the natural course—the restoration of the equipoise of nature. It is true that the robin, as we call him, now and then steals a cherry, and has been blamed as though he were nothing more than a cherry-thief; but surely we can spare him a little fruit for his dessert, when we remember that his meal has been composed mainly of the deadly enemies of that very fruit! Swallows are accused of breeding lice, which, if true, would not be a serious charge, considering that their nests are generally in the loftiest and least accessible corner they can find; but when we consider how many millions of noxious flies and poisonous mosquitoes they destroy, how they hover over the swamps and meadows for this especial purpose, and how much annoyance their labors save to human kind, we owe them gratitude instead of abuse.

Every tribe of birds has its allotted part to play; and if destroyed, not only will its pleasant songs and bright feathers, gleaming amid the green leaves, be missed, but some species of bug or insect, some disgusting caterpillar or injurious fly, will escape well merited destruction, and increasingly visit upon man the punishment of his cruelty and folly.

The beautiful blue-birds, the numerous woodpeckers, the tiny wrens, the graceful swallows and noisy martins, are sacred to the sportsman, and constitute one great division of the creatures that he desires to protect. It is true that enthusiastic foreigners, with cast-iron guns, are seen peering into trees and lurking through the woods, proud of a dirty bag half filled with robins, thrushes, and woodpeckers; but let no ignorant reader confound such persons with sportsmen. Their satisfaction in slaying one beautiful little warbler, as full of melody as it is bare of meat, with a deadly charge of No. 4 shot; or in chasing from tree to tree the agile red squirrel, who, with bushy tail erect, leaps from one limb to another, emulating the very birds themselves with his agility, is as unsportsmanlike as to kill a cheeping quail, that, struggling from the thick weeds in September before the pointer's nose, with feeble wings, skirts the low brush; or to murder the brooding woodcock, that flutters up before the dog in June, and, with holy maternal instinct, endeavours to lead the pursuer from her infant brood.

From such acts the veritable sportsman turns with horror; they are cruelty—the slaughter of what is useless for food, or what, by its death, will produce misery to others; and no persons in the community have done more to repress this wantonness of destruction than the Sportsmen's Clubs. It was at their request that the killing of song-birds was prohibited altogether; and they are the most earnest to restrict the times of lawful sport to such periods as will not, by any possibility, permit its being followed during the season of incubation.

Not alone by obtaining the passage of appropriate laws and their vigorous enforcement, have these clubs effected a great reform; but by their personal example and social influence, often, too, at considerable loss to themselves. For while the poacher, taking the chance of a legal conviction as an accident of business, and but a slight reduction of his unlawful profits, anticipates the appointed time, true sportsmen, restrained by a feeling of honor and self-respect, although they know that the birds are being killed daily in defiance of the statute, wait till the lawful day arrives, and thus often, especially in woodcock shooting, sacrifice their entire season's sport for a principle.

This honorable spirit, if encouraged and extended, is the best protection for song-birds and game that can be had. The laws are only necessary to deter those who are dead to honor and decency, and to fix the proper times—which ought to be uniform throughout our entire country. But to enforce them requires the assistance of public opinion. Every encouragement should be given to sportsmen's associations. The absurd prejudice that has originated from confounding them with a very different class of the community should be overcome, and their efforts to have good laws passed, and to make them effectual, should be sustained. The vulgar idea, that confounds laws for the protection of the wild creatures of wood, meadow, lake, and stream, with the monstrous game-laws of olden time—that made killing a hare more criminal than killing a man— should be corrected.

In this country, where every man is expected to be a sort of volunteer-policeman, all should unite in enforcing the laws; and then, in spite of the irrepressible obstinacy of the German enthusiast, and the mean cunning of the sneaking poacher, our cities would soon be rid of the disgusting worms that make their trees hideous, our farms protected from the devastations of the curculio, the weevil, the borer, and the army-worm; the country would once more be populated with its native feathered game, and our fields would resound with the glad songs of the little birds that there build their homes.

So long as the ignorant of our *nouveaux riches*, imagining themselves to be epicures, will pay for unseasonable game an extravagant price, so long will unscrupulous market-men purchase, and loafing, disreputable, tavern-haunting poachers shoot or otherwise kill their prey. It must be made a disgrace, and if necessary punished as a crime, for any modern Lucullus to insult his guests by presenting to them game out of season; and eating-house keepers should not only be taught—by persistent espionage, if necessary—that illegal profits will not equal legal punishments; but their customers should also discourage, by withdrawing their patronage, conduct that is so injurious to the public interests. Woodcock would not be shot in spring, nor quail in summer, unless the demand for them were sufficiently great to pay both the expense of capture and the danger of exposure; and, with a diminution of purchasers, will be an increased diminution of the number of birds improperly killed.

Birds and fish, except in their proper seasons, are always tasteless, and often unhealthy food. A setting quail or a spawning trout is absolutely unfit to eat, and to do without them is no sacrifice; but for the sportsman to restrain his ardor as the close-time draws towards an end, and when others less scrupulous are filling their bags daily, or when in the wilder sections of country there is no one to complain or object, requires the heroism of self-denial. Nevertheless, the effect of example should not be forgotten, and the duty of the true sportsman is clear and unmistakable: he must abide by the law; or, where there is no law, must govern himself by analogous rules.

In the wilderness, it is true, where birds are abundant to excess, he may without blame supply his pot with cheeping grouse or wood-duck flappers, if he can offer hunger as an excuse; but not even there, unless driven by extremity, can he slay the parent of a brood that will starve without parental care. In the settled regions, no matter how great the provocation, the true sportsman will never forget the chivalric motto, *noblesse oblige.*

The close-times of the present statutes are not altogether correct; and in so extensive a locality as the United States, where diverse interests are to be considered, it is nearly impracticable to make the laws perfect. For instance, where quail are abundant, as in the South, there is no objection to killing them during the entire month of January; but, as at that period they are often lean and tough, and have to contend, in the Northern States, against dangers of the elements and rapacious vermin, with not too favorable a chance for life—it is undesirable, where they are in the least scarce, to continue the pursuit after December.

If it were possible to make a uniform law for the entire Union, and to enforce it everywhere, English snipe and ducks should not be killed at all during the spring. The latter at the time of their flight northward are poor and fishy; but if they can be slain in New Jersey, it is hardly worth while to protect them in New York. For every duck or snipe that passes towards the hatching-grounds of British America in the early part of the year, four or five return in the fall and winter. Could proper protection, therefore, be enforced, the sport in the latter season would be four times as great as in the former.

As matters stand, however, the seasons for killing game birds should be: For woodcock, from July fourth to December thirty-first; for ruffed and pinnated grouse, from September first—and quail from November first—to the same period, both days inclusive; for wood-duck from August first till they migrate southward. It is desirable to fix upon anniversaries or days that are easily remembered. Woodcock are often young and weak in early summer, and the three days gained between the first and the fourth of July are quite an advantage. Although the first brood of quail may be fully grown in October, a vast number of the birds are too small, and the brush is too dense and thick before the first of the ensuing month; whereas it is simply monstrous to slay pinnated grouse, put up by the panting, overheated pointer from the high grass of the western prairie, in the month of August, ere they can half fly. But the migratory birds of the coast—the waterfowl and snipe, the waders and plovers—may continue to be shot when they can be found, till their rapidly diminishing numbers shall compel a more sensible and considerate treatment.

The bay-snipe lead the advancing army of the game birds that have sought the cool and secluded marshes of Hudson's Bay and the Northern Ocean to raise their young, and are hastening south from approaching cold and darkness to more congenial climes. Next come the beautiful wood-duck, and, almost simultaneously, the English snipe; then the swift but diminutive teal; after him the broad-bill or the blue-bill of the west; and then a host of other ducks, till the hardy canvas-backs and geese bring up the rear. From July, when the yellow-legs and dowitchers abound; throughout August, in which month the larger bay-birds are continuously streaming by; during September, when the English snipe are on the meadows and the wood-ducks in the lily-pad marshes of the fresh-water lakes; in October, when the teal and blue-bills are abundant in the great west; all through the fall and into winter, when the geese and canvas-backs arrive, the bayman finds his sport in perfection.

Many of the upland birds are disappearing; the quail is being killed with merciless energy, and his loved haunts of dense brush are cleared away from year to year; the woodcock can hardly rest in peace long enough to rear her young, and finds many of her favorite secluded spots drained by the enterprising farmer; the ruffed grouse disappears with the receding forest, and the prairie chicken with the cultivation of the open land. But although innumerable ducks, snipe, and plovers are killed every season, and by unjustifiable measures are driven from certain localities, their vast flights throughout the whole country—amounting to myriads in the west—are apparently as innumerable as ever.

From the first of August to the last of December they stretch athwart the sky from the Atlantic to the Pacific; and although in localities they may appear scarce, still constitute countless hosts. Were it possible to stand on some peak of the Rocky Mountains, and take in at a glance the vast stretch of heavens from ocean to ocean, with the moving myriads of migratory flocks, the mind would be astonished; and it would seem impossible ever to reduce their numbers. This is to a certain degree true; for so long as the lagoons of the South shall remain undisturbed, and the shores of the bays and rivers unoccupied to any great extent, this abundance of the migratory birds will continue.

But who can tell how long this will last? The methods of destruction are being perfected, the number of destroyers is increasing, until now the reverberation of the fowling piece accompanies the water-fowl from the rocky shores of Maine to the sandy coasts of North Carolina with the unceasing roar of threatened death. Twenty years ago, and "batteries," as they are called, the sunken floats which are the most fatal ambushes of the gunner, were almost unknown south of Havre de Grace; now they are so abundant throughout the waters of North Carolina that the migratory bird is never out of ear-shot of them during his entire journey.

It would be better for the permanence of wild-fowl shooting never to use batteries where fair sport can be obtained from points or blinds. Ducks, geese, and, above all, swans have great faith in the sharpness of their eyes and the acuteness of their noses. Dangers that they can see they are rather tempted to scorn. They learn to shun points where man may conceal his murderous propensities, and are not to be inveigled by the apparent security of the deceitful likenesses of themselves which are innocently nestling near by. They seek the safety of the open water, and feed in the narrow bays and marsh-encompassed ponds during moonlight nights, if they belong to the tribes that are compelled to gain their living by grubbing at the bottom, with heads down and tails up. And no matter how they are harried in certain places, they feel safe in others close at hand. But the battery, sunken to a level with the water and hidden by the stand of decoys around it, placed on their favorite feeding grounds and in the broad bosom of the open bays, is too much for their courage or sagacity. To see a man, a merciless and murderous mortal, arise in all his horrid aspect from the depths of the sea, from the middle of a body of their fellows, is a terror that custom never stales. After a few such experiences, they lose faith in themselves, and, if possible, take flight to safer and more propitious realms.

To those who are accustomed to it, there is no more delightful method of shooting than from a battery, but a novice will find much trouble in becoming accustomed to the confined position and the awkwardness of motion. I remember, years ago, hearing Mr. Dominy, who then kept the famous sporting hostelry at Fire Island, say that if he was to shoot on a wager for his life, he would prefer to shoot from a battery rather than in any other way. To one not used to the narrow box and constrained position, lying on one's back does not seem to be the most cheerful manner of killing any species of game. There is everything in habit, and certainly the exhilaration of watching the approach of the birds as they come nearer and nearer, and grow larger and larger, from mere specks on the horizon to the size of broad-bills, canvas-backs, or perhaps brant or geese, is hardly to be surpassed by any kind of sport. In most of the Southern waters the destructive nature of these machines is so well recognized, that non-residents are not permitted to use them, and the natives keep this method of wild-fowling to themselves.

The shooter lies on his back in this modified coffin, and whenever a flock approaches he rises to a sitting posture and fires. He cannot leave his floating home, and is unable to retrieve his ducks without the aid of an assistant. There have been many accidents arising from carelessness or inexperience, not merely in the use of the machine itself, but from the fault of the tender; and so many guns have blown holes in the bottom of the box, that it is the habit of the gunners on the south side of Long Island always to warn green hands, and instruct them how to rest and hold their guns. In two instances within my own knowledge, the sailing boat that accompanies the shooter, and serves as his tender and protector, was unable to return to him. In one case it was driven to leeward, and could not work back to windward, and in the other it went aground on a falling tide just before dark, when the thermometer ranged but little above zero. In both cases the sportsmen were saved, but in both the hand of death grazed them closely.

Night shooting is a still more deleterious practice. Wild fowl must be allowed to rest at night; indeed, the same might be said of most other animals, including the human family. If they are not, they will inevitably wend their way elsewhere. The discharge of one shot at night, with its accompaniment of flame, and its noise reverberating more horribly in the still and silent hours, will do more to frighten away the marsh ducks than any amount of daylight shooting. As the night begins to fall, the fowl begin to seek the marshes. They rise from the open water where they have been resting, perhaps without being able to feed at all, and move towards the shore, coming on in a steady unbroken flight, until they have all found nesting and feeding grounds in the shoal water. Drive them from such places in the night, and there will be no shooting during the day.

The use of pivot-guns is another reprehensible practice that has been so earnestly condemned, even among market-gunners, that it has been in a great measure abandoned. Still, however, in some quiet bay of one of the great lakes of the West, where there is no one to observe the iniquity, or of a moonlight night on the Chesapeake, the poaching murderer, sculling his boat down upon an unsuspicious flock crowded together and feeding or asleep, will discharge a pound or two of coarse shot from his diminutive cannon; and wounding hundreds, will kill scores of ducks at the one fatal discharge. The noise, however, reverberating over land and water, scatters the tidings of the guilty act far and wide;

and often brings upon the criminal detection and punishment. To avoid this the pivot-shooter will sometimes, as soon as he has fired, throw his gun overboard with a buoy attached to it, and if pursued, pretend he has used nothing but his small fowling-piece. The practice of pivot-shooting, however, has almost ceased, never having been extensively adopted; and has nothing whatever sportsmanlike about it, being a mixture of cruelty and theft.

Another mode of pursuing ducks, which is at the same time attractive, exciting, and injurious, is by the use of a sail-boat. Not only is there the excitement of the pursuit, the rushing down wind with bellying sail and hissing water—the crested waves parting at the prow and lengthening out behind in two long lines of foam—but there is the free motion and the pleasant breeze to stimulate the sportsman. This is really a delightful sport, combining the excitement of shooting with the exhilaration of sailing; but as it disturbs the flocks upon their feeding-grounds, as it gives them no rest during the noontide hours, when it appears that ducks—like all other sensible people—love to indulge in a quiet nap, it eventually drives them away; and not only makes them shy of the locality, but injures the sport of the point-shooter, who depends upon their regular flights for his success. It is not often very remunerative, but is uncommonly attractive, and is only condemned with great reluctance on proof of its injurious results.

But while sailing for ducks is wisely forbidden by the laws of New York and of most of the older States, that prohibition should not be stretched beyond the true meaning and intent of the statute. Coots, the big black sea coot of the coast and his congeners, not the little mud coot or blue peter of the fresh waters, may be ducks from a scientific point of view, but they were never intended to be included in the prohibition. These dusky gentlemen are wonderful divers, they swim under water almost as readily and rapidly as they fly above it, and seek their food at the bottom. They do not so much live on fish, in fact I have never noticed fish in their stomachs, although some authorities say that they feed on them, but they devour incredible numbers of small clams and oysters. They are not content to take the full grown bivalve, two or three of which would make a solid meal even for a voracious coot, but they invariably select the tiny fellows just starting in life, and of whom it takes a great many to furnish forth a breakfast or dinner. There is little sport in shooting these tough fellows, and no sport except in killing them from a sailboat when underway.

In this chapter on the obligations that man owes to his feathered friends, his naturalized assistants must not be forgotten. The imported sparrow, though small in himself, has done a great work for our country, and still more for our cities. We all know that gratitude is a fleeting sentiment, and looks rather to things hoped for than to those which have already been conferred, and it is somewhat the fashion to decry the bustling busy immigrant from abroad; but those who remember the condition of our streets and parks, hung full with disgusting measuring worms pendent from every tree and branch, till to pass through them was an annoyance, will not wholly forget our debt to the English sparrow. He has been, wrongfully I think, accused of driving away our native birds, but before we condemn him it will have to be shown, not only that he has done so, but in addition that he has driven away birds more useful than himself.

It is but a few years since he was first brought among us, and already have the caterpillars so thoroughly disappeared, that one is rarely seen in our streets, and the trees are allowed to bear their foliage in peace, instead of being reduced to bare boughs, as was their invariable fate in old times. The sparrow has been accused, and has been compelled to plead guilty of the crime of not eating the hairy as well as the smooth-skinned caterpillar, but it ought to be urged in mitigation, before he is condemned to condign punishment, that his adversaries do not do so either, while they are guilty of the further crime of not even eating the smooth-skinned kinds.

CHAPTER II.

GUNNERY—MUZZLE-LOADERS AND BREECH-LOADERS.

To the young sportsman, armed with the finest of implements, and trusting much to them for his success, it is a matter of mortification and surprise how well a bad gun will shoot in good hands; nevertheless, no true sportsman ever lived but, if he were able by any self-denial to scrape the means together, would purchase a valuable and necessarily expensive fowling-piece. Not only is a well made and handsomely finished gun safer and lighter than a cheap affair manufactured for the wholesale trade; not only does it ordinarily carry closer and recoil less; but it needs fewer repairs, lasts infinitely longer, and is always a matter of pride and delight to its owner.

Many guns of inferior workmanship throw shot as strongly as those turned out by the best makers—although this is not the fact in general—but greater weight has to be given to insure tolerable safety, and the locks, if not the barrels, are sure to give out in a few years; whereas the high-priced article will be as perfect at the end of a dozen years—which have accustomed its owner to its easy, rapid, and effective management—as it was in the beginning, and will endure until failing sight, wasting disease, or accumulating years, shall compel its transfer into younger hands.

Unless a man has continual practice, or is an excellent shot, it is a serious undertaking to change his gun and accustom himself to another, which, although apparently identical in weight and shape, will inevitably differ in some slight point that will be sufficient to destroy, for a time, accuracy in aim and prompt execution in cover. Some persons require months to acquire the effective use of a new gun under difficult circumstances; and in those dense thickets where so much of our shooting is done, and where it is by instinct founded upon long habit that the sportsman is enabled at all to kill his game, and where he cannot indulge in the deliberate care that more open shooting allows—this deficiency will be most painfully apparent. For such persons to purchase a new piece, is equivalent to throwing away the sport of an entire summer or fall, and when we consider that few of us can expect to average more than forty summers or falls, the loss of one-fortieth part of life's enjoyment is no trivial deprivation.

A very cheap gun is dangerous; but it is not expected that any person reading these lines will trust his life with an instrument that common sense tells him is manufactured to kill at both ends. A gun of moderate price, that is, from forty to fifty dollars, is as safe as the most expensive—the iron is not so tough, but more of it is used; but in a short time the barrels will wear away; the locks, losing their original quick spring and sharp click, will become dull and weak, till they will scarcely discharge the cap; and the stock, warping with the weather, will exhibit yawning fissures between itself and the iron lock-plates or false breech.

In lightness, however, is the great superiority of the highly wrought implement; and in hard tramping through a dense swamp of a hot July day, or deep wading in a soft snipe-meadow, or in a wearisome trudge over hill and dale after November quail, a pound will make itself felt in the additional weight of the fowling-piece, and not only so, but a light gun can be handled more readily. In open shooting, especially for the wild fowl of our bays and coasts, mere weight is a positive advantage; but in the tangled thickets, where birds flash out of sight like gleams of party-colored light, and the instantaneous use of the piece can alone secure success, a light gun is an absolute necessity.

Moreover, on certain occasions, when the barrels are exposed to an extraordinary strain, when the piece built for light charges and upland shooting is used temporarily upon the larger game of the coasts or woods, and the two and a half drachms of powder and ounce of fine shot are replaced by a dozen buckshot, or an ounce and a half of No. 3 driven by five drachms of powder—then it is pleasant to feel that the iron is of the utmost possible tenacity and the workmanship in every way faultless.

A learned dissertation on the science of gunnery is neither appropriate to the occasion nor possible to the author, and would probably prove as little entertaining as instructive to the reader. The majority of purchasers cannot form an exact opinion relative to the merits of a gun prepared with the utmost skill and ingenuity to deceive them, and must rely mainly on the word of the seller or reputation of the maker. There is something, to be sure, in the smooth working of the locks, and still more in the perfect fitting of the stock; but after all, even to the experienced sportsman, there is little difference in appearance between the Shamdamn and the purest laminated steel.

American importers have a peculiarly moral and respectable habit of vending German guns stamped with the names of English makers, and pacify their consciences with the idea that the manufactures of Germany are not inferior to those of England; but they would give more satisfaction to the public and more ease to their consciences by proving this in open contest, and establishing the reputation of the German makers, than by appropriating the names and reputations that good work has made famous. So far is this deception carried, that some houses even order from the Belgian manufacturers a certain number, nominally, of each of the leading gun-makers. It may be that there is little real difference, although on the continental guns you sometimes pay for useless ornament, money that should have been expended where it would tell, on locks and barrels; but the mode of proceeding is certainly not creditable.

In a highly finished article the locks usually work with a smooth oiliness that can be distinguished with a little practice, and are fitted with great accuracy into the stock, so that projections of wood will be left standing not thicker than a piece of blotting-paper. The barrels will be without flaw or indentation, and if looked through with the breech removed, will exhibit a perfect ring of light flowing up evenly, as they are raised or lowered. The mountings will be faultless, and the cuts in all the screw-heads will point in the same direction; the screws will work easily and yet perfectly, and the triggers and trigger-plate, which are invariably neglected in a poor gun, will be admirably finished and fitted. Examine all these particulars, but especially the last, and you can form some judgment whether the piece comes from a good maker or a spurious imitator.

The greatest attention, however, in the selection of a gun should be paid to the form of the stock and the pull of the triggers; if the former is unsuited to the shape of the purchaser, or the latter are stiff or dissimilar, the consequence will be utter failure that no amount of practice will remedy. If the purchaser's arms and neck are long, the stock may be long and crooked; but if the contrary is the case, the stock must be short and straight.

If possible, the person intending to use a gun should select it for himself; and if it does not "come up right" the first time he brings it to his eye, he should refuse it positively. He must not allow himself to be persuaded to try it again and again; for after one or two trials he will instinctively adapt his eye to its construction, and will imagine the gun suits him—an impression that the rapid flight of the first quail he endeavors to cover will dissipate. The triggers should give back at a weight of four or five pounds; the hammers of a muzzle-loader at ten or twelve, and of a breech-loader at twelve or fourteen. For the former, the best cone is what is called the inverted, where the bore is larger at the top and receives the entire flame from the cap.

The shape of the breech for the muzzle-loader formerly gave rise to much learned disquisition and many plausible theories; but, in all probability, had no influence on the shooting, which is due mainly to the form and quality of the barrels. Joe Manton founded his fame on the idea that the lines of force, if reflected from a hollow cup, like rays of light from a reflector, would be directed parallel to one another and lengthwise of the barrel; but later experiments have tended to destroy this theory. The simple fact appears to be, that powder exerts just so much force, and, as it cannot escape sideways, it must go out at the end of the barrel; and that the shape of the breech, except so far as it may affect the rapidity of ignition, has no influence whatever.

These questions, however, are being effectually disposed of by the march of events and the general diffusion of breech-loaders; to the latter, as they are not universally known or appreciated in our country —to which, by its nature and its game, they are peculiarly adapted—the writer's remarks will be mainly confined. Feeling entirely convinced, even from a short experience, of their superiority in most particulars, and their equality in all, he regards the consequence as inevitable that they will utterly supersede the old-fashioned fowling-piece; the few defects that were originally alleged to exist in them having been either removed or remedied, and the supply of ammunition for them in this country having become sufficient. They have won their way slowly into public favor against the interested opposition of gun-makers on one hand, and the ignorance and superstitious dread of change of gun-users on the other.

They are a French invention of forty years' standing, and proved their superiority long ago; but prejudice was too strong for them, as it has been for many another good thing. Their merits, nevertheless, slowly conquered opposition, convinced the intelligent, and confounded the obstinate; till at last in England—the very hot-bed of prejudice and the favorite abiding-place of antiquated ideas—there are now sold fifty breech-loaders to one muzzle-loader. As they are not universally used with us, the description of them will have to be somewhat minute, and would be better understood if the reader would take the trouble to examine one for himself.

The best and most generally adopted of the various kinds is the *Lefaucheux*, or some slight modification of it; and to that the attention will be principally directed. In this gun the breech, which in the muzzle-loader screws into the barrel, is omitted, and the barrels are open at both ends; they are fastened to the stock by a pin and joint a few inches beyond the guard. When free, the muzzle hangs down, and the breech end presents itself several inches above the stock, so that the cartridge can be readily inserted; when the barrels are pressed back into their place for firing, they are caught by a bolt that can be opened or closed by a lever lying along the under part of the stock, between the guard and the joint. The false breech is flat, solid, and heavy, and completes the barrels, taking the place and performing the duty of the breech in the muzzle-loader. The hammers have a flat surface on the striking end, and the locks are back-actioned, to avoid interfering with the other mechanism.

The pin cartridge is made of paper, shaped like a short section of the barrel, with a brass capsule on one end and open at the other; it is two or three inches long, and has a pad of thick paper beneath the capsule. In this pad a hole is punched on the inside and the percussion-cap is inserted, with a brass pin resting in it and projecting above the capsule on the outside. The percussion-cap is entirely within the cartridge-case, and the brass pin passes through a hole drilled in one side of the capsule, just large enough to admit it and exclude moisture entirely. A blow on the projecting end of the pin drives the other end into the cap, and discharges the latter. The cartridge-case is prepared already capped, and is sold in England for from thirty to fifty shillings the thousand; it may be recapped by an instrument made for the purpose with a peculiar cap, and may be used, on an average, three times.

The cartridge must be loaded as the gun would be, only by the use of a short ramrod or a special loading implement; the powder is poured in, a wad placed above it, and the shot and another wad follow. The cartridge may then be trimmed down and the end bent over, so as to retain the load securely, if it is to be carried for a considerable distance; but where the shooting is from a boat or stand, the case should be left untrimmed and of full length. A chamber is cut away in the lower part of the barrel, which corresponds exactly with the cartridge-case, so that the latter fits perfectly in it; but, if there is an interval between the end of the cartridge and the shoulder in the barrel, no injury to the charge or the shooting appears to result. A small notch is cut in the upper edge of the barrel to contain the brass pin, and allow it to project so as to receive the blow from the hammer.

When the bolt is withdrawn and the barrels are allowed to fall so as to bring the open breech fairly into view, the loaded cartridge is inserted, the barrels are sprung back to their place with a sharp snap that sends them home at once, and are ready to be discharged. To allow the cartridge to be inserted, the hammers must be drawn to half or full cock; and when the trigger is pulled, they fall upon the pin, which penetrates the cap and fires the load. The entire mechanism is so simple that it can hardly become deranged, and will last as long as the barrels. The greatest care is necessary in making the chamber that receives the cartridge of a proper shape, for if this is faulty the cartridges are apt to stick after explosion.

There is no decided improvement on the original Lefaucheux model, except in the modification of the machinery, and a convenient method of separating the barrels from the stock; and no other innovation of a like character need be particularly described. The needle-gun, which is made on a somewhat similar principle, is more curious than valuable, being both dangerous and complicated, and possesses no advantages over the other pattern. In it the cartridge has a percussion-cap so disposed at its base that it is penetrated by a needle, which is projected by a spring through a hole in the lower end of the cartridge; but the composition of the cartridge, and the manner of its insertion, are altogether different from the same in the Lefaucheux gun.

According to the arrangement of some English guns, on a plan invented by Jeffries, the lever, instead of closing forward, lies under the trigger-guard, when the barrels are closed; and provision is made for tightening the bolt, in case it wears loose by long usage. This invention permits of the use of forward-action locks, and the easy separation of the barrels from the stock, and has come into vogue in England; it is undoubtedly convenient in both these particulars, and has as yet developed no corresponding drawbacks.

Personally, the writer has always preferred British to French or Belgian guns, although chance has compelled him to own as many of the latter as the former. The English gun is made for work; even when cheaply manufactured, it will be found effective where efficiency is necessary; and it is far more beautiful to the eye of a true sportsman, with its plain blued lock-plates, and total deficiency of ornament, than the Continental weapon, covered with engraving and ornamentation, but defective in some of those minutiæ that lend nothing to its beauty, but add much to its usefulness. This is particularly the case with breech-loaders, which, if not manufactured carefully, are almost useless, and which, although originally invented in France, are at this day produced in more serviceable style—unless where the highest-priced article is obtained—in England than in the country of their origin. Great discredit was brought upon breech-loaders among us at their first introduction, in consequence of the importation of inferior articles, and they still labor under the disadvantages of that failure, although rapidly overcoming all objections.

There are a few implements that are necessary to the use of a breech-loader, which are much simpler than they at first appear. To load the cartridge is required either a short ramrod and a machine for turning over the edges of the case upon the wad, to retain it in its place, or an apparatus, also invented by Jeffries, that combines all the requisites for loading, and by the aid of which a hundred cartridges can be loaded in an hour. As the case can be used several times, and the cap, which is of a peculiar size, has to be placed in its exact position to receive the pin, a capper invented for the purpose is employed, by which the cap is inserted, and the pin pressed into it without the least difficulty; a pair of tweezers are used to withdraw the pin after a discharge, in order to free the old cap and make room for the new, and a large gimlet will be found useful for extracting any discharged caps that may happen to stick.

A cleaning-apparatus is also occasionally used, consisting of a brush at one end of a string and a small weight at the other; the weight is dropped through the open barrel and the brush drawn after it; but, as the gun may be fired ten times as often as a muzzle-loader without fouling, a plain rag and cleaning-rod will answer. Cartridge-cases, of course, cannot be obtained like powder and shot at every country store, and to obviate the danger of finding oneself, after extraordinary good-luck with a gun, without the means of firing it, it is well to carry a couple of brass cases, which can be used with a common French cap, and reloaded indefinitely almost as quickly as a muzzle-loader.

The sportsman, by the aid of these implements and a couple of scoops with handles for powder and shot, recaps the cartridges which have been discharged, loads them as he would a gun, only much more rapidly, and lays them aside for future use. In the field, he carries them in a leather case, or, which is the preferable plan, in a belt round the waist, or in his pockets, being able to store in the pockets of his vest alone at least twenty. The English sportsmen carry them loose in the pockets of their shooting-coats; but a belt is convenient and commodious, holding from thirty to fifty, and distributes the weight pleasantly. Where the shooting is to be done from a boat or stand, of course they will be kept in an ammunition-box, without having their edges turned over, as there will be nothing to loosen the wads.

The reader may naturally suppose that there is risk in carrying a number of loaded cartridges about the person; but in this he is entirely mistaken. In the first place, the difficulty of discharging a cartridge, except in the gun, is surprising; no pressure will explode the cap, and no ordinary blow, unless the cartridge is retained in a fixed position; and if one falls, the weight of the shot compels it inevitably to fall on the end: but in case these difficulties are overcome, the result is merely the discharge of a large fire-cracker.

The writer instituted a number of experiments, and having succeeded, after many trials, in setting off the cartridge, found that the powder burst the paper, but failed to drive the wad out of the case. This was tried with cartridges in all positions, horizontal and perpendicular, but produced invariably the same result, with unimportant modifications; and it was further ascertained that the fire from one would not communicate to another. So that, if a cartridge does explode accidentally, it may scorch the clothes or even burn the person slightly, but can inflict no serious injury. These remarks, however, do not apply to the brass cartridge-cases, which must be handled more carefully. The common paper-cases may therefore be carried with perfect impunity, and transported, if carefully packed, without risk.

A more curious idea—for the dread of danger from the loaded cartridge is natural—prevailed at one time, that the barrels were weakened because they were open behind, instead of being closed by the breech-screw; as if a cylinder would be rendered more cohesive by screwing another piece of metal into one end. In fact, if the breech-screw has any effect whatever upon the strength of the gun, its presence is probably an injury. The charge, it will be observed, presses against the shot on one side and the false breech on the other, and would not be retained any more securely by the addition of a breech-screw, which tends to separate instead of closing the barrel. So, also, it must be borne in mind there is no strain worth mentioning on the hinge-bolt, and no danger of the barrels blowing away with the charge; while the disposal of the metal at the false breech, and the omission of the ramrod, tends to make the gun light at the muzzle—a great advantage in snap-shooting.

There is absolutely no escape of gas at the break-off; none can escape unless the brass capsule, which closes the joint hermetically, can be driven out, and this is a sheer impossibility. The gas cannot penetrate the paper of the cartridge, and if it bursts the latter, still cannot escape except through the brass; and although the least perceptible amount may come out alongside of the pin, it is scarcely traceable, and nothing like what is lost at the percussion-cap in the common gun. These cartridges are wonderfully close, as the reader may conclude when he is informed that a loaded breech-loader, left entirely under water for fifteen minutes, was discharged as promptly as though it had never been wet; while a muzzle-loader, that had not been half so long exposed, would not go at all, and required an hour's cleaning. In fact, the breech-loader is entirely impervious to any ordinary wetting, will not fail in the worst rain, and the average number of miss-fires, in well made cartridges, is one in a thousand.

In the handling of this gun there is one peculiarity: the pins rise from the middle of the cartridge, and not at one side, like the ordinary cones, thus bringing the hammers closer together. To the beginner this may appear awkward, but is no real disadvantage. It would seem also desirable to use more powder with a breech-loader, although this is not necessary to so great an extent as it was formerly; but, on the other hand, the weight at the breech appears either to diminish the recoil or reduce its effects on the shooter; as the testimony of persons using breech-loaders is unanimous that the recoil is less perceptible than with muzzle-loaders, although the scales have refused to verify their impression.

One immense advantage of the breech-loader is its safety in loading, especially in a confined position, as on a boat or in a battery. Whereas, in the muzzle-loader, immediately after the discharge, while the smoke is still pouring from the barrel, and while the fire may be smouldering invisible below, the sportsman deliberately pours in a fresh charge of powder, holding his hand and the entire flask over the muzzle, endangering his life, and incurring injury far more frequently than most persons suppose; with the breech-loader, the barrels are opened and fall into such a position that no discharge can take place, and never point towards the person of their owner.

Several of the writer's friends have been maimed for life by the premature discharge of a load in the muzzle-loader from a spark remaining in the barrel; the risk connected with it has always seemed very great; and even with the patent flasks, which are hardly practical inventions, more or less unavoidable. This danger is entirely obviated by the breech-loader, which cannot go off until the barrels are restored to position after the charges are inserted; cannot leave hidden sparks to imperil the owner's life or limb; never expose the hand over the loaded barrel, that may have been left at half-cock, if the sportsman is liable to thoughtlessness or over-excitement; and which can be loaded without difficulty in the most confined position. So, not only do we have rapidity, but entire safety in loading.

GATES OF ST. AUGUSTINE, FLORIDA.

The objections, however, urged against breech-loaders have not been few, and, if well founded, forbid the use of the gun; if, as has been said, the target is not so good, nor the shot sent with as much force, the requisites of a first-class sporting implement are wanting. These charges, freely advanced, have been sustained in a measure by the wretched performance of poor guns, but were early been brought to the only true test—actual experience, under equal conditions; and by this test have been so utterly annihilated that their discussion is only necessary on account of popular ignorance of the experiments. When breech-loaders first came prominently before the English public, their supposed merits and demerits were discussed in the sporting papers in an animated and violent manner; and in order to settle the questions at issue, the editor of the London *Field* determined to have an open trial, where the breech-loaders and muzzle-loaders could be fairly matched against one another. The contests took place in 1858 and 1859, and being carefully conducted, settled the dispute for the time being, and, even before the latest improvements, established more fully the superiority of the breech-loader. The best guns and gun-makers of England were represented; and in spite of occasional variation and accidental luck—as in the pattern of the first muzzle-loader—the prejudices against the modern arm were so entirely dissipated that the old-fashioned guns are at present rarely sold.

Since that trial considerable advance has been

made in the minutiæ of the manufacture; and now it is the general impression of those acquainted with the arm, that the breech-loader, with a slight additional increase of powder, shoots both stronger and closer than its rival. In the pigeon-matches, with scarcely an exception, held both in this country, of late years, as well as in Great Britain, where it is to be supposed that the best implements the country could furnish would be used, and where some of the shooting was done at thirty yards, the favorite and most successful weapons have been breech-loaders. With all allowance for the quality of the marksman, the quality of the gun that wins a match at English "blue-rocks" must unquestionably be good; and this, the universal experience of those matter-of-fact John Bulls, who test everything by success, has entirely confirmed.

A trial of guns was made in 1859, and the results were published in tabular form in *The Shot-Gun and Sporting Rifle*, by Stonehenge, p. 304. The targets were made of double bag-cap paper, 90 lbs. to the ream, circular, thirty inches in diameter, with a centre of twelve inches square, and were nailed against a smooth surface of deal boards. The centres were composed of forty thicknesses for forty yards, and twenty for sixty yards, and weighed eighteen and nine ounces respectively, with such slight variation as will always occur in brown paper. The powder was Laurence's No. 2, the shot No. 6, containing 290 pellets to the ounce, and the charges were weighed in every instance.

TABLES OF THE FIELD TRIAL.

Kind of Gun.	Bore.	Length of Barrel.	Weight of Gun.	Charge of Powder.	Charge of Shot.	No. of Marks on Face of Targets.				No. of Sheets pierced.		No. of shots through 20 sheets.		Total on face of 4 targets.	Tot'l thro'gh 4 targets.	Recoil in pounds.	
		in.	lb. oz.	drs.	oz.	at 40 yds.		at 60 yds.		at 40 yds.		at 60 yds.					
Muzzle-loader	12	30	6.11	2¾	1¼	158	119	63	60	29	33	5	2	399	68	68	62
"	12	30	7.6	2¾	1¼	148	98	52	65	28	22	1	2	363	53	66	65
"	12	29½	6.8	2¾	1¼	116	120	46	40	25	24	1	1	381	55	63	64
Breech-loader	12	30	7.8	3	1¼	141	90	32	58	28	30	0	9	324	60	untested.	
"	12	30	7.2	3	1¼	108	98	60	62	24	31	2	4	3 8	61	"	
"	12	30	7.0	3	1¼	132	93	55	38	26	33	2	3	318	64	70	68
Muzzle-loader.....	13	30	7.0	2¾	1¼	117	71	47	61	29	37	4	8	296	73	untested	
Breech-loader.....	13	29	6.10	3	1⅛	65	135	24	54	29	39	0	1	278	69	64	62
Muzzle-loader.....	13	28	6.14	2¾	1⅛	113	118	24	46	23	34	0	1	296	58	63	68
"	12	29½	6.10	2½	1 3/16	106	103	35	31	22	32	0	0	275	54	59	61
Breech-loader.....	16	30	7.4	3	1¼	95	105	50	31	20	27	2	0	281	49	untested	
"	16	28	7.4	2¾	1	73	99	22	42	30	40	0	1	236	71	64	66
"	13	28½	7.4	3	1⅛	97	95	31	20	22	26	0	0	243	49	65	61
"	12	31	7.8	3	1⅛	100	77	32	29	33	25	0	0	237	58	72	69
"	12	30	7.4	3	1⅛	88	91	37	[illegible]	[illegible]	27	2	1	247	52	76	73
"	13	28	5.4	3	1	90	87	20	29	20	31	1	0	225	52	64	68
"	14	29½	7.8	3	1⅛	60	48	31	40	25	23	0	0	179	48	74	64
Averages.....						106	97	33	43	26	30	1	1½	285	59	67	66

TABLES OF THE FIELD TRIAL.

Kind of Gun.	Bore.	Length of Barrel.	Weight of Gun.	Charge of Powder.	Charge of Shot.	No. of Marks on Face of Targets.				No. of Sheets Pierced.		No. of shots through 20 sheets.		Total on face of 4 targets.	Total through 4 targets.	Recoil in pounds.	
		in.	lb. oz.	drs.	oz.	at 40 yds.		at 60 yds.		at 40 yds.		at 60 yds.					
Muzzle loader......	15	30	6.14	2¾	1⅛	101	121	48	55	88	22	3	5	325	68	63	58
"	14	28½	6.11	2¾	1⅛	147	85	42	48	24	19	0	0	322	43	53	54
"	14	27	5.14	2½	1	130	92	80	60	25	27	2	0	31[illegible]	54	65	68
"	16	31	6.12	2½	1	122	86	86	57	27	28	2	0	301	57	64	62
"	14	29	6.0	2¾	1⅛	101	103	81	55	21	25	0	1	289	47	60	44
Breech-loader.....	15	30	6.14	3	1¼	105	106	63	26	29	33	6	1	300	69	69	76
"	15	29	6.8	3	1¼	129	57	45	52	20	28	0	3	283	51	64	60
Muzzle-loader.....	11	29	6.4	2¾	1⅛	99	99	34	42	32	27	0	8	274	67	68	74
Breech-loader	15	30	7.0	3	1	77	100	41	31	33	26	5	0	249	64	71	73
Muzzle-loader	14	30	7.0	2¾	1	71	92	52	27	20	29	0	0	242	49	69	64
"	15	30½	6.8	2¾	1⅛	83	55	44	24	28	29	5	0	206	62	68	67
Breech-loader	15	28	6.4	2¾	1⅛	83	101	34	7	18	28	0	0	225	46	68	72
Averages......						104	92	42	40	26	27	2	1½	277	56	65	64

The guns were classified according to their weight. The breech-loaders, which used one quarter of a drachm more powder, showed about an equal recoil; the recoil differed surprisingly, ranging from 44 to 76 lbs., and was no indication of the power with which the shot was driven—a greater number of sheets being pierced where the recoil was under the average. The patterns produced by the muzzle-loaders varied from those of the breech-loaders less than they did from one another, and far less than that of one barrel differed from that of the other; in fact, the right-hand barrel seems to have shot much the best, and some of the guns that excelled at 40 yards fell far behindhand at 60 yards.

In penetration, which is a more valuable quality in a gun than even pattern, the breech-loaders took the lead; one pierced through 40 sheets and another through 39 sheets, so that the vaunted superiority of the old gun in this particular was found not to exist. It was further noted that a great improvement in this particular had taken place in the breech-loaders since the trial of the year previous, which improvement has been going on steadily since. The trial also proved that, although the breech-loaders required an extra amount of powder to give them force, it caused in them no additional recoil, and was objectionable in so far only as it entailed extra expense and weight of ammunition. The muzzle-loader was left, to offset its numerous inferiorities, nothing more than a claim to diminished weight of gun and ammunition, and a trifling saving in expense; in force and pattern it was equalled; in safety and handiness it was far surpassed by its competitor.

These trials were continued afterwards, but none were or could be more conclusive than the first which I have given, and there is no need of troubling the reader with them. Indeed, it would almost seem unnecessary to give time and space to the consideration of the superiorities of breech-loaders over muzzle-loaders at this day, so universally are the former accepted in the better informed localities, but in so extensive a country as ours, there are parts which are late to learn and hard to be convinced. To-day, while the muzzle-loader has nearly disappeared from the Northern and Eastern States, it still holds its own in the South and far West, and there are at present as many of them in service throughout the length and breadth of our land, as there are of breech-loaders.

One change that was early made in the cartridges was to do away with the pin and substitute a central fire, and so much was this change admired, that pin-fire guns have almost gone out of use. Nevertheless, I have never been convinced that this was any improvement, and believe, that if the pin-fire gun had come into general use before it was introduced, it would not have been accepted. However, admitted facts cannot be ignored, and to-day the pin-fire system has been almost as fully and far less intelligently relegated to the past, as the muzzle-loader itself. I am also no admirer of the snap-action, which has to a certain extent been substituted for the lever, on the ground that, while the lever never gets out of order, the spring of the snap often breaks. I may say, that no guns could have been more severely tried than mine that were manufactured by *Lefaucheux*, one of which was the second that was ever permanently used in this country, and that they have never given out in their working parts, while the oldest and most hardly used has never given out at all, although shot in all weathers and under very trying circumstances.

Indeed I go farther and insist that there have been no important improvements made in breech-loaders since the original *Lefaucheux* pattern until the introduction of the hammerless guns. These are still imperfect, but they will probably be soon perfected, so that the last serious danger from a breech-loader will be removed, that of premature discharge in the field. Were it not for this discovery, it is my belief that sportsmen would yet give up the central-fire, and return to the pin-fire, there being no advantages in a central fire, while there are several disadvantages. The principal of these consists in the fact that no one can tell whether it is loaded or not, and a secondary danger lies in the loading of the cartridges, which has already cost several lives. As yet, however, the hammerless gun is not entirely safe. It is thrown back to full cock in opening, and when closed with a hard snap it will sometimes jar off. This happens very rarely, but often enough to make the gun dangerous.

It will foul about the working parts of the breech when it is used hard without cleaning, so that the springs will not act, and a premature discharge may follow, and it sometimes catches on the edge of the bent in the tumbler without slipping into it. As soon as these defects are absolutely remedied, the graceful and convenient hammerless gun will take the place of all others. I know very well it is claimed that these, and all other defects have been removed by the introduction of the safety block, which interposes before the tumbler, and thus between the strikers and the cap, and I do not intend to enter into an argument which would lead to no practical result. There are men ever ready to take certain risks in order to be ahead of their fellows. Let such disregard the advice, which common sense suggests, and make experiments, from which they cannot be dissuaded, and by which others may profit. I would, however, say that I am sustained in my objections by so high an authority, as "Stonehenge," but am willing to admit that even as they are, I think a hammerless gun is safer than a central fire, for they avoid one of the greatest risks which the sportsman runs, that of the trigger catching on a twig as he is going through the bushes. Those who have used them sufficiently to get accustomed to them, say that they can shoot better with them than with the old gun, a fact which they attribute to the absence of the hammers.

CHAPTER III.

BAY-SNIPE SHOOTING.

THE various writers on the different kinds of sport in our country have generally devoted their attention to upland shooting; to the quail, woodcock, English snipe, ruffed grouse of the hills, dales, and meadows, to the prairie-chicken of the far west, or to the larger game—the ducks, geese, and swans of our coast; and the few suggestions to be found in *Frank Forester's Field Sports*, or *Lewis's American Sportsman*, are of little assistance in discussing the mode of capture of their less fashionable and less marketable brethren called bay-snipe. I shall inevitably make mistakes and omissions. The later works on water-fowl shooting are limited to the consideration of ducks, geese, and brant, as though bay snipe belonged to the upland. But I consider them nearly as much of a water-bird as the black duck, for, like the latter, they are shot mostly at pond holes in the marshes or from sedgy points.

The birds that are shot along our shores upon the sand-bars or broad salt meadows, or even upon the adjoining fields of upland, are among sportsmen termed bay-birds or bay-snipe; and although including several distinct varieties, present a general similarity in manners and habits. They are ordinarily killed by stratagem over decoys, and not by open pursuit; different varieties frequent the same locality, so that many species will be collected in the same bag; they are for the most part, except the upland birds, tough and sedgy, and at times hardly fit for the table; and they arrive and may be killed at certain periods in vast numbers.

Although despised by the upland sportsman, who regards the use of the dog as essential to the pure exercise of his art; and by the pot-hunter, because they do not generally bring high prices in market;— to the genuine lover of nature and the gun they furnish splendid sport, requiring, if not as high a degree of skill as may be needed to cut down a quail in the dense coverts, at least as many fine qualities in the sportsman, and as thorough a knowledge of their habits as any other bird. In upland shooting the dog does the largest part of the work, and invariably deserves the credit for a super-excellent bag; and truly glorious is it to follow the dog that can make that bag, and wonderful to watch his powers;— but in bay-snipe shooting there is no trusty dog to look to, who can retrieve by his superiority his master's blunderings. The man relies upon himself, and himself alone; he it is that must, with quick observant eye, catch the faint outline of the distant flock, and with sharp ear distinguish the first audible call; his experience must determine the nature of the birds, his powers of imitation bring them within gun-shot, and his skill drop them advantageously from the crowded flock. To excel in all this requires long patience, much experience, and great qualities of mind and body; and few are the sportsmen who ever deserve the compliment paid by old Paulus Enos of Quogue, when he remarked, " Colonel P. is a werry destructive man—a werry destructive man in a flock of birds."

It is true that quail-shooting is almost a certainty; and day after day of fair weather, with well-trained animals and good marksmen, will produce nearly the same average, so that an entire failure will be almost impossible; whereas, with bay-snipe everything, in the first instance, depends upon the flight; and if there are no birds, the result must be a total blank; but when the season is propitious—and this can be determined by the experienced sportsman with tolerable accuracy—the sport is prodigious, and the number of shots enormous.

Nor is it so easy to kill the gentle game that approaches the decoys with such entire confidence, and often at so moderate a pace. The upland sportsman, who can cover the quail through the thick scrub-oaks, or the woodcock in the dense foliage of the shady swamp, and send his charge after them with astonishing precision, and who will expect easy work with the bay-snipe, will find himself wonderfully bothered by their curious motions and irregular flight, till he has acquired the knack of anticipating their intentions. He will learn that their speed is irregular; that while at times they will hang almost motionless in the air, at others they will dart past at the rate of a hundred miles an hour;

that although usually flying steadily, they will frequently flirt and twist as unexpectedly as an English snipe; and that often they will either suddenly drop from before his gun and alight, or, taking the alarm, will whirl fifty feet into the air; and when one barrel has been discharged into a flock, the rest will "skiver" so as to puzzle even the best marksman. It is not enough to kill one bird with each barrel from a flock, as in quail-shooting, but a number must be selected at the moment they cross one another, so that several may be secured with each barrel; to do this will require much practice and entail many total misses, and is rarely thoroughly learned by the upland sportsman. It will not answer to follow the example of an enthusiastic French gentleman, whom I once left in the stand while I went to the house for dinner; and who, on my return, in an excited way remarked:

"Ah! I have vun beautifool shot, I make ze lovely shot; tree big birds come along—vat you call him?"

"Willet?" I suggested.

"No, no; ze big brown birds."

"Sickle-bills!"

"No, not ze seeckle-bills."

"Jacks?"

"No, no; not ze jacks."

"Marlin!"

"Yes, yes; tree big marlin come close by, right ovair ze stool; zay all fly near ze other; I am sure to kill zem, it was such beautifool shot. I take ze gun and miss zem all!"

Moreover, the excitement of a rapid flight is intense; the birds arrive much faster than the muzzle-loader can be charged, and a flock will hover round the stand, returning again and again in the most bewildering manner; as there are usually two sportsmen in each stand, and the stands are often in sight of one another, a sense of rivalry is added to the other difficulties of the position.

As the birds approach, great judgment is required in selecting the proper time to fire, both as regards the condition of the flock and their position relative to the associate sportsman; they must be allowed to come well within the reach of both, and yet be taken when they are most together, and not allowed to pass so far as to endanger the success of the second barrel. Each sportsman must invariably fire at his side of the flock, and wait till it is well abreast of him, and never either shoot over his neighbor's corner of the stand or at his portion of the birds. Nothing is so disagreeable as to have a gun discharged close to one's head, except perhaps to have it discharged at one's head; the noise and jar produce painful and dangerous effects, and unsettle a person's nerves for hours. No man who will fire by his associate without presenting his gun well before him, can know the first principles of gunnery —or who, if knowing them, wilfully disregards their effects, is a fit companion. The concussion from the explosion is exceedingly unpleasant, even if the gun is several feet off, and will produce a slight deafness.

Of the number of birds which can be bagged, it

is hardly possible to speak within bounds— more than a hundred having been killed at one shot—but probably a hundred separate shots are occasionally fired by each sportsman in the course of a day, and with the breech-loader even more. There have been times when twenty-five pounds of shot have been expended by one gun, but those days exist no longer, and it is rare to use more than five pounds where the load does not exceed an ounce and a quarter.

The uncertainty of the flight is the principal drawback to bay-snipe shooting, although experience can in a measure overcome the difficulty; but to the citizen confined to certain days, a selection of time is an impossibility. The height of the season extends from August 15th to the 25th for the bay-birds proper; and from August 28th to September 8th, for golden plover; and if a north-easterly storm should occur at this period, it will be followed by an immense flight.

Dry seasons are never good, and so long as the weather remains warm the birds will tarry in their northern latitudes; when the meadows are parched for want of rain, they become too hard for the birds to perforate, and the latter, being unable to feed, must migrate elsewhere; but when they are soft with moisture, the older snipe that have left their progeny at the far north, linger on the feeding-grounds and wait for the latter to arrive. They seem to make it a point to send back portions of their number from time to time to look after the young; and on such occasions, both the messengers and the young stool admirably. Thus flocks of old birds will frequently be seen wending their way towards the north, while the main flight is directed southward; and these flocks will invariably come to the decoys, although the main body will take no notice of them.

Of course when the meadows are too parched to furnish food, the birds cannot return on their tracks, but must continue their flight to more hospitable shores, and in this way one of the best chances for good shooting is lost. There are probably, in addition, many ease-loving gluttons among the troupe, who if they find the feeding-grounds well supplied, stop for a time to enjoy the luxury after their long abstinence in the inclement north; and in passing to and from their favorite spots, are said by the native human species to have established " a trade" to those places. These birds, of course, wherever they see a flock apparently partaking of a plentiful repast, naturally pause to obtain their share, and thus fall a prey to their appetites.

Bay-snipe fly during the day and night high up in the heavens, or close to the earth, in rain or shine, but especially during a cold north-easterly storm, which, from its direction, is favorable to their southerly migrations; and they have a vigor of wing that enables them to traverse immense distances in a short time. In proceeding with the wind, it is usually at a considerable distance from the earth; but when facing an adverse current, they keep close to the surface, and consequently are apt to be attracted by the stools. They do not move much during foggy weather, for the simple reason that they cannot see their course, but do not seem to be troubled by a rain. Although clear—that is to say, not rainy—weather is preferable on many accounts, for their pursuit, good sport is frequently had, especially on Long Island, during a rain.

Their line of flight is peculiar. Except the plover, they do not follow the entire coast, and are not found to the eastward of Massachusetts, but appear to strike directly from their northern haunts to Cape Cod, where, in the neighborhood of Barnstable, there was in former times excellent shooting; thence they proceed to Point Judith, or even somewhat to the westward of it, and then they cross Long Island Sound, rarely much to the eastward of Quogue; from Long Island they make one flight to Squan Beach, and so on along the bays and lagoons of the southern coast to the Equator, or perhaps beyond it to the Antarctic region. The plovers follow the coast more closely, and strike the easternmost end of Long Island in their career.

It is very remarkable, that these birds which generally pass northward in May, and require only three months for incubation and growth of young, live the other nine months apparently in comparative idleness at the south. This peculiarity has led to the suggestion that they may travel to the Antarctic ocean during their absence from the north—which, although probable, is as yet, from our entire ignorance of their habits, a mere suggestion.

During the northward flight in May, there is often good sport, but the time is more uncertain than in August; nor do the birds, which are old and wary, stool quite so well as on their return. In the spring they pursue the same course as in the autumnal flight; which, although it is the most direct line, and follows the principal expanse of salt meadow, necessitates considerable journeys far out at sea. But it is doubtless the fact that these birds, in consequence of their stretch and power of wing, could sustain an unbroken flight from north to south, and accomplish the distance in a wonderfully short space of time. Unabated speed of one hundred miles an hour is equivalent to twenty-four hundred miles in a day, and portions of the flock may not pause between Labrador and the swamps of Florida.

When the wind is strong and continuous from the westward, it is supposed that they pass far out to sea; and during these seasons there will be no flight of birds either at Long Island or on the Jersey coast. At such periods sportsmen often conclude that the entire race has been destroyed, till the easterly winds and soaking rains of the following year, bring them back more numerous than ever. As they must migrate, and are not to be found anywhere on the land, it is clear that they must have the power of completing their journey in one unbroken flight.

The principal varieties are the sickle-bill, jack-curlew, the marlin and ring-tailed marlin, the willet, the black-breast or bull-head, and golden plovers, the yelper, yellow-legs, robin-snipe, dowitchers, brant-bird, and kricker. The upland or grass-plover is pursued in a different manner, and the smaller birds are not pursued for sport at all.

The sickle-bills, so named after the beautiful sweeping curve of the bill, which has been known to measure eleven inches in length, are the largest of them all. They are colored much like a marlin, have a beautiful bright eye, a short reed-like call, and a steady, dignified flight. In stretch of wings they exceed three feet, and nothing can be more impressive than the approach of a large flock of these birds with wings and bills extended and legs dropped in preparation for alighting amid the stools.

They are often shy in the first instance, but as soon as one of their number is killed, they return again and again to the fatal spot—apparently in blind confidence that he must have alighted instead of fallen, or out of brotherly anxiety for his fate. I have on several occasions attracted a large flock that was hesitating whether to approach or not, and almost resolving to depart, by killing one of their number that incautiously ventured within long range—for immediately on seeing him fall, they approached, in spite of the report, with full confidence.

They are easily killed, by reason of their moderate speed and customary steadiness, although they can dart rapidly when alarmed, and will often, like all the bay-birds, carry off much shot. Their flesh is tough, very dark, and scarcely fit for the table, except perhaps when they first come on from feeding on the more dainty repasts furnished by the uplands of Labrador.

The jack-curlew is a still more wary bird, and although he comes to the stools, rarely pauses over them, and never returns after being once fired at. He is seldom seen in large flocks, and flies rapidly and steadily. His cry is longer than that of the sickle-bill, and, like it, easy to imitate. From his wariness and rarity he is regarded as the greatest prize of the sportsman, although his flesh is little better than that of the sickle-bill.

The marlin is quite common, very gentle, stools admirably, and goes in large flocks. In color it is similar to the sickle-bill, but it is much smaller and has a straight, if not slightly recurved, bill. It is attracted by the same call, and is equally tough and sedgy as food. The ring-tailed marlin differs from it entirely in color, resembling a willet—except that its wings are darker, and its tail black with a white ring—but it has the long, straight, marlin bill. It is a rare bird, seldom collects in large flocks, and is often fat and tolerable eating. It does not stool as well as its plainer brother, but from its scarcity and higher gastronomic claims, it is more highly prized.

The willet is greyish in general color, with a white belly and broad bands of black and white across its wings. It has a loud, shrill shriek, stools well, flies steadily, congregates in large flocks, and when fat is quite eatable. It often associates with marlins and sickle-bills, where its light colors make a beautiful contrast.

The last four varieties are nearly similar in size and greatly exceed the following, but are far less desirable in an epicurean point of view.

The golden plover is one of the finest birds that flies; it associates in flocks of a thousand, stools well, is extremely fat, is delicious on the table, and has a peculiarly musical whistle. It frequents the uplands, and feeds on grasshoppers. Its back is marked with a greenish red that faintly resembles gold, and gives rise to its name. The young are quite different in plumage.

The black-breast or bull-head is a shy and rather solitary bird—although it occasionally collects in large flocks—but it is quite fat, and frequently killed in the salt marshes over the stools used for the ordinary bay-birds.

The yelper has a strong, rapid, and often irregular flight, and a loud cry. It stools well, but escapes rapidly as soon as shot at, darting from side to side in a confusing way, and returns less confidently than the willet or marlin. It pursues its course generally high in the clouds, whence it will drop like a stone when coming to the stools. On Long Island it goes by the name of big yellow-legs; its call can be heard at an immense distance, and is repeated continually as it flies. Gastronomically considered, it is passable, and, when fat, really excellent.

The yellow-legs, or little yellow-legs, as it is termed on Long Island, is similar in appearance to the yelper, but has a softer and more flute-like note, and congregates in larger flocks. It stools admirably, and is killed in immense numbers. Its flight is rapid and irregular, especially when it is frightened; and, as food, it ranks with the yelper.

The brant-bird is a beautiful bird, and stools well; it rarely consorts in large flocks, and is quite acceptable on the table.

The robin-snipe is a graceful, beautiful, and delicious bird; its favorite localities are the meadow-islands of the salt bays and lagoons; its flight is steady, and it does not collect in such immense flocks as the last named variety. Its whistle consists of two clear shrill notes, by which it is readily attracted; and its predominant colors are grey on the back and red on the breast.

The dowitcher, which is considered ornithologically as the only true snipe of them all, has the habits of the sandpiper and the distinctive attributes of the *scolopax;* it is abundant, extremely gentle, and excellent eating. It stools admirably, coming to any whistle whatever; and although it can skiver when alarmed, it usually flies steadily. It associates with the smaller birds.

The kricker feeds on the meadows, remains till late in October, becomes extremely fat, and is an epicurean delicacy; it utters a creaking cry, but will not stool at all. It also flies with the smaller snipe.

Having thus mentioned the peculiar distinctive qualities and characteristics of each bird, of which a fuller description will be given in another place, we will now pass to a consideration of the best mode of their pursuit. This being by stratagem, the more thorough the deception, the more favorable will be the result; and although they can frequently be attracted by an accurate imitation of their call within reach of their destroyer, crouched in the open field and unaided by decoys, they will approach much better to the concealed sportsman and well made stools. A stand is usually erected near some pond or bar where the birds are in the habit of alighting—and this can be built in half an hour of bushes or reeds—high enough to conceal the sportsman comfortably seated in his arm-chair; and as the grass has become by the latter part of August a dull yellowish green, he may even shelter himself from the sun's rays by a brown cotton umbrella, if he be delicate or ease-loving. His clothes should assimilate to the color of the landscape, and be as cool as possible—for the temperature is often oppressively hot; and a waterproof should always be at hand in case of rain, to cover, not so much the sportsman as his gun and ammunition, which may be seriously injured by dampness and salt air combined.

If it is impracticable to build a stand, and the locality is sandy, a hole may be dug, with the excavated sand banked around it, and the sportsman may deposit himself upon his Mackintosh at the bottom. However, to one unaccustomed to the posture, it is difficult to rise and shoot from such a position, and a comfortable seat is far preferable; and besides, the mosquitoes are thicker near the earth; the breeze has less effect and the sun more.

The stools should be so placed that they can be readily seen from the line of flight, not too high above the water, and the farthest not more than thirty-five yards from the shooter. If too near a bank, they will be confounded with the grass, and be invisible even to the keen eye of the snipe. They should be scattered sufficiently to allow each one to be distinct, and must be headed in different directions, so that some may present their broadsides to every quarter of the heavens. They should tail down wind, in a measure, from the stand, as the birds, no matter what direction they come from, head up wind in order to alight, and will make a circle to do so. In this way they reach the lower end of the imitation flock first, and are led safely close to the sportsman, giving him an admirable opportunity to make his selection from their ranks.

As the tide varies according to the wind and moon, and will often cover with several feet of water places usually dry, it is well to have two sets of sticks—one set for deep water much longer than those for ordinary use; otherwise, it will occasionally be found impossible to set out the stools at all, or they will stand so high above the ground as to resemble bean-poles more than birds.

It is customary to have in the flock, which should not be less than forty, imitations of the different species—some being brown to represent marlin, others grey, with white breasts and a white and black streak over the tail to stand for willet, and so on; but a more important point is to have them large.

Small stools cannot be seen far enough to attract a yelper sailing amid the clouds, or a marlin sweeping along the distant horizon; and although it is pretty and appropriate to have them of suitable colors, size is more necessary. A sickle-bill is a large bird, and I have seen one tethered among the stools towering above them, so that the imitations looked puny by comparison, although larger than they were usually made. The word stool is derived from the Danish *stoel*, and signifies something set up on less than four legs, but of the mode or reason of its adoption we have no record; it is in universal use, to the exclusion of the more elegant and appropriate term, decoy, which is confined to imitation of wild fowl. Stools are ordinarily made of wood, and occasionally painted with great artistic care and skill; and although a rough affair, coarsely daubed, seems often to answer nearly as well, there are times when the birds, rendered wild by many hair-breadth escapes, look sharply ere they draw near, and will not approach unsightly blocks of wood, no matter how sweetly they seem to whistle.

As wooden stools take up much room and are troublesome to carry for any distance, tin ones have been made that will pack together in a small space. By heading these, different ways, they present a good view to the snipe, except when the latter are high in air, from which position they are invisible. To remedy this defect, it has been suggested that a strip of tin of the width of the body may be soldered along the upper edge; and thus, while they pack snugly, a section of the object is presented in every direction.

Wooden stools are decidedly the best, especially where it is desirable that the birds should alight, and are in general use. They are made of pine, and painted the distinctive colors of their prototypes; thus sickle-bills, marlin, and jacks, are all brown with dark spots on the back and wings; willet, as heretofore described; yellow-legs, dark mottled grey on the back and wings, and white beneath; dowitchers brown on the back and wings, and yellowish-white below; bull-head plover light on the back, with dark breasts; robin-snipe light grey on the back and side, and reddish beneath. But the snipe are not always discriminating, and a few varieties will answer every purpose.

Stools are easily made and moderate in cost, and every sportsman should have not less than twenty-five of his own, so that in case those that he finds at the country taverns for the public use are engaged, he may have some to fall back upon—although twenty-five are not a full supply. They may be carried in a bag or basket, with their feet and bills removed; and the basket will be useful to hold lunch, ammunition, or game.

Extempore representations can be made from the dead birds, although they are not quite so good as the wooden ones, by cutting a forked stick with one end much longer than the other, and thrusting the longer point into the bird's neck and the shorter one into its body. It may then be stood up in the sand,

and will make a decoy scarcely distinguishable by man from the living prototype, but apparently more unnatural to the birds—which are sometimes alarmed at its ghastly appearance—than the ordinary stools.

Very perfect stools are made of India-rubber, which, being compressible and light, can be readily transported, and are a deceptive imitation; their principal defects are their liability to injury from shot—which is also the case with wooden ones—and the facility with which the hole where their long leg is inserted becomes torn—an accident that entirely destroys their usefulness. They can be packed in a small compass, and are infinitely the best article where they are to be carried long distances. Although of necessity undersized, their full plump shape makes them visible at a considerable distance.

To prevent the bills, which are the most delicate part, from being injured, it is necessary to make them rather thicker than those of the living bird; they are to be painted dark-brown, blue, or grey, according to circumstances; and their loss, although it may not diminish the attractiveness, destroys the beauty of the fictitious flock. More important than perfection of decoys, is accuracy in whistling; this should be a perfect imitation and answer to the call of the bird, and will often allure him to the fowler without any decoys whatever. It is impossible to describe the calls on paper, and long practice will alone give a thorough knowledge of them; they are generally shrill and loud; the shriller and louder the better—for man's best efforts will rarely equal the bird's natural powers. The yelper has a clear, bold cry, and the willet a fierce shriek that can be heard for miles; and if listened to from a distance, it will be found that the bird's call can be heard twice the distance of the man's answer. It is true that when the snipe are near at hand and about alighting, a lower whistle is better, for the reason that it is more perfect, and because the cry changes to a note of welcome when the flock receives its fellows. And often, when the birds once head for the stools, if not distracted by neighboring stands, or alarmed, they will come straight on without any whistling, although this is by no means invariably the case.

Many persons find insuperable difficulty in whistling the clear, shrill, sharp calls; and for them artificial whistles have been manufactured with a hole at the lower end, which, being opened or closed by the finger, like the holes in a flute, regulates the sound. These artificial whistles are not so good as a perfectly trained natural one; the sound is not sufficiently reed-like, and they occupy and confine one hand when it should be free to seek the gun. They are suspended from the button-hole by a string, so that they can be dropped in an instant; but are only used out of necessity.

A curious one, to be held in the mouth, has been invented of a wedge-shaped piece of tin in the form of an axe-head, with two holes through the sides. The sound is regulated by the tongue, and is altogether more correct than that of any other whistle;

but more time and patience are required to learn the use of this invention than of the lips. It will be far better for the sportsman who intends to pursue this sport, to practise with the organs that nature has given him, however much time or perseverance may be necessary, and then there will be no danger of leaving his whistle at home.

As before remarked, the great drawback to the sport of shooting bay-snipe is its uncertainty; if the flight has not come on, or a westerly wind has driven the birds to sea, or a heavy north-easter carries them with it high in air and prevents their stopping—there will be no shooting; and the most experienced hand will often receive the comforting assurance which is always bestowed upon the inexperienced, that if he had only come two weeks sooner, or deferred his visit two weeks longer, he would have been sure of fine sport. There are nevertheless certain general rules that furnish a tolerable criterion; and laying aside the spring shooting, which occurs in May, and is extremely uncertain, the main flight of small birds—such as dowitchers and yellow-legs—commences about the tenth of July, and of large birds about the fifteenth of August. Each lasts about two weeks.

The flight of large birds usually terminates with a short flight of yellow-legs, and is followed by the plover, which are succeeded by the krickers. An easterly storm generally brings the birds, either by bearing them from their northern homes, or by forcing them in from the sea, where the main body is supposed to fly; and if such a storm occur at either of these periods, and be succeeded by a south-westerly wind, it will surely be followed by an abundance of the appropriate birds.

During an easterly blow they will be seen passing by Point Judith in an almost unbroken line; and after it, they abound throughout the whole length of the coast, as though they had been carried to all parts of it at once. But if no such storm occur, the catching the flight is a mere chance; and where the summer has been dry, the snipe will be scarce. If the meadows have been kept moist by continual showers, there will be a moderate supply of game the summer through; but if there has been a drought, the surface becomes too hard for the snails and insects to inhabit, or for the birds to penetrate; a scarcity of food results, and there will be no flight whatever.

Scattering birds, wandering away from their fellows and exhausted with hunger, delighted at beholding their friends apparently feeding, will be killed perhaps in numbers sufficient to make now and then a decent bag; but what is known as the "flight"—when the great army moves its vast cohorts, division after division, regiment after regiment, company after company—will not take place. How they reach the south no one can accurately tell; they either fly inland or out at sea high in the air, or late at night; but their returning myriads in the spring following, prove that in some way they did reach their southern winter homes.

Notwithstanding the greatest experience, and despite the most favorable signs, the oldest gunner will find that more or less uncertainty exists in obtaining sport, and that his unlucky expeditions generally outnumber his lucky ones. Often a flight will commence unexpectedly and without any apparent reason; and a change of weather, after a long continuance of wind from one quarter, will be followed by good shooting for some days, although such weather is not intrinsically favorable. The follower of baybirds must therefore make up his mind to disappointment, and on such occasions live on his hopes for the future, or his recollections of the past.

For this sport a heavy gun, such as is commonly employed for ducks, is not at all necessary; inasmuch as many of the birds are small and the flocks frequently scattered, it is rarely desirable to use two ounces of shot and five drachms of powder; and to fire such a charge at a solitary dowitcher, as is often done, is simply ridiculous. A light field-gun, with an ounce and a quarter of shot and three drachms and a half of powder, (or, as I prefer, an ounce of shot and three drachms of powder,) is amply sufficient—will confer more pleasure and require more skill in the use, will cut down a reasonable number from a flock, and will kill a single bird handsomely.

The gun should be kept at half-cock, and may be laid upon a bench beside the sportsman; there is always time to cock it, even if a flock is not seen till it is over the stools; and a gun at full cock in a stand, is a danger that no reasonable man will encounter.

In field-shooting, I do not approve of carrying the gun at half-cock, believing, for certain reasons unnecessary here to repeat, that it is less dangerous at full-cock; but in a stand or in a house, or in fact anywhere but in the field where it is always in the sportsman's hand, it should be never otherwise than at half-cock. It is common to pass in front of guns lying on the bench in the stand, and they often fall off, and are usually reached for by the sportsman while his eye is on the advancing flock, and does not note whether his hand grasps the barrel or the triggers; and there is an excitement, when the flight is rapid, sufficiently perilous of itself in connexion with fire-arms, without uselessly increasing it. Every precaution should therefore be taken; and if by accident the gun which cannot go off at half-cock shall be discharged in cocking or uncocking it, it will point forward, away from the stand, and in such a direction that injury to human life cannot follow.

Next in importance to care in preventing the gun's injuring a fellow-creature, is care in preventing its being injured. The least dampness, whether from fog or rain, and even the salt air alone, will rust the delicate steel and iron, and, penetrating farther and farther, make indentations that will spoil its beauty and injure its effectiveness permanently. To prevent this, oil frequently applied is the only remedy; a rag well oiled, and a bottle to replenish from, should be among the ordinary equipments, and invariably taken to the shooting-ground; the first symptom of rust or even discoloration should be removed, and every portion of the iron-work kept well lubricated. At night a waterproof covering should be used, and the charge invariably left undrawn, as the dirt prevents oxydization for a time; and during a rain the utmost care should be taken to protect, if not the entire gun, at least the locks and trigger-plate. Kerosene oil is excellent to remove rust, but is too thin to form a coating, and not so good a protection as sweet or whale oil. Varnish is highly recommended, but I have never known any one to try it; and in case no oil can be obtained, the gunners on Long Island are in the habit of shooting a small snipe, which is often extremely fat, and using its skin as an oiled rag.

Of course with a breech-loader the charge is withdrawn, and the cleaning apparatus may be forced through every evening, although this is unnecessary, as the dirt is rather a protection; and after the cleaning, whether of the muzzle-loader or breech-loader, the barrels should be well oiled both inside and out. If, however, the gun is to be left for a long time unused and exposed to salt air, a piece of greasy rag wound upon a stick may be thrust into the barrels to the bottom, and oil should be liberally applied to the exposed parts. Moreover, the locks, however well they may fit, will be injured after a while, and should be removed and examined occasionally. The size of shot used should be changed according to the season and character of the flight; in July, when the yellowlegs and dowitchers are the principal victims, No. 8 is abundantly large; but in August, when curlews, marlin, and willets are flying, all of which are able to endure severe punishment, No. 6 is preferable. Eley's cartridges are often useful with grass-plover, although they ball so frequently that the majority of sportsmen have lost faith in them.

Favorable seasons for snipe, when heavy or repeated rains have saturated the meadows, and filled every hollow with stagnant pools of dirty water, are also favorable for mosquitoes. Persons who suffer from the bites of this pestiferous insect—and the difference between individuals upon this subject is remarkable—should prepare themselves with mosquito-nets and ill-scented oils, as they would for a visit to the wild woods; while those who are much affected by the sun should bring unguents with which to temper its intensity and assuage the pain that its burning rays inflict.

Shoes are the proper things for the feet, as boots become heated and uncomfortable; and a brown linen jacket with white flannel pantaloons, thick enough to resist the attacks of a mosquito, and with the necessary underclothes for an exceptionally cold day, constitute the most practical rig.

If the sportsman use a muzzle-loader—which he should not do if he can afford to buy a breech-loader—he must have a loading-stick which he can extemporize from his cleaning-rod by substituting a ramrod head for the jag. This he does by simply having a piece of brass of the proper size and shape to screw into the place of the latter. He should also have two guns, or he loses the chance at the returning flock, which is the most exciting, as it is often the most successful shot.

The powder should be coarse; the large grain of the ducking-powder being alone fitted to withstand the deleterious effects of the moisture that is an invariable concomitant of the salt atmosphere of the ocean.

One great difficulty that the writer has encountered in preparing this work, is a proper selection of names—the natural history of our country is popularly so little understood; to copy English names and apply them to creatures bearing a faint resemblance in general coloring, though neither in habits nor scientific distinctions, was so natural to the first immigrants, and the introduction of a proper appellation is so nearly impossible, that the confusion in nomenclature of our birds, beasts, and fishes is hardly surprising. This confusion existing in every department of natural history—confounding fish of all varieties, leaving birds nameless, or giving them too many names—culminates among the bay-snipe.

Although the bony-fish or mossbunkers of New York become the menhaden of the Eastern States, and king-fish are transformed into barb in New Jersey, and perch become pickerel in the west—there are rarely more than two names, and every fish has some designation; but with bay-snipe, after an infinite multiplication of names for certain species, others are left entirely unnamed. Many that are frequently killed are without a popular designation, and more still are called frost-birds, and meadow-snipe, and beach-birds—names that might with justice be applied to the entire class, and which are so utterly confused, that persons from different sections of the country do not know what others are talking about. To make matters worse, the scientific gentlemen have stepped in, and after indulging in plenty of bad Latin, have added fresh English appellations, more unmeaning and less appropriate if possible than the common ones.

From this mass of incongruities the writer has endeavored, while preserving the best name, to select the one in general use, bearing in mind that names are mere substitutes, and not descriptive adjectives. The name frost-bird or frost-snipe—which belongs to entirely different creatures—is applicable to every bird that appears after a frost, and as nearly a hundred varieties are in this category, it is not distinctive; the names meadow-snipe and beach-bird are ridiculous, but the latter, being applied to an unimportant class, is allowed to stand. The snipe that is herein called a krieker, or, as it may be spelled, creaker, which utters a hoarse, creaking note, is called in various places meadow-snipe—although most of the bay-birds haunt the meadows; fat-bird, whereas others are equally fat; and short neck, in spite of the fact that its neck is longer than some species; while ornithologists call it pectoral sandpiper, probably because it has a breast. So also with the brant-bird, which is called on the coast of New Jersey horsefoot-snipe, because it feeds on the spawn of the horse-foot; notwithstanding that the yellow-legs and several others do the same. The name, however, is not satisfactory on account of its similarity to the brant or brent-goose; and probably the scientific designation, turnstone, if it were at all in common acceptation, would be better. It is to be hoped these names will at some day be harmonized by universal consent, and these pages will at least make mutual comprehension open the way for that desirable result. The sickle-bill, jack-curlew, marlin, willet, golden-plover, yelper, dowitcher, and kricker, are excellent; and the ring-tailed marlin, black-breast plover, yellow-legs, and robin-snipe, are at least descriptive. Were these generally accepted, a simple and tolerably accurate system of nomenclature would be obtained; and it has been my effort, while placing the preferable name at the head of the description of each variety, to collate all the other names that in any section of our vast territory are applied to the same bird. In this attempt I can only be partially successful; for the ingenuity of the American people in coining new names, added to a profound ignorance of ornithology, has produced a confusion that no one man can reduce to order.

Bay-snipe, except the plovers, krickers, and a few others, are not considered delicate eating, contracting along the salt marshes a sedgy flavor; but on the shores of the western lakes, where the fresh water appears to remove this peculiarity, the yellow-legs and yelpers—which are often found in considerable numbers, and are called by the general appellation of plovers—are almost equal in tender,

FORT MARION, ST. AUGUSTINE, FLORIDA.

juicy delicacy to the English snipe. Whether the same change is noticeable in the larger varieties, I cannot say of my own knowledge.

The gunners have an ingenious way of stringing them in bunches of a half dozen each, on the longest feathers taken from their wings, a pair of these being tied together by the feather ends, and the quillpoints thrust through the nostrils of the birds. It is desirable to put them up in small bunches, as under the warm temperature of summer they will, unless every precaution is exercised, soon become tainted. To prevent this, the entrails should also be carefully removed without disturbing the plumage; and a little salt, or, as many persons recommend, coffee, rubbed inside, and they should be at all times carefully protected from the sun. Their sedgy flavor grows stronger with every day they are kept; and being extremely oily, the least taint renders them, together with all the wild inhabitants of the coast, unfit for food.

Bay-snipe are essentially migratory, rarely stopping on our shores to build their nests and rear their young; during the spring months they pass to or beyond the coast of Labrador, and attend to the duties of maternity in the vast levels and swamps that surround Hudson's Bay, and constitute a large portion of the northern part of British North America. In my ramblings through the Provinces, I was frequently informed that they abounded during the latter part of summer on the marshes near the Bay Chaleur in New Brunswick. This must evidently have been during their return flight; but whether they were our bay-birds in their vast variety, or whether they were merely the flocks of golden plover that follow the winding of the coast and subsequently visit Nantucket and Montauk Point, I had no opportunity to determine by personal experience.

With us they make their appearance in the neighborhood of Boston Bay, and thence they are found, with various intermissions, caused by the nature of the ground, all the way to the State of Texas. The innumerable bays, sounds, and lagoons of our Southern States, inclosed by broad meadows and including thousands of marshy islands, are their favorite feeding-grounds, and are visited by them in unnumbered thousands. The larger varieties may be seen there all through the fall quietly feeding, and scarcely noticing the approach of man. In Texas they seem to congregate in vast bodies, and probably move off to or beyond the equator in the early winter months, although this has never been positively ascertained.

They are not killed as game south of Virginia, and rarely south of New Jersey; in fact, it may be said that only on Cape Cod, Long Island, and the shore line of New Jersey, are they scientifically pursued. At these places the sport has greatly diminished of late years; a few years ago Barnstable beach was a celebrated resort; and at Quogue, parties used no stools, but stationed themselves along the narrow neck that connects the beach with the main land, and fired till their guns were dirty or their ammunition exhausted. Then it was no unusual thing to expend twenty-five pounds of shot in a day, where now the sportsman that could use up five would be fortunate.

Of all the locations on this extent of meadow and beach, no place is so famous, from its natural advantages and its ancient reputation, as Quogue. Once on a time the best pond was permanently occupied by a famous Governor, a still more famous General, and a notorious Colonel—although the latter was not " in the bond ;" but there are other good stands, and for small birds—yellow-legs, dowitchers, and robin-snipe —it has no equal. Although many flocks pass it high in air, all those that follow the coast, low down to the earth, must cross the meadows that are compressed to a narrow strip at this point, which is the dividing-ground between the two great bays on the south side of Long Island.

Unfortunately, a watering-place for the summer resort of the exquisites of New York has been established in the vicinity, and the consequent advantages of comfortable beds and a good table are more than overborne by the annoyance of such companionship. If there be a flight of birds, every unfledged sportsman takes out his elegant fowling-piece, and, daintily dressed, proceeds to the meadow, where he would be comparatively harmless, and dangerous only to himself, were there room for him and his fellows. But as the ground is limited, and the favorable points few, he is sure to interfere ; and, while killing nothing himself, ruins the prospects of those who could do better. At Quogue, decoys were first used about the year 1850, and the best day's sport of late was one hundred and thirty-eight birds.

West of Quogue there are some snipe, and occasionally a good flight at South Oyster Bay, and more rarely still at Rockaway; but the large birds are not numerous north of New Jersey. Squan Beach, Barnegat, Egg Harbor, and Brigantine Beach are famous for the large birds—the sickle-bills, curlews, willets, and marlins—that visit them; the same number of shots cannot be obtained as at Quogue, but the bag is larger. At the former places there is also a flight, of greater or less extent, of dowitchers and yellow-legs, but these are not so abundant as along the margin of the Great South Bay of Long Island. On the other hand, a bag of one hundred of the larger varieties is not unusual; while at Egg Harbor the robin-snipe, which affect marshy islands are exceedingly numerous.

Twenty years ago there was good bay-snipe shooting at what is termed "Fire Island," and even in the year 1883 there was a remarkable flight late in the fall. But the cry of old George, which the gunners of "long ago" welcomed in their youth, is never heard now; George and his salutation have departed, and "Wake up, all them as is goin' sniping" is a thing of the past.

CHAPTER IV.

THE JERSEY COAST.

"*A Girl from New Jersey.*"

Why is it that every one who visits New Jersey comes away with an ecstatic impression of Jersey girls that he never can forget? Lovely they are, it is true, but not more beautiful than other fair ones of America; affable, gentle, graceful, sprightly—but these qualities are common in our angel-favored country. Yet no one that has been blessed with their company can forget them, but carries for ever in his heart the image of one, if not two or three, Jersey girls.

These reflections were suggested to the writer by the recollection of his first trip, many years ago, to the Jersey coast. The summer had been oppressively hot, and being detained in town during the fore part of August, he was glad to avail himself of the first chance to escape from the city and betake himself to the cool, invigorating breezes of the seashore. Not knowing precisely what route to follow, he trusted himself on board the train without any definite destination, and, upon inquiry, was informed that a good place for bay-shooting was at Tommy Cook's, near the coast, and about four miles from one of the last stations on the road, where, under the charge of the Quaker host, considerable comfort could be had.

To Cook's, therefore, upon reaching the station, the writer told the driver of what seemed to be a mongrel public coach, that he wanted to go; but in thoughtlessness, never conceiving that there could be two Cooks, he omitted the Tommy that should have preceded the direction. His surprise was by no means moderate to find, upon reaching his destination, the supposed Quaker host slightly inebriated, dancing a solitary hornpipe to an admiring circle. Thinking perhaps that that was the custom of Jersey Quakers—for the State is exceptional in certain things—he took a glass of bad whiskey with the jovial landlord, made proposals, much to every one's surprise, to go shooting the day following, and retired early.

Next morning a short walk dissipated all idea of finding game, and having made the discovery that he was still fifteen miles from the proper shooting-ground on the beach, he returned to the house, and in order to enjoy a few hours ere the wagon for his further transportation would be ready, joined a bathing party. It was quite a sociable affair; both sexes, dressed in their bathing clothes—the girls without shoes—crowded down in the bottom of an open wagon. But surely it is not fair to tell how one of the flannel-encased nymphs nearly fell from the wagon, and was caught in the arms of the writer, who had jumped out for the purpose; nor how the rest drove off to leave them; nor how he bore his lovely burden—plastic grace and beauty personified—bravely in pursuit; nor how his foot chanced to trip—accidentally, of course—and they fell and rolled in the sand together. If he would tell, he could not; words do not exist for the purpose.

He had, however, all he could do to explain the accident and pacify the nymph. If she had known how much of solidity there was in her loveliness, and how little of romance in the deep yielding sand, she might have more readily accepted the excuse of weariness. If the grasshopper becomes a burden under certain circumstances, why may not a naiad?

The road to the beach lay through a village formerly known by the euphonious and distinctive title of Crab Town—a village of a thousand inhabitants. It was evening ere Crab Town was reached, and just beyond, the driver came upon a bevy of female acquaintances. In a moment the suggestion was made that they should ride; after a little demur they accepted, and were crowded in. The stage was not large, but there would have been room if they had been twice as numerous; they filled every seat, and every lap besides.

There are days in one's lifetime that should be celebrated as anniversaries; and if any gentleman has carried in his arms, albeit with true tenderness, one charming Jersey girl in the morning, and has had another equally charming sit on his lap in the evening, he may look upon that day as never likely to repeat itself.

There was a hum of pleasant voices—words like, "Oh! Deb, we should not have got in;" "Why, Mary, we may as well ride—it's all in our way." "But these gentlemen are strangers, and may think it wrong of us." "Oh, Lib, don't talk that way; they know better." We assured them that nothing could be more perfectly proper. So situated, the ride appeared very short, and the next mile, which was as far as our delightful freight would go, was passed seemingly in about a minute and a half, decidedly the fastest time on record. At the end of it, on a suggestion from the driver, who lived in that section and knew the country, toll was taken of their rosy lips as passage-money. Jersey is a glorious place.

Passing Charley's, as he is generally called, the son of the old man, who for years was famous as the first hunter in that land, we turned off beyond, down the beach. The bay between the mainland and the sand-bar, known everywhere as "The Beach," was narrow, widening slowly as we advanced, until, at the end of our seven miles' journey, it was nearly three miles across. There was little vegetation beside salt grass and bay-berry bushes; but of the animal kingdom the only representatives—the mosquitoes—were thicker than the mind of man can conceive; they rose in crowds, pursuing us fiercely, covering the horses in an unbroken mass, settling upon ourselves, flying into our eyes, crawling upon our necks, stinging through our clothes, and filling the air. Although small, they were hungry beyond belief, and, following their prey relentlessly, compelled us to fight them off with bushes of bayberry for our lives.

Mosquitoes are found plentifully at our summer watering-places, and still more numerously in the wild woods, grow abundantly in Canada, and are over-plentiful at Lake Superior; but nowhere are they so merciless, fierce, and numerous, as, on occasions, at the New Jersey beach. They are a beautiful little creature, delicate, graceful, and elegant, but obtrusive in their attentions; although the ardent lover was anxious to be bitten by the same mosquito that had bitten his lady-love, that their blood might mingle in the same body.

One good effect they had, however, was to compel the driver to urge on his weary team, and leave him no time to gossip at Jakey's Tavern, over the beach party that was to be held there next day. A beach party is another delightful institution of the Jerseyites, and consists of a congregation of the youths of both sexes, especially the female, collected from the main shore, and meeting on the beach for a frolic, a dance, and a bath. As it rarely breaks up till daylight, the pleasantest intimacies are sometimes formed, and soft words uttered that could not be wrung from blushing beauty in broad day.

The establishment of the "old man"—the sporting "old man," not the political one—since he has been gathered to his forefathers, is kept up by his son-in-law, usually known by the abbreviation—Bill. It is not an elegant place; sportsmen do not demand elegance, and willingly sleep, if not in the same room, in chambers that lead into one another; but it is situated within a hundred yards of the best shooting ground, and is as well kept as any other tavern on the beach. Sportsmen do not mind waiting their turn to use the solitary wash basin, drawing water from the hogshead, or wiping on the same towel, but are thankful for good food, and the luxury of a well filled ice-house.

In addition to the general directions heretofore given, it may be well in this connexion to describe more particularly the mode of killing bay-snipe. A number of imitation birds, usually called stools, are cut from wood, and painted to resemble the various species; they have a long stick, or leg, inserted into the lower part of the body, and a sufficient number to constitute a large flock are set up in shallow water, or upon some bar where the birds are accustomed to feed. They are made from thin wood, or even from tin, and are headed various ways so as to show in all directions; the coarsest and least perfect imitations will answer.

The most remarkable trait of the shore birds, or bay-snipe, is their gregarious nature and sociability. A flock flying high in air, apparently intent upon some settled course, will, the moment they see another flock feeding, turn and join it. Their natural history, or the object which they evidently have in thus joining forces, does not seem to be understood; but the baymen, by imitation-birds and calls, take advantage of this instinct. Farther south, along the shores of Florida and Texas, these snipe collect in crowds; and either this is the first step towards that purpose, or they are merely attracted by the feeding birds to a promising place for a plentiful repast.

Although ordinarily they will come to the stools of themselves, if they happen to be at a distance flying fast and high, the gunner must trust to the shrillness of his whistle and the perfection of his call, to attract their attention. If they turn towards the decoys and answer the whistle—which they will do at an immense distance—they are almost sure to come straight on, and their confidence once gained, rarely wavers.

There is a common expression among the baymen, that birds have a trade, or are trading up and down over a certain course, by which they mean that they fly backward and forward at regular hours, and to and from regular places. Snipe that are thus engaged trading are not only in the finest condition, but come to the decoys, or stool, as it is termed, the most readily. They are probably stopping on the meadows, and fly to their feeding-grounds in the morning and back at night. The great migratory bodies, which frequently stretch in broken lines almost across the horizon, and which are pursuing their steady course to their southern homes, rarely heed the whistle, or turn to the silly flock that is eating while it should be travelling.

The best days are those with a cloudy sky, and a south-westerly wind. On such occasions the birds often come in myriads, delighting the sportsman's heart, testing his nerves, and filling his bag to repletion. When the object is to kill the greatest number possible, they are permitted to alight among the stools and collect together before the gun is fired; then the first discharge is followed rapidly by the second, which tears among their thinned ranks as they rise; and, if there be a second gun, by the third and fourth barrel, till frequently all are killed. The scientific and sportsmanlike mode is to fire before they alight, selecting two or three together and firing at the foremost.

It is a glorious thing to see a flock of marlin or willet, or perhaps the chief of all, the sickle-bills, swerve from their course away up in the heavens, and after a moment's uncertainty reply to the sportsman's deceitful call and turn towards his false copies of themselves. As they approach, the rich sienna brown of the marlin and curlew seems to color the sky and reflect a ruddy hue upon surrounding objects; or the black and white of the barred wings of the willet makes them resemble birds hewn from veined marble. The sportsman's heart leaps to his throat, as crouching down with straining eye and nerve, grasping his faithful gun, he awaits with eager anxiety the proper moment; then, rising ere they are aware of the danger, he selects the spot where their crowding bodies and jostling wings shut out the clouds beyond, and pours in his first most deadly barrel; and quickly bringing to bear the other as best he may among the now frightened creatures as they dart about, he delivers it before he has noticed how many fell to the first. Dropping back to his position of concealment, he recommences whistling, and the poor things, forgetting their fright and anxious to know why their friends alighted amid a roar like thunder, return to the fatal spot, and again give the fortunate sportsman a chance for his reloaded gun.

It was for such glorious sport as this, with fair promise of success—for the flight was on, as the saying is, when the snipe are moving—that I prepared myself the next morning. Rising at earliest daybreak, a friend, the gunner, and myself sallied out to the blind, and having set out our stools, possessed our souls in patience for what might follow. A blind is another ingenious invention of the devil—as personified by a bayman, in pursuit of wild fowl—and is constructed by planting bushes thickly in a circle round a bench. Seated upon this bench and concealed from the suspicious eyes of the snipe by the dense foliage of the bayberry bushes, the sportsman, in comparative comfort, awaits his prey. In less civilized localities he hides himself among the long sedge grass, or scoops out a hole in the sand and lies at length upon a waterproof blanket.

The wind had hauled, in nautical language, to the south'ard and west'ard, and the sun's rays driving aside the hazy clouds, illuminated the eastern sky with fiery glory. The land and water, dim with the heavy night fog, stretched out in broad, undefined outline, and the heavens seemed close down upon the earth. Through the hazy atmosphere and sluggish darkness the rays of light penetrated slowly, bringing out feature after feature of the landscape, lighting the tops of distant hills, and revealing the fleecy coursers of the sky.

Amid the fading darkness we soon heard the welcome cry of the bay-snipe pursuing his course, guided by light that had not yet reached our portion of the earth's surface. Instantly we responded with a vigor and rapidity on behalf of each, that must have impressed the travelling birds with the belief that we constituted an immense flock. Again and again, long before our straining eyes could catch the outline of their forms, came the answering cry. Our eagerness increased with the approaching sound, until from out the dim air rushed a glorious flock of marbled willet, and swooping down to our stools dropped their long legs to alight—we feeling as though little shining goddesses were descending upon us.

Without pausing to discuss their angelic character, but mercilessly bringing our double-barrels to bear upon the crowded ranks, we poured in a destructive broadside that hurled a dozen upon the bloodied sand. Startled at the fearful report and its terrible consequences, they rose, darting and crossing in their alarm, and fled at full speed; but hearing again the familiar call, after flying a few hundred yards, they turned and came once more straight for the decoys. Then my friend thought highly of me and my breech-loading gun, for ere he had reloaded I had discharged my two barrels three times, adding six birds to those already upon the sand. Eighteen willet from the first flock, and ere the sun was fairly up, gave us a good start; and after the birds were gathered, the favorable send-off was duly celebrated in a few drops of water with enough spirit to take the danger out.

And now myriads of swallows made their appearance, skimming close along the water, but in one steady course, as though they were going out for the day, and would not be back till night-fall. They were followed by scattering snipe that furnished neat but easy shooting till six o'clock, when the regular flight began with a splendid flock of marlin that came rapidly from the south'ard, and after hovering over the stools and giving us one chance, returned for two more favors from the breech-loader, and left sixteen of their number.

Sportsmen of any experience know that nothing is easier than to select from a flock a single bird with each barrel; but in bay-shooting, a man who claims to excel, must kill several with the first barrel, and one, at least, with the second. If, however, to the ordinary excitement be added the natural emulation arising from the presence of several sportsmen in the same stand, the foregoing desirable result is not always attained. If, therefore, the reader shrewdly suspects we should have killed more birds than we did, let him place himself in a similar position, and record his success.

Shore birds of the various species, beginning with the magnificent sickle-bill, and including the wary jack-curlew, the noisy, larger yellow-legs or yelper, and the smaller one, down to the pretty simple-hearted dowitcher, went to make up our morning's bag. The scorching sun when it hung high over our heads stopped the flight, and, aided by venomous mosquitoes, drove us to the shelter of the house, and turned our thoughts towards dinner.

The stands being convenient to the tavern, we had run in and snatched a hasty breakfast, but now collected to clean guns, load cartridges, and talk over results. The breech-loader being at that time something of a novelty, attracted considerable attention, and was accused of that defect popularly attributed to it, of not shooting strongly. As there were several expensive guns present—among them one of William Moore—in all of which the owners had great faith, the question was soon tested and settled to the satisfaction of the most sceptical.

That being concluded, black-breast, or bull-head plover, was the occasion of a terrible contest over the entire plover family—some of the sportsmen insisting there were three, others four or five well-known kinds. They all agreed as to there being the grass-plover, the bull-head, and the golden-plover; but some claimed in addition, the frost bird and the red-backed plover. At last one burst forth:

"There is Barnwell; he ought to know: what does he say?"

As they turned inquiringly, feeling the momentous nature of the occasion, and that now was the chance to establish my reputation for ever, with an air of deep learning, I commenced:

"In the first place, you are mistaken in including among plovers the grass or grey-plover, as it is commonly called; it is not a plover at all——"

"Oh! that is nonsense," they burst forth unanimously; "you don't know what you're talking about."

Never was a growing reputation more suddenly nipped. Instantly reduced to a state of meekness, and only too glad to save a shred of character, I mildly suggested that Giraud's work on the birds of Long Island was in my valise, and probably contained the desired information.

"Well," said one, "let's hear what he says."

So I procured the book and read as follows:

"'TRINGA BARTRAMIA—WILSON.
BARTRAM'S SANDPIPER.

Bartram's Sandpiper, Tringa Bartramia, Wil. Amer. Orn.
Totanus Bartramius Bonap. Syn.

Totanus Bartramius Bartram Tatler, Su. & Rich. Bartramian Tatler, Nutt. Man.

Bartramian Sandpiper. Totanus Bartramius Aud. Orn. Biog.'

"After giving the specific character, and a spirited account of the well-known manner of shooting them from a wagon, which is not followed with any other bird, as you well know, he proceeds as follows:

"'In Massachusetts, Rhode Island, New Jersey, and on the Shinnecock and Hempstead Plains, Long

Island, it is common, where it is known by the name of "gray," "grass," "field," or "upland" plover. It is very wary, and difficult to be approached. On the ground it has an erect and graceful gait. When alarmed it runs rapidly for a short distance before taking wing, uttering a whistling note as it rises; its flight is rapid, frequently going out of sight before alighting. It usually keeps on the open, dry grounds—feeding on grasshoppers, insects, and seeds. In the month of August it is generally in fine condition, and highly prized as game. When feeding, for greater security, this species scatter about; the instant the alarm is given, all move off. In the latter part of August it migrates southward, and, it is said, performs the journey at night. Stragglers frequently remain behind until late in September.'"

"It is evident he knew the bird," replied one of the objectors; "but as he calls it by six or seven names—the English ones being both sand-piper and tatler—he evidently did not know what it should be called."

"That is the way with naturalists," replied another; "they each give a name to a species, but in this case all agree that it is not a plover. What is the name plover derived from?"

"It comes from the French word *Pluvier*, rain-bird, because it generally flies during a rain. But naturalists found distinctions more upon the shape of bill and claws than on the habits of any species. According to them, plovers proper have no hind toe, or, at most, only a knob in its place."

"Do you know what Frank Forester says on the subject?"

Feeling my reputation rising a little, I resumed: "He confuses frost-bird and grass-plover, quoting Audubon as his authority; but he points out the distinctive peculiarity of the plover."

"If he thinks a grass-plover and a frost-bird are alike, he knows very little of his subject. Why, the frost-bird stools admirably, while the plover never stools at all."

"Not so fast! Frank Forester was a splendid writer, and upon matters with which he was familiar he was thorough. He has conferred an immense favor upon the American sporting world; but where he had not personal experience—and no one can know everything—he had to rely upon others. He has done as much to correct and elevate sportsmanship in this country, to introduce a proper vocabulary, and to enforce obedience to gentlemanly rules, as any man possibly could. As a body, we owe it to him that we are sportsmen, and not pot-hunters. Probably in some places the grass-plover is called a frost-bird."

"I have more faith in Giraud, and would like to hear what he can tell us about the golden-plover, unless he says that is a sandpiper also."

"He begins with a description of the black-bellied plover, which is known to us as bull-head, the *charadrius helveticus*, and then describes the American golden-plover, or *charadrius pluvialis*, and uses these words: 'It is better known to our gunners by the name of frost-bird, so called from being more plentiful during the early frosts of autumn, at which season it is generally in fine condition, and exceedingly well flavored.' Then follow the ring-plover, or ring-neck—*charadrius semipalmatus*, Wilson's plover; the piping-plover, or beach-bird—*charadrius melodius;* and the kildeer plover—*charadrius vociferus*, these being all the varieties of American plover."

Bill could stand it no longer; but rising as the book was closed, burst forth at once:

"Those writers are queer fellows; they put the oddest, hardest, longest names to birds that ever I heard. Who would have thought of their calling a two-penny beach-bird, a radish mellow-deuce! What I have to say is—we baymen will never learn these new-fangled names."

"That is exactly the trouble," I replied. "You baymen will, in different sections of the country, call the same bird by various names, till no one can tell what you are talking about; and the man of science has to step in and dig up a third name, usually some Latin affair, which nobody will accept. Thus it is that the older frost-birds, which, strange to say, invariably arrive before the young, are known as golden-plover, and their progeny as frost-birds."

"Speaking of the seasons," replied Bill, evasively, "have you noticed that they are changing every year? The springs are later than they used to be. In old times the English snipe arrived from the south early in March; now they hardly come till June; so, the ducks come later and stay later. The springs are colder, and the autumns warmer, than when I was young, and the bay-snipe appear in September instead of August, as it once was."

"As to the English snipe you are undoubtedly correct, but this is due probably to their increasing scarcity; and although we have no spring, and the summer extends frequently into September, this appears to result from the changes in climate effected by clearing the woods. As the forests are cut down, the cold winds of spring, and the burning suns of summer, produce a greater effect, and each in its turn lasts longer. Altogether, however, our seasons seem to be moderating."

At this interesting point in our discussion, some one discovered by the aid of a telescope that a flock of willet had settled on the sand-bank among the stools. The announcement was followed by a general seizure of weapons and rush for the blinds. My friend and myself hastened to the little boat, used in floating quietly down upon ducks, and called a "sneak box," and embarking, glided silently towards our stand. The tide had left bare a long bank of sand, upon which was collected a glorious flock, or, more properly speaking, two flocks united, one of marlin and the other of willet.

All unconscious of approaching danger, the pretty creatures were busily engaged, some in feeding, others in washing—dipping under and throwing the water over their graceful bodies—others in running actively about, or jumping up and taking short flights to dry their wings. A happy murmur ran through the flock, and so innocent and beautiful were they that we remained watching them in silent admiration, unwilling to disturb the romance of the charming scene. The rich brown feathers of the imposing marlin formed an exquisite contrast to the white and black of the elegant willet, as the different species mixed unreservedly together.

They did not exhibit the slightest alarm when our boat, after we had ceased rowing, was borne towards them by the wind, and allowed us to approach till it grounded on the flat. Having feasted our eyes on the magnificent spectacle, we at last gave the word to fire. At the report they rose wildly, and receiving the second discharge, made the best of their way to safer quarters. Both barrels of my friend's gun missed fire, and we gathered only seven birds, as the flock, although numbering at least seventy birds, was widely scattered and offered a poor mark.

No sooner were we again ensconced in our blind, than the exhilarating sport of the morning was renewed—sport such as only those who have tried it can appreciate—sport that makes the heart beat and the nerves tingle—sport that overweighs humanity and compels the remorseless slaughter of these beautiful birds. Flock after flock, seen at great distance, and watched in their approach through changing hopes and fears, or darting unexpectedly from over our heads and first noticed when rushing with extended wings down to our stools, presented their crowded ranks to our delighted gaze. From the very clouds, would come the shrill whistle of the yelper, or from the horizon, the long shriek of the willet, or nearer at hand would be heard the plaintive note of the gentle dowitcher; they appeared from all quarters, sailing low along the water or pitching directly down from out the sky.

Towards evening the flight diminished, and when the horn announced that supper was ready, the different parties met once more at the house to compare notes and relate adventures. All had met with excellent success, but our stand carried off the palm.

"Bill," commenced some unhappy person, after we had left the close, hot dining-room, "why do you not enlarge your house?"

"Bill is waiting for another wreck," was the volunteer response; "the whole coast is fed, clothed, and sheltered by the wrecks. The house is built from the remnants of unfortunate ships, as you perceive by the name-boards of the Arion, Pilgrim, Samuel Willets, J. Harthorn, and Johanna, that form so conspicuous a part of the front under the porch. When a vessel is driven ashore, and the crew and passengers who are not quite dead are disposed of by the aid of a stone in the corner of a handkerchief, which makes an unsuspicious bruise, the prize is fought for by the natives, and not only the cargo, but the very ribs and planks of the vessel appropriated."

"Now that's not fair," replied Bill, aroused; "no man, except my father-in-law, has done more to save drowning men than I have. I tell you it's an awful sight to see the poor creatures clinging to the rigging and bowsprit, to see them washed off before your eyes, sometimes close to you, without your being able to help them, and their dead bodies thrown up by the waves on the sand. You don't feel like stealing or murder at such times; and besides, I never knew a dead man come ashore that had anything in his pockets."

A peal of laughter greeted this naïve remark, together with the ready response: "Bill, you were too late; some Barnegat pirate had been before you."

"No, the Barnegat pirates are kinder than the Government. We do our best to save the poor fellows, but the Government puts men in charge of their station-houses that know nothing about their business. My father-in-law was the first man that threw a line with the cannon over a ship, and he was presented with a medal by the Humane Society. He never was paid a dollar for taking charge of the station, the life-boat, and the cannon. Since he died I kept it for five years, and was paid two years; now men are selected for their politics. One lives back on the main land two miles from his station-house, another never fired a gun, and a third never rowed a boat. The last got a crew of us together once to go out to a ship in the life-boat and undertook to steer, but we told him not one of us would go unless he stayed on shore. It is a dangerous thing to have a green hand at the helm, or even at an oar, in times like that."

"How far can you reach a ship with the cannon?" we inquired.

"The line, you know, is fastened to the ball with a short wire, so that it won't burn off, and is coiled up beside the gun, and of course it keeps the ball back, and then people forget we always have to fire against the wind, as vessels are never wrecked with the wind off shore; so although the guns are expected to carry five hundred yards, they will not carry more than one hundred and eighty. That is enough, though, if they only have the right sort of men to manage them; but how is a landsman to tell whether he must use the cannon or is safe in going off in the boat? In one case, while the station-master was trying to drag his cannon down to a ship, a party of us took a common boat and landed her crew and passengers before he arrived. I don't care about the pay, for I kept it three years without; but I hate to see lives sacrificed for politics. Would you like to see the medal they gave to the old man?"

We responded in the affirmative; and he soon produced a silver medal, with an inscription on one side recording the circumstances, and on the other an embossed picture of a ship in distress, a cannon from which the ball and rope attached had been discharged and were visible in mid air, several men standing around the gun, and a life-boat climbing the seas.

"But, Bill, tell us about the Barnegat pirates leading a lame horse with a lantern tied to his neck over the sand hills in imitation of a ship's light, and thus inveigling vessels ashore."

"I can only say I have never heard of it. As quick as a vessel comes ashore, the insurance agent is telegraphed for, and he takes charge of everything. Why, we even buy the wrecks and pay well for them, too. Now and then something is washed up like that coal in front of the house, but it is not often."

"What do you mean by the stations?"

"They are houses built by the Government and placed at regular distances along the beach. The gun, and rope, and life-boat, and life-car, and all other things that are needed in case of shipwreck, are kept in them. Then there is a stove and coal ready to make a fire, for if a poor wretch got ashore in mid-winter he would soon freeze if he couldn't get to a fire. And if the man who has charge of the station lives two miles off across a bay that he can't cross in a bad storm, what can the poor half-drowned fellows do, if they are too much benumbed to break open the door? I'd stave it in for them pretty quick if I was there, law or no law."

"It is a shame that a matter like that should not be free from politics."

"So it was once," Bill went on fluently; for on this subject he felt that his family had a right to be eloquent; "at one time some department had it in charge that never would either appoint or remove a man on political account; but that is all changed now, and the men are expected to go out with every administration, and shipwrecked passengers die while political favorites draw the two hundred dollars a year pay for the station-master."

"Now, Bill, stop your talk about the public wrongs, and tell us something more interesting. Have you ever heard one of Bill's ghost stories?" This inquiry was addressed to the public.

Bill's face lengthened; he sat silently nursing his leg and smoking his brierwood pipe, while a shadow seemed to settle on his countenance. "Come, Bill," we responded, "let's have the story."

Bill answered not, and the shadow deepened, and the smoke was puffed in heavier masses from his lips.

"Bill is afraid; he don't like ghosts, and don't dare to talk of them."

"I am not easily skeered," he answered at last; "but if you had seen what I have on this shore, you would not talk so easy about it. 'Lige, do you remember the time we saw that ship? There had been a heavy storm, and when we got up next day early, there lay a vessel on the beach; she must have been most everlastingly a harpin' it."

"What is that?" was asked wonderingly, on the utterance of this peculiar expression.

"Why, she had come clear in over the bar, and must have been going some to do that; for there she lay, bow on, with her bowsprit sticking way up ashore, just below the station yonder. Her masts were standing, and we clapped on our clothes and started for the beach. The wind was blowin' hard, and the sand and drizzle driving in our faces as we walked over, and we kept our heads down most of the time. When we got to the sand-hills we looked up, and the ship was gone. I thought that likely enough, for she must have broken up and gone to pieces soon in that surf, so we hurried along as fast as we could; and sure enough, when we rounded the point, the little cove in which she lay was full of truck. 'Lige was there, and he saw it as plain as I did. The water was full of drift-boxes, barrels, planks, and all sorts of things, pitching and rolling about; and some of them had been carried up onto the sand and were strewed about in all directions.

"It was early, and the day was misty, but we could see plain enough, and we saw all that stuff knocking about as plain as I see you now. There was a big timber in my way—a stick—well, thirty feet long and two feet or two and a half square, so that I had to raise my foot high to clear it; I stepped one leg over, and drew the other along to feel it, but it didn't touch anything; then I stopped and looked down—there was no timber there; I looked back towards the sea—the drift had disappeared, the barrels and boxes and truck of one sort or another was gone. There was nothing on shore nor in the water. Now you may laugh, but 'Lige knows whether what I've told you is true."

"Bill, that is a pretty good story, but it is not the one I meant," persisted the individual who had commenced the attack.

"Well, another time, Zeph and I were at work

getting the copper bolts out of an old wreck, when we happened to look up and saw two carriages coming along, up the beach. I spoke to Zeph about it, but as they came along slowly, we went on with our work, and when we looked up again there was only one. That came on closer and closer till I could tell the horses; they were two bays of squire Jones' down at the inlet; they drove right on towards us till they were so near that I did not like to stare the people in the face, and looked down again to my work. There were two men, and I saw them so plain that I should know 'em anywhere. Well, I raised my head a second after, and they were gone; and there never had been any wagon, for Zeph and I hunted all over the beach to find the tracks in the sand."

"I guess that was another misty day, and you hadn't had your eye-opener," was the appreciative response.

"No, it was three o'clock in the day, and bright sunshine; but at that time, as near as can be, Tommy Smith was drowned down at the inlet, and the very next day at the very same hour, the 'Squire's wagon did come up the beach, with the same two men driving, and the body in a box in the back part."

"Now, Bill," continued the persistent individual, "this is all very well, but it is not the story. Come, out with it; you know what I mean."

Bill fell silent, again looking off into the distance as though he saw something that others could not see; he pulled away nervously on his pipe, which had gone out, but answered not.

"Bill's afraid;" was the tantalizing suggestion.

"There's Sam," said Bill suddenly; "he's not afeard of man or devil; ask him what he saw."

The person referred to was a large, broad-shouldered, pleasant-faced man, with a clear blue eye that looked as though it would not quail easily, and he responded at once:

"I never saw anything; but one night when I was coming by the cove where the Johanna was cast away, and where three hundred bodies were picked up and buried, I heard a loud scream. It sounded like a woman's voice, and was repeated three or four times; but I couldn't find anything, although I spent an hour hunting among the sand-hills, and it was bright moonlight. It may have been some sort of animal, but I don't know exactly what."

"Bill's adventure happened in the same neighborhood, so let's have it," continued the persistent man.

"As Sam says," commenced Bill, at last, "the Johanna went ashore one awful north-easter in winter about six miles above here, near Old Jackey's tavern; she broke up before we could do anything for her, and three hundred men, women, and children—for she was an emigrant ship—were washed ashore during the following week; most of them had been drifted by the set of the tide into the cove, and they were buried there; so you see it ain't a nice place of a dark night.

"I was driving down the beach about a year after she was lost, with my old jagger wagon, and a heavy load on of groceries and stores of one kind or other. It was about one o'clock at night, mighty cold, but bright moonlight; and I was coming along by the corner of the fence, you know, just above Jackey's, when the mare stopped short. Now, she was just the best beast to drive you ever saw. I could drive her into the bay or right over into the ocean, and she was never skeered at anything. But this time, she come right back in the shafts and began to tremble all over; I gave her a touch of the whip, and she was just as full of spirit as a horse need be, but she only reared up and snorted and trembled worse than ever. So I knew something must be wrong, and looked ahead pretty sharp; and there, sure enough, right across the road, lay a man. Jackey was a little too fond of rum at that time, and I made up my mind he had got drunk and tumbled down on his way home; it was cold, and I didn't want to get out of the wagon where I was nicely tucked in, and thought I would drive round out of the road and wake him up with my whip as I passed. I tried to pull the mare off to one side to go by, but she only reared and snorted and trembled, so that I was afraid she would fall. She had a tender mouth, but although I pulled my best I could not budge her; at last, getting mad, I laid the gad over her just as hard as I could draw it. Instead of obeying the rein, however, she plunged straight on, made a tremendous leap over the body, and dragged the wagon after her. I pulled her in all I knew how, and no mistake; but it was no use, and I felt the front wheels strike, lift, and go over him, and then the hind wheels, but I couldn't stop her. That was a heavy load, and enough to crush any one, and as soon as I could fetch the mare down—for she had started to run—I jumped out quick enough then, you may bet your life. I tied her up to the fence, although she was still so uneasy I daresen't hardly leave her, and hurried back to see if I could do anything for Jackey. Would you believe it, there was nothing there! I tell you I felt the wagon go over him, and what's more, I looked down as I passed and saw his clothes and his hair straggling out over the snow, for he had no hat on; though I noticed at the time that I didn't see any flesh, but supposed his face was turned from me. There was no rise in the ground and not a cloud in the sky; the moon was nearly full, and there wasn't any man, and never had been any man there; but whatever there was, the mare saw it as plain as I did."

"Now let's turn in," said a sleepy individual, who had first been nodding over Bill's statement of public wrongs, and had taken several short naps in the course of his ghost story; "and as there was something said yesterday about a smoke driving away mosquitoes, for heaven's sake let's make a big one; the infernal pests kept me awake all last night."

This was excellent advice, and not only was an entire newspaper consumed in our common sleeping apartment, but a quantity of powder was squibbed off, till the place smelt like the antechamber of Tartarus. The mosquitoes were expelled or silenced at the cost of a slight suffocation to ourselves, but we gained several hours sleep till the smoke escaped and allowed the villains to return to their prey.

One sporting day resembles another in its essential features, although not often so entirely as with the Englishman, who, having devoted his life to woodcock shooting, and being called upon to relate his experiences, replied that he had shot woodcock for forty years, but never noticed anything worth recording. Our next day, however, was enlivened by sport of an unexpected kind. We had heard there was some dispute about the ownership of the stands; in fact, that the one occupied by my friend and myself belonged to the Ortleys, a family represented as decidedly uninviting; while both Bill and the Ortleys claimed that, where another party was located.

In the disputed stand were Bill, a New York gentleman, who, as events proved, seemed to be something of an athlete, and a sedate, unimpassionable Jersey lawyer of considerable eminence. Elijah was with us, when two villanous, red-haired, freckle-skinned objects presented themselves, and, after some preliminary remarks and a refusal on their part of a friendly glass, which is a desperate sign in a Jerseyman, mildly suggested that they would like a little remuneration for the use of the stand. As their suggestion was moderate, reasonable, and just, and they undoubtedly owned the land, we complied, and beheld them proceed, to Elijah's great delight, for the same purpose towards the other stand. Elijah prophetically announced they would probably get more than they demanded.

The other stand was distant about a hundred yards, in full view, and we perceived at once that a commotion was caused by the unexpected arrival. The athletic man was shortly seen outside the blind, flinging his arms wildly about in front of the two Ortley brothers, and, as we were afterwards informed, offering to fight either or both of them. Matters then seemed to progress more favorably, till suddenly Bill and the younger Ortley emerged, locked in an unfriendly embrace, and commenced dragging each other round the sand-bank, while the demonstrative sportsman was seen dancing actively in front of the other Ortley, and preventing his interference.

Of course we dropped our guns and hastened across the shallow, intervening water, having just time to perceive that Bill had thrown his adversary and remained on top. The first words we heard were: "Take him off! Oh, my God! take him off. Enough, enough, take him off," from the one on the ground, whose eye—the only vulnerable part to uninstructed anger—Bill was busily endeavoring to gouge out, while the other shouted frantically: "He is killing my brother; let me get to him; he is gouging his eye out. He will kill him, he will kill him."

"Never mind," answered the athletic man, swinging his arms ominously, and dexterously interposing between the victim and his brother, whenever the latter attempted to dodge past him. "Let him be killed, it would serve him right; he came over here for a fight, and he shall have enough of it if both of his eyes are gouged out."

Elijah arrived in time to prevent the latter catastrophe, and being of a peaceable and humane disposition, pulled off his brother before anything more serious than a little scratching had occurred. In fact, there is no position in which ignorance renders a person more pitiably inefficient, than in fighting; and, while a skilful man could have killed his opponent during the time Bill had enjoyed, the latter had really effected nothing worth mentioning. The ugly wretch was awfully frightened, however; his face being ghostly pale, streaked with bloody red, and he commenced whining at once:

"I am nothing but a boy, only twenty-two last spring, and he's a man grown."

"You know boys have to be whipped to keep them in order," was the consolatory response; for we naturally took part with our landlord.

"Gentlemen, just look at me."

"Don't come so close, you're covered with blood; keep back, keep back."

"But look at me; he's bigger than I am, and I am only a boy."

"Then you shouldn't strike a man."

"Oh! gentlemen, I didn't strike him first, indeed I didn't; he struck me when I wasn't thinking; indeed he did."

"Yes," broke in his brother, who was just recovering from the spell first put upon him by our athlete's continual offers to accommodate him in any way he wished. "Yes, it will be a dear blow for you; I saw you strike him."

"No," said the lawyer, advancing for the first time from behind the blind where he had been an unmoved and impartial umpire of the fray, "you should not say that; your brother certainly struck first; I saw him distinctly." His manner was solemn, and convincing, and conclusive, taken in connexion with his perfect equanimity during the affair; but, of course, he was met by contradiction and protestation from the two brothers. This dispute would have been endless, but at that moment a fine flock of willets was descried advancing towards the stools.

"Down, down," every one shouted, and, true to the bayman's instinct, friend and foe crowded down on the sand together, waiting breathlessly the arrival of the birds. The latter came up handsomely, were received with four barrels, and left several of their number as keepsakes or peace-offerings; for, of course, anger was dissipated, and the defeated enemy retired amid a few merry suggestions, and the excellent advice that they had better not repeat their joke.

Such squabbles—for it can be called nothing graver—lower one's opinion of human kind, and it makes one ashamed to think that two men may hug and pull one another about, and roll on the sand for

fifteen minutes, with the best will in the world to
do each other all the damage possible, and only inflict, in the feebleness of uneducated humanity, a few
miserable scratches. Any of the lower animals
would, in that time, have left serious marks of its
anger; but the pitiful results of these human efforts
were, that Bill's beard was pulled and Ortley's face
scratched. It makes one blush to think he is a
man.

As our party returned to the blind we had left,
Elijah spoke, softly ruminating aloud:

"Well, it only costs thirty-five dollars anyhow,
and it was worth that."

Our humane, peaceable friend, it seems, had been
cast in a similar case, and had to pay six cents
damages and thirty-five dollars costs of court.
There is probably nothing that has so soothing and
pacifying an influence on the New Jersey mind as
costs of court. The words alone act like a charm upon
a Jerseyman in the acme of frenzy, and are as effective as a policeman in uniform. If a man commits
assault and battery, he is fined six cents damages
and costs of court; if he is guilty of trespass it is
the same; if he kisses his neighbor's wife against
her will, if he slanders a friend's character, it is
always six cents damages and costs of court; and
Jerseymen will probably expect in the next world
to get off with six cents damages and costs of court.

The shooting was excellent during the whole day,
and evening found us collected in the bar-room, well
satisfied and particularly jocose over the amusing

pugilistic encounter we had witnessed. It lent point to many a good hit at Bill's expense; even his wife, who is a fine, resolute-looking woman, saying that if she had seen it sooner, she would have taken a broomstick and flogged them both. The general impression was, she could have made her words good.

The pleasure of indulging in fun at the expense of a fellow-creature is very great, and Bill's adventure was certainly fair game. When our wit was exhausted, and the craving for tobacco mollified by the steady use of our pipes, our thoughts and voices turned to our never-wearying passion, and one of the party commenced:

"I have shot a number of the birds you call krickers; they are a fat bird, but do not seem to stool. I have never before shot them, except occasionally on the meadows."

"They don't stool," said Bill, "and only utter a kricking kind of cry; but in October they come here very thick, and we walk them up over the meadows. Why, you can shoot a hundred a day."

"A most excellent bird they are, too—fat and delicate. They are the latest of the bay-snipe in returning from the summer breeding-places; and as they rise and fly from you, they afford extremely pretty shooting. They are sometimes called short-neck, and are, in a gastronomic point of view, the best bay-snipe that is put upon the table."

"We call the bay-birds usually snipe," said the first speaker; "but I have been told they are not snipe at all. Refer to Giraud again and give us the truth."

This fell, of course, to my share, and I commenced as follows:

"I read you yesterday about the plovers, and immediately after them we find an account of the turnstone, *strepsilas interpres*, which is nothing else than our beautiful brant-bird or horse-foot snipe, as it is called farther south, because it feeds on the spawn of the horse-foot. This pretty but unfortunate bird belongs to no genus whatever, and has been to the ornithologists a source of great tribulation. They have sometimes considered it a sandpiper and sometimes not, so you may probably call it what you please; and as brant-bird is a rhythmical name, it will answer as well as *strepsilas interpres;* if you have not a fluent tongue, perhaps somewhat better. Of the snipes, or *scolopacidæ*, the only true representative is the dowitcher, *scolopax noveboracensis*.

"Hold on," shouted Bill; "say that last word over again."

"*Noveboracensis.*"

"That is only the half of it; let's have the whole."

"*Scolopax noveboracensis.*"

"Scoly packs never borrow a census; that is a good sized name for a little dowitch, and beats the radish altogether. Go ahead, we'll learn something before we get through."

"Why, that is only Latin for New York snipe."

"Oh, pshaw!" responded Bill, in intense disgust, "I thought it meant a whole bookful of things."

"The sandpipers, however, come under the family of snipes, and are called *tringæ*. Among these are enumerated the robin-snipe and the grass-plover, as I told you before, the black-breast, the kricker, or short-neck, and several scarcer varieties. The yelpers and yellow-legs, the tiny teeter, and the willet are tattlers, genus *totanus*, while the marlin is the godwit *limosa*. The sickle-bills, jacks, and futes are curlews, genus *numenius*."

"And now that you have got through," grumbled Bill again, "can you whistle a snipe any better or shoot him any easier? Do you know why he stools well in a south-westerly wind, why one stools better than another, or why any of them stool at all? Do you know why he flies after a storm, or why some go in flocks and others don't, or why there is usually a flight on the fifteenth and twenty-fifth of August? When books tell us these things, I shall think more of the writers."

"These matters are not easy to find out; even you gunners, who have been on the bay all your lives, where your fathers lived before you, do not know. But now tell us what other sport you have here."

"On the mainland there are a good many English snipe in spring, while in the fall we catch bluefish and shoot ducks. The black ducks and teal will soon be along; but ever since the inlet was closed, the canvas-backs and red-heads have been scarce."

"What do you mean by the inlet's closing?"

"There used to be several inlets across the beach—one about ten miles below—and then we had splendid oysters and ducks plenty. There came a tremendous storm one winter that washed up the sand and closed the inlet, and so it has remained ever since."

"Can't they be dredged out?"

"The people would pay a fortune to any man who did that, if he could keep it open. In the fall, we go after ducks twenty miles when we want any great shooting; but we kill a good many round here."

"How do you catch the blue-fish that you spoke of?"

"They chase the bony-fish along the shore, and when they come close in, you can stand on the beach, and throw the squid right among them. I took sixteen hundred pounds in half a day."

"Phew!" was the universal chorus.

"'Lige was there, and he knows whether that is true. They averaged fifteen pounds apiece. On those occasions, the only question is whether you know how to land them, and can do it quick enough."

"Your hands must have been cut to pieces."

"Not at all; you'll never cut your hands if you don't let the line slip."

"Did you run up ashore with them?"

"No, I had no time for that; I landed them, hand over hand."

"Well, after that story it's time we went to bed; so good-night."

During that night the mosquitoes, bad as they had been, were more terrible than at any time previous. Favored by the late frequent rains, they had become more numerous than had ever been known on the beach; and being consequently compelled to subdivide to an unusual degree the ordinarily small supply of food, they were savagely hungry. Sleep was out of the question, and after trying all sorts of devices from gunpowder to mosquito-nets, the party wandered out of doors, and, scattering in search of a place of retreat, afforded an excellent representation of unhappy ghosts on the banks of the Styx. The shore, near the surf, and the bathing-houses had heretofore been tolerably secure resorts, but, on this unprecedented night, a special meeting of mosquitoes seemed to have been called in that neighborhood.

Those that tried the ground, and covered themselves carefully from head to foot, found that the enterprising long-legs disregarded the customary habits of their race, and consented to crawl down their sleeves, up their pants, or through the folds of the blanket. The sand-fleas also were numerous and lively, bounding about in an unpleasantly active way; and where there were neither mosquitoes nor sand-fleas, the nervous sufferer imagined every grain of stray sand that sifted in through his clothes to to some malignant, blood-sucking, insect.

One great advantage, however, followed from this discomfort—that we were up betimes next morning and ready for sport that soon proved equal to any we had experienced. In fact, so steady and well sustained a flight of large birds was extremely rare; before our arrival the shooting had been good, and since excellent. There was a repetition to a great extent of the day previous, in many particulars of flight, number, and character of birds; in infinite modification of circumstance, there was an incessant variety of bewildering sport.

No two birds ever approach the sportsman's stand in precisely the same way, and there is one round of deliciously torturing uncertainty; the flock we are most certain of may turn off, the one that has passed and been given up, may return; the bird that has been carefully covered may escape, another that seems a hopeless chance may fall: it is these minute differences, and this continual variety, that lend the principal charm to the sportsman's life.

At midday came again the congregation at the house, the discussion over sporting topics, the joke or story, and the comparison of luck. Thus passed the days, alike, yet different, affording undiminished pleasure, excitement, and instruction, with sport admirably adapted to the hot weather, when the cool, shady swamps are deserted by the woodcock. The English snipe have not yet arrived upon the meadows, and the fall shooting is still in prospective;

the labor is easy, the body can be kept cool by wading for dead birds, and to those who are, at the best, not vigorous, bay-snipe shooting is a delightful resource.

Never did mortals pass a pleasanter week than that week at the beach, and it is impossible to chronicle all the good shots, to repeat all the amusing stories or merry jokes, or to record all the valuable instruction; and to obtain an inkling even, the reader had better make a firm resolve that next August will not pass over his head without his devoting at least one week to bay-snipe shooting. When at last the time came to part, and the baggage was packed, and the guns reluctantly bestowed in their cases, we bade our farewell with sincere regret, praying that often thereafter might we have such sport, and meet such companionship.

It is a long journey to the beach, but it is a longer one back again; no high hopes buoy up the traveller, regrets accompany him instead—no anticipation of grand sport, but the gloomy certainty that it is over for the year; and although the conveyance to the beach is irregular, there is absolutely none away from it. It is true there are several different routes to and from it, but all by private conveyance, and, rendered by the mosquitoes nearly impracticable.

Bill harnessed his ponies—for, wonderful to say, a few horses and cattle manage to live on the beach and sustain existence in spite of the mosquitoes—and we stowed ourselves and our luggage in his well worn wagon. The road lay over the barren beach, deep and heavy with sand, and hardly distinguishable after a heavy rain; the one-story shanty, that had been our resting-place, soon faded from view, and we had nothing in prospect but the dreary journey home.

At the head of the beach we encountered a bathing-party, and were sorely tempted to join the rollicking girls in a frolic among the breakers; but, by exerting great self-denial, and shutting our eyes to their attractions, much to my companion's disgust, we kept on our course. We dined at the tavern on the road, and having bade farewell to Bill, and engaged another team, we reached Crab Town by dusk.

How changed the village seemed to us! Where was the precious and beautiful freight that had paid us such delicious toll? Our eyes peered up and down the road, and into the windows of the scattered houses; our ears listened sharply for the music of merry voices and ringing laughter; our thoughts reverted to that crowded stage, which had so lately borne us through the village. The road was vacant and desolate; all sound was hushed and still; graceful forms, clad in yielding drapery, were nowhere to be seen; the dull lights in the windows revealed nothing to our earnest gaze. Our lovely companions were invisible, although we pursued our search persistently till late at night, when, weary and disconsolate, we crawled up to bed in a dismal hostelry kept by Huntsinger. Going sporting into Jersey is delightful, but returning is sad indeed.

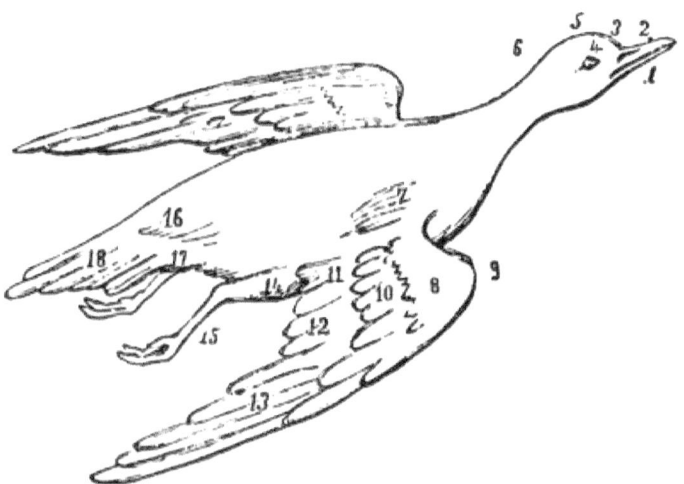

1. Lower mandible.
2. Upper mandible.
3. Forehead.
4. Loral space.
5. Crown of the head.
6. Hind part of the head.
7. Scapulars — long feathers from shoulders over sides of back.
8. Smaller wing coverts.
9. Bend of the wing
10. Larger wing coverts.
11. Tertials, arising from the second bone of the wing at the elbow-joint.
12. Secondaries, from the second bone of the wing.
13. Primaries, from the first bone of the wing.
14. Tibia, the thigh.
15. Tarsus, the shank.
16. Upper tail coverts.
17. Lower tail coverts.
18. Tail feathers.

The length of a bird is measured from the extremity of the bill to the end of the longest tail feather; the length of the wing is measured from the bend to the tip of the longest quill.

CHAPTER V.

BAY-BIRDS.

ALTHOUGH a cursory account of the various bay-birds, their habits and peculiarities, has been given in a previous chapter, it seems desirable to add a more complete, exhaustive, and specific description. This is attempted in the following pages, and although the ornithological characteristics are taken from *Giraud's Birds of Long Island*, which seems to have been the resource of all our sporting writers, nothing else is derived from him; but the facts are stated, either upon personal knowledge, which is generally the case, or upon reliable information.

As to the abundance or scarcity of any particular species, the experience of sportsmen will differ according to the accident of flight, or the locality of their favorite sporting-ground; and in relation to their shyness or gentleness, much depends upon the time of year and the condition of the weather. In consequence of the confusion of nomenclature, it has been deemed advisable to give the scientific description of the common species, each one being placed under its most appropriate name, and to collect together as many designations as could be found to have been applied to them respectively. Nevertheless, many names will no doubt be omitted, and there will be other birds, and some quite common varieties, that, among bay-men, have no names whatever.

It is not intended to furnish a description of all the species of shore-snipe that occasionally are killed, but to supply such information as will enable the sportsman to distinguish the ordinary varieties; and such facts as have not been fully stated, which are more especially applicable to certain members of this great class, are grouped together under separate heads. Nothing is expected to be added to the ornithological learning of the world, and only such portions of that science are given as may be considered desirable for the ready use of the sportsman in the intelligent pursuit of his pleasures.

Plovers.

Genus Charadrius, Linn.

Generic distinctions.—Bill short, strong, straight, about the length of the head, which is rather large and prominent in front; eyes large; body full; neck short and rather thick; wings long; tail rounded and of moderate length; toes connected at the base; hind toe wanting, or consisting of a small knob.

Black-Breast.

Bull-Headed Plover. Beetle-Headed Plover. Black-Bellied Plover.

Charadrius Helveticus, Wils.

This bird is killed along our bays indiscriminately with the other snipe, although it does not stool as well as the marlin or yellow-legs. It passes north early in May, when it is often called the black-bellied plover, and regarded from its plumage as a distinct variety from the fall bird; it is then quite shy. In August or September it returns, being more plentiful in the latter month, and is often found in great numbers especially at Montauk Point; and at that period the young, being quite fat, are regarded as delicious eating. It is then greyer in appearance and not so strongly colored as when in full plumage. Before the main flight arrives, scattering individuals are heard uttering their peculiar beautiful and shrill cry, and are seen shyly approaching the stools, or darting round not far off, and yet afraid to draw close to them. Its head is large and round, giving rise to the name of bull-head, which is common on the coast of New Jersey, although in New York it is generally known as black-breast.

"*Specific Character.*—Bill stout, along the gap one inch and five-sixteenths; length of tarsi one inch and five-eighths. Adult male with the bill black, strong, shorter than the head; cheeks, loral space, throat, fore-neck, breast, with a large portion of the abdomen black; hind part of the abdomen and flanks white; forehead, with a broad band passing down the sides of the neck and breast, white; crown, occiput, and hind-neck greyish white, spotted with dusky; upper parts blackish-brown, the feathers broadly tipped with white; eye encircled with white; tail and upper tail-coverts white, barred with black, the former tipped with white; lower tail-coverts white, the outer feather spotted with black; primaries and their coverts blackish-brown, the latter margined with white; primary shafts about two-thirds from the base, white, tips blackish-brown; part of the inner webs of the outer primaries white; both webs of the inner primaries partially white; secondaries white at the base, margined at the same; feet black; toes connected by a membrane. Female smaller. Young with the upper plumage greyish-brown, the feathers spotted with white; throat, foreneck, and upper part of the breast greyish-white, streaked with dusky; rest of the lower parts white. Length of adult male eleven inches and three quarters, wing seven and a half."—*Giraud's Birds of Long Island.*

American Golden Plover.

Frost Bird, Greenback.

Charadrius Pluvialis, Wils.

This bird furnishes great sport at Montauk Point, when the fortunate sportsman happens to arrive after a fierce north-easter early in September and during one of those wonderful flights that occasionally occur. They come readily to the decoys which are placed in the open upland fields, and were once killed in great numbers on Hempstead plains before cultivation ejected them. A large number of decoys should be used, for they are not so easily seen as when set in the water. After alighting, the golden plover runs with great activity in pursuit of the insects, mostly grasshoppers, on which it feeds; and when killed it constitutes a prime delicacy for the table, and brings a high price in market. It passes to the northward in the latter part of April, and returns in the early part of September. Its general color on the back is greenish, and it has a distinct light stripe alongside of the eye. They often congregate in immense numbers, and I have certainly seen a thousand in a flock.

"*Specific Character.*—Bill rather slender; along the gap one inch and an eighth; tarsi one and nine-sixteenths. Adult with the bill black, much slighter than *C. helveticus ;* forehead, and a band over the eye, extending behind the eye, white; upper parts, including the crown, brownish-black, the feathers marked with spots of golden yellow and dull white; quills and coverts dark greyish-brown; secondaries paler —the inner margined with yellowish-white; tail feathers greyish-brown, barred with paler, the central with dull yellow; shafts of the wing quills white towards the end, which, with their bases, are dark brown; lower parts brownish-black, though in general we find them mottled with brown, dull white, and black; lower tail-coverts white, the lateral marked with black; feet bluish-grey. Late in autumn, the golden markings on the upper parts are not so distinct, and the lower parts are greyish-blue. Length, ten inches and a half, wing seven and one-eighth."— *Giraud.*

Beach-Bird.

Piping Plover.

Charadrius Hiaticula, Wils.

The beach-bird, as its name implies, prefers the beaches to the meadows, and follows each retreating wave of ocean surf in pursuit of its prey, escaping with amazing agility from the next swell. It is a pretty little bird, not often associating in flocks, and on hazy days coming well to the decoys, which should be placed near to the surf, while the sportsman conceals himself by digging a hollow in the loose sand. Although these birds are small, they are plump and well flavored, and when flying rapidly on a level with the flashing breakers, amid the noise and confusion of old ocean's roar, are by no means easy to kill. They are present with us more or less all summer, their diminutive size tending to protect them from destruction.

" *Specific Character.*—Bill shorter than the head; at base orange color, towards the end black; foreneck and cheeks pure white, bordered above with black; rest of the head very pale brown. Adult male with the bill short, orange at the base, anterior to the nostrils black; forehead white, with a band of black crossing directly above; upper part of the head, hind neck, back, scapulars, and wing coverts, pale brown; rump white, the central feathers tinged with brown; tail brown, white at base, tipped with the same; lateral feathers pure white—the next with a spot of blackish-brown near the end; upper tail coverts white; primaries brown; a large portion of the inner webs white; a spot of the same on the outer webs of the inner quills; secondaries white, with a large spot of brown towards the ends; lower surface of the wings white, a black band round the lower part of the neck, broadest on the sides where it terminates; entire lower plumage white. Female similar, with the band on the neck brown. Length seven inches, wing four and a half."—*Giraud.*

Kildeer.

Charadrius Vociferus, Wils.

A worthless bird, furnishing no sport, and poor eating.

"*Specific Character.*—A band on the forehead passing back to the eye; a line over the eye, upper part of the neck all round, and a band on the lower part of the fore-neck, white; above and below the latter, a broad black band; rump and upper tail-coverts orange red. Adult with the bill black; at the base a band of blackish-brown; on the forehead a band of white passing back to the eye; directly above a band of black; rest of the head brown, with a band of white behind the eye; throat white; a broad band of the same color encircling the upper part of the neck; middle of the neck encircled with black, much broader on the fore-neck; below which, on the fore-neck, a band of white, followed by a band of black on the lower neck, the feathers of which are tipped with white, of which color are the breast, abdomen, under tail-coverts, and sides, the latter faintly tinged with yellow; tail rather long, rounded; the outer feathers white, barred with brownish-black, their tips white, with a single spot of blackish-brown on the outer web; the rest pale reddish-brown at the base, changing into brownish-black towards the ends, which are white; some of the inner feathers tipped with yellowish-brown; the middle feathers are plain brown, with a darker spot towards the ends, which are slightly tipped with white; upper tail-coverts and rump reddish-brown, the latter brighter; upper parts brown, the feathers margined with reddish-brown; primaries dark brown, with a large portion of the inner web white; a spot of the same color on the outer webs towards the tips, excepting the first two; their coverts blackish-brown tipped with white; secondaries white, with a large spot of brown towards the ends; their tips, with those of the primaries, white; secondary coverts brown, broadly tipped with white. Length ten inches, wing seven inches."—*Giraud.*

Sanderling.

Charadrius Rubidus, Wils.

"*Specific Character.*—Bill straight, black, along the gap one inch and one-eighth; length of tarsi one inch; hind toe wanting. Adult with the bill straight, about as long as the head. Spring plumage, upper parts, with the throat, fore-neck, and upper part of the breast rufous, intermixed with dusky and greyish white; deeper red on the back; lower part of the breast, abdomen, and sides of the body pure white; tarsi and feet black; claws small, compressed; primaries, outer webs, black; inner webs light brown; shafts brown at the base, tips black, rest parts white; secondaries light brown, broadly margined with white. Winter dress, lower parts white; upper parts greyish-white, intermixed with black or dusky, darkest on the back. Length seven inches and three-quarters, wing four and seven-eighths."—*Giraud.*

TURNSTONE.

Genus Strepsilas.

Generic Distinctions.—Bill shorter than the head, strong, tapering, compressed, and blunt; neck rather short; body full; wings long, of moderate breadth, and pointed; tail round, rather short, and composed of twelve feathers; tarsus equal to the middle toe, and rather stout; hind toe small, fore-toes free, with a narrow margin.

BRANT-BIRD.

Horse-foot Snipe, Turnstone, Beach-Robins.

Strepsilas Interpres.

This is a beautiful bird, and stools pretty well, but is rare and mostly solitary; its young are at Egg Harbor sometimes termed beach-birds. The brant-bird is considered good eating. It feeds on the eggs of the king-crab or horse-foot, which it digs up by jumping in the air and striking with both its feet at once into the sand, thus scratching a hole about three inches deep and an inch and a half across.

"*Specific Character.*—Bill black; feet orange; the head and sides of the neck streaked and patched with black and white; fore part of the neck and upper portion of the sides of the breast, black; lower parts, hind part of the back, and upper tail-coverts white; rump dusky; rest of the upper parts reddish-brown, mottled with black; primaries dusky; a band across the wings and the throat white. Young with the head and neck all round, fore part of the back, and sides of the breast, dusky brown, streaked and margined with greyish-white; wing-coverts and tertials broadly margined with dull reddish-brown. It can at all times be identified by its having the throat, lower parts, hind part of the back, and the upper tail-coverts white, and the feathers on the rump dusky. Adult with the bill black, throat white, sides of the head mottled with black and white; crown streaked with black on white ground; on the hind neck a patch of white; a patch of black on the sides of the neck, of which color are the fore-neck and the sides of the breast; lower parts white; tail blackish-brown, white at the base, of which color are the lateral feathers, with a spot of black on the inner vanes near the end—the rest margined with reddish-brown, and tipped with white; upper tail-coverts white; hind part of the back white; the feathers on the rump black; fore part of the back mottled with black and reddish-brown; primaries dark brown, inner webs white;

secondaries broadly edged with white, forming a band on the wings; outer secondary coverts reddish-brown, inner black; outer scapulars white, with dusky spots; inner scapulars reddish-brown. In winter the colors are duller. Length nine inches, wing five and three-quarters."—*Giraud.*

Sandpiper.

Genus Tringa.

Generic Distinctions.—Bill straight, slender, and tapering, compressed towards the end, and but little longer than the head; body rather full; wings very long and pointed; tail rather short and nearly even; tarsi moderate; hind toe very small, and sometimes wanting; fore toes slender, of moderate length, and generally divided.

Robin-Snipe.

Red-breasted Sandpiper.

Tringa Cinèrea, Wils.   Winter.

Tringa Rufa, Wils.   Spring.

This delicious and beautiful bird, although far from plentiful, furnishes excellent sport, coming readily to stool, and flying regularly and steadily. It mostly affects the marshy islands lying between the salt water creeks, and derives its name from a fancied resemblance to the robin, as he is termed among us. It is always gentle, occasionally abundant, and generally fat and tender; by reason of its steady flight it is not difficult to kill; and its food, mostly shell-fish, does not contribute an unpleasant flavor to its flesh. It arrives from the north about the middle of August, and often lingers for some time on the meadows. As the season advances its plumage becomes paler, till it acquires the name of white robin-snipe—although I have often seen them late in August of the most beautiful and strongly marked coloring, the breast being a rich brownish red and the back a fine grey.

The robin-snipe is of about the size of the dowitcher, with a shorter and more pointed bill, and is killed indiscriminately on the stools with the other bay-birds. Its call consists of two notes, and is sharp and clear; when well imitated, it will often attract the confiding snipe to the gunner, exposed in full view, and without decoys. This bird is very beautiful, and a great favorite.

"*Specific Character.*—Bill straight, longer than the head; tarsi one inch and three-sixteenths long; rump and upper tail-coverts white, barred with dark brown; region of the vent and the lower tail-coverts white, with dusky markings. In spring the upper parts are ash-grey, variegated with black and pale yellowish-red; lower parts, including the throat and fore-neck, brownish-orange. In autumn the upper parts are ash-grey, margined with dull white; rump and upper tail-coverts barred with black and white; lower parts white; the sides of the body marked with dusky; a dull white line over the eye. Adult in spring—bill black; a broad band of reddish

THE LIFE CAR.

brown commences at the base of the upper mandible, extends half-way to the eye, where it changes to reddish-brown; upper part of head and the hind neck dusky, the feathers margined with greyish white—a few touches of pale reddish-brown on the latter; throat, fore-neck, breast, and abdomen reddish-brown; vent white; lower tail coverts white, spotted with dusky; upper plumage blackish-brown, upper tail-coverts barred with black and white; tail pale brown, margined with white; primary coverts black, tipped with white; secondary coverts greyish-brown, margined with white. Young with the upper parts greyish-brown; the feathers with central dusky streaks, a narrow line of cinnamon-color towards their margins, which are dull white; the lower parts ash-grey. Length of adult, ten inches; wing, six and three-quarters."—*Giraud.*

Upland Plover.
Grey, Grass, or Field Plover.
Bartram's Sandpiper.
Tringa Bartramia, Wils.

This bird, although scientifically not a plover, is, by its habits, entitled to an appellation that common consent has bestowed upon it. It is found upon the uplands, never frequenting the marshes except by crossing them while migrating, and feeds, not on shell-fish or the innumerable minute insects that live in sand and salt mud, but on the grasshoppers and seeds of the open fields. It never takes the slightest notice of the stools, is comparatively a solitary bird, and although continually uttering its melodious cry, does not heed a responsive call.

On the eastern extremity of Long Island, and along the coast of New England, are vast rolling and hilly stretches of land, where there are no trees and little vegetation, besides a short thin grass, and here the plovers rest and feed. They migrate to the southward in August, and appear about the same time scattered from Nantucket to New Jersey. In spite of their shyness and the difficulty of killing them, they are pursued relentlessly by man with every device that he finds will outwit their cunning or deceive their vigilance.

Rhode Island has long been one of their favorite resorts, but has been overrun with gunners, who follow the vocation either for sport or pleasure, and there, for many years, the grey plover were killed in considerable quantities. Many are still found in the same locality, or further east, as well as at Montauk Point; but at Hempstead Plains, where they were once found quite numerous, they appear no longer; and the eastern shore of New Jersey being unsuited to their habits, they rarely sojourn or even pause upon it. They travel as well by night as by day; and in the still summer nights their sweet trilling cry may be heard at short intervals; while during the day they will often be seen in small bodies, or singly, winging their way rapidly towards the south.

They are wary, fly rapidly, and are difficult to shoot, and, were it not for one peculiarity, would escape almost scatheless. Alighting only in the open fields, where the thin grass reveals every enemy and exposes every approaching object to their view; readily alarmed at the first symptom of danger, and shunning the slightest familiarity with man, they are impossible to reach except with laborious and painful creeping that no sportsman cares to undertake. Not sufficiently gregarious or friendly in their nature to desire the company of wooden decoys, they cannot be lured within gunshot; and it is only through their confidence in their fellow-beasts that their destruction can be accomplished.

A horse, they know, has no evil design, does not live on plover, and may be permitted to come and go as he pleases; a horse drawing a wagon is to be pitied, not feared; and, most fortunately, the birds cannot conceive that a man would be mean enough to hide in that wagon, and drive that horse in an ingenious manner round and round them, every time narrowing the circle till he gets within shot. Man, however, is ready for any subterfuge to gain his plover; and, seated on the tail-board, or a place behind prepared for the purpose, he steps to the ground the moment the wagon stops, and as the bird immediately rises, fires—being often compelled, in spite of his ingenuity, to take a long shot.

Even in this mode no large number of birds is killed, and by creeping or stalking few indeed are obtained. One inventive genius made an imitation cow of slats and canvas painted to represent the living animal, and, mounting it upon his shoulders, was often able to approach without detection; when near enough, or if the bird became alarmed, he cast off his false skin and used his fowling-piece. This was certainly an original and successful mode of modifying an idea derived from the times of ancient Troy.

This bird is so delicious and so highly prized by the epicure, that no pains are spared in its capture; it is by many superior judges regarded as the richest and most delicately flavored of the birds of America; while its timid and wary disposition renders it the most difficult to kill. It is, therefore, justly esteemed the richest prize of the sportsman and the gourmand, and holds as high a rank in the field as in the market.

It is not, properly speaking, a bay-bird; but as it is frequently shot from the stand when passing near the decoys, these few remarks concerning it are inserted. It is essentially an upland bird, although from the nature of its migration it passes along the coast and occasionally far out at sea.

"*Specific Character.*—Bill slender, rather longer than the head; tarsi one inch and seven-eighths; neck rather long, slender; axillars distinctly barred with black and greyish-white; upper parts dark brown, margined with yellowish-brown; fore-neck and fore part of the breast with arrow-shaped markings; rest of the lower parts yellowish-white. Adult with the bill slender, yellowish-green, dusky at the tip; upper part of the head dark brown, with a central yellowish-brown line, the feathers margined with the same color; hind part and sides of the neck yellowish-brown, streaked with dusky; fore part of the neck and breast paler, with pointed streaks of dusky; sides of the body barred with the same; rest of lower parts yellowish-white; lower wing-coverts white, barred with brownish-black; upper plumage dark-brown, margined with yellowish-brown, darker on the hind part of the back; primaries dark-brown; coverts the same color; inner webs of the primaries barred with white, more particularly on the first—the shaft of which is white; the rest brown, all tipped with white; secondaries more broadly tipped with the same; coverts and scapulars dark-brown, margined with yellowish-brown, and tipped with white; tail barred with black and yellowish-brown, tipped with white; middle feathers darker, tipped with black. Length ten inches and a half, wing six and five-eighths."—*Giraud.*

RED-BACKED SANDPIPER.

Winter Snipe.—Black-breast.

Tringa Alpina, Wils.

This bird absolutely has no common name.

"*Specific Character.*—Bill about one-third longer than the head, bent towards the end; length of tarsi, one inch. Adult with the bill black—one-third longer than the head, slightly bent towards the end, and rather shorter than that of T. Subarquata; upper part of the head, back, and scapular, chestnut-red, the centre of each feather black, which color occupies a large portion of the scapulars; wing-coverts and quills greyish-brown; the bases and tips of the secondaries and parts of the outer webs of the middle primaries, white; forehead, sides of the head, and hind neck, pale reddish-grey, streaked with dusky; fore neck and upper part of breast greyish-white, streaked with dusky; on the lower part of the breast a large black patch; abdomen white; lower tail coverts white, marked with dusky; tail light-brownish grey, streaked—the central feathers darker.

"Winter dress, upper parts brownish-grey; throat, greyish-white; fore part and sides of neck, sides of the head, and sides of the body, pale brownish-grey, faintly streaked with darker; rest of the lower parts white. Length, seven inches and a half; wing, four and an eighth."—*Giraud.*

LONG-LEGGED SANDPIPER.

Peep, Blind Snipe, Frost Snipe, Stilt.

Tringa Himantopus.

This bird also is nameless: it is rare, although I have killed quite a number of them, and I believe its numbers are increasing; it rarely consorts in flocks of more than five or six, stools readily, and is often mistaken for the yellow-legs.

"*Specific Character.*—Bill about one-third longer than the head, slightly arched; length of tarsi, one inch and three-eighths. Adult, with the upper parts brownish-black, the feathers margined with reddish white; the edges of the scapulars with semiform markings of the same; rump and upper tail-coverts white, transversely barred with dusky; tail, light grey, the feathers white at the base and along the middle; primary quills and coverts brownish-black—inner tinged with grey; the shaft of the outer primary, white; secondaries, brownish-grey, margined with reddish-white, the inner dusky; a broad whitish line over the eye; loral space dusky; auriculars, pale brownish-red; fore part and sides of neck, greyish white, tinged with red, and longitudinally streaked with dusky; the rest of the lower parts, pale reddish, transversely barred with dusky; the middle of the breast and the abdomen without markings; legs long and slender, of a yellowish-green color. In autumn, the plumage duller, of a more greyish appearance, and the reddish markings wanting, excepting on the sides of the head, and a few touches on the scapular. Length, nine inches; wing, five."—*Giraud.*

RING-NECK.

American Ring Plover.

Tringa Hiaticula, Wils.

This is a small, but delicate, fat, and pretty bird; it does not stool well, and accompanies the small snipe.

"*Specific Character.*—Bill shorter than the head; base, orange color, towards the point, black; a broad band on the forehead white, margined below with a narrow black band, above with a broad band of the same color; rest part of the head wood-brown; lateral toes connected by a membrane as far as the first joint; inner toes, about half that distance. Adult male with the bill flesh color at base, anterior to the nostrils black; a line of black commences at the base of the upper mandible, passes back to the eye, curving downward on the sides of the neck; a band on the fore part of the head pure white; fore part of crown, black; occiput, wood-brown; chin, throat, and fore neck, passing round on the hind neck, pure white; directly below, on the lower portion of the neck, a broad band of black; upper plumage, wood-brown; primaries, blackish-brown; shafts, white—blackish-brown at their tips; secondaries slightly edged with white on the inner webs; outer webs, nearest to the shafts, an elongated spot of white; wing-coverts wood-brown; secondary coverts broadly tipped with white; breast, abdomen, sides, and lower tail-coverts, pure white; tail brown, lighter at the base; outer feathers white—the rest broadly tipped with white, excepting the middle pair, which are slightly tipped with the same. Female similar, with the upper part of the head and the band on the neck brown. Length, seven inches and a quarter; wing five."—*Giraud*.

Krieker.

Meadow Snipe, Fat Bird, Short Neck, Jack Snipe, Pectoral Sandpiper.

Tringa Pectoralis, Aud.

This is an excellent bird, remaining in the meadows till October, and becoming fat, rich, and fine flavored, but unfortunately it will not come to the stools. Although frequently associating in flocks, it can hardly be said to be truly gregarious, and is as often found with the different varieties of small snipe as with its own number. It is quite a difficult bird to kill when on the wing, its flight being rapid and irregular, and its size small; but when it becomes fat and lazy, after a long residence in well supplied feeding-grounds, not only is its flight slower and itself easier to hit, but it is often shot sitting. Its general color is grey, with white on the abdomen; and its size varies greatly according to its age and condition, some being of more than double the size of others. As a natural consequence, considerable practice is required to distinguish it readily from the ox-eyes by which it is often surrounded, when the meadow grass hides it, in a measure, from view. It feeds and dwells altogether in the meadows, finding its food in the stagnant water collected upon their surface, and is only plentiful when these are wet. When alarmed, it rises rapidly, and makes off in a zigzag way, that reminds the sportsman of the flight of English snipe; and early in the season it is wild and shy. It occasionally passes over the stools, but never pauses or seems to notice them; and for this reason, in spite of its epicurean recommendations, it is generally neglected. In the cool days of September and October, when the mosquitoes have succumbed in a measure to the frost, its pursuit over the open meadows is pleasant and exhilarating. It is often killed to the number of eighty in a day, and is so fat that its body is absolutely round.

"*Specific Character.*—Bill straight, base orange-green; length of tarsi one inch and one-sixteenth; upper parts brownish-black, edged with reddish-brown; throat white; fore part of neck and upper part of the breast light brownish-grey, streaked with dusky; rest of lower parts, including the lower tail-coverts, white. Adult with the bill straight; top of the head dark-brown, intermixed with black; sides of the head, neck, and a large portion of the breast, greyish-brown, streaked with dusky; chin white; a streak of dark brown before the eye, continuing to the nostril, directly above a faint line of white; back dark-brown; feathers margined with white; primary quills dark-brown—shaft of the first white; outer secondaries slightly edged with white; tail-feathers brown, margined with brownish-white —two middle feathers darker, longest, and more pointed; lower part of the breast, abdomen, and sides of the body and under tail-coverts white; feet dull yellow; tibia bare, about half the length. Female, the general plumage lighter. Length nine inches and a half, wing five and a quarter."— *Giraud.*

Ox-Eye.

Tringa Semipalmata, Wils.

"*Specific Character.*—Bill rather stout, broad towards the point; along the gap about one inch; length of tarsi seven-eighths of an inch; bill and legs black; toes half webbed. Adult with the bill slender, about the length of the head—dark-green, nearly approaching to black; head, sides, and hind-part of neck ash-grey, streaked with dusky; upper parts blackish-brown, the feathers edged with greyish-white; secondary coverts tipped with white; primary coverts brownish-black, as are the feathers on the rump; upper tail-coverts the same; wing-quills dusky, their shafts white; tail-feathers ash-grey, the inner webs of the middle pair much darker; over the eye a white line; lower parts white; legs black. Length six inches and a half, wing four."—*Giraud.*

This and the following variety are generally confounded by bay-men; and being too small to demand much consideration, and never shot unless huddled together, so that a large number may be bagged, they are called promiscuously by the odd name ox-eye. They are fat, and almost as good eating when in prime order as the reed-bird.

Ox-Eye.

Wilson's Sandpiper.
Tringa Pusilla, Wils.

" *Specific Character.*—Bill along the gap three-quarters of an inch, slender; tarsi three-quarters of an inch; legs yellowish-green. Adult with the bill brownish-black; upper part of the breast greybrown, mixed with white; back and upper parts black; the whole plumage above broadly edged with bright bay and yellow ochre; primaries black —greater coverts the same, tipped with white; tail rounded, the four exterior feathers on each side dull white—the rest dark-brown; tertials as long as the primaries; head above dark-brown, with paler edges; over the eye a streak of whitish; belly and vent white. Length five inches and a half, wing three and a half. With many of our birds we observe that individuals of the same species vary in length, extent, and sometimes differ slightly in their bills, even with those which have arrived at maturity.—On consulting ornithological works, we notice that there are no two writers whose measurement is in all cases alike. With specimens of the Wilson's sandpiper, we find in their proportions greater discrepancy than in many other species—and out of these differences we are inclined to the opinion that two spurious species have been created."—*Giraud.*

TATLER.

Genus Totanus.

Generic Distinctions.—Bill longer than the head, straight, hard and slender; neck slender, and both it and body rather long; wings long and pointed; tail short and rounded; legs long; hind-toe very small, and the anterior ones connected at the base by webs, the inner being slightly webbed.

WILLET.
Semipalmated Tatler.
Totanus Semipalmatus, Lath.
Scolopax Semipalmata, Wils.

This is a fine, large, and beautiful bird; the sharply distinct white and black of its wings contrasting admirably with the reddish-brown tints of the marlin and sickle-bills with which it often associates; it stools well, flying steadily, and often returning after the first, and even second visit; but even when fat, it is tough and ill-flavored. It congregates in large flocks, and reaches the Middle States on its southern journey in the latter part of August. Its cry is a fierce wild shriek, which is rarely, if ever, accurately imitated; but it responds to the call of the sickle-bill, and when once headed for the stools, rarely alters its course. In exposed situations it is shy and difficult of approach, like most of the shore-birds, which, although they come up so unsuspiciously to the decoys, are wary of the gunner, and rarely permit him to crawl within range of them.

"*Specific Character.*—Secondaries and basal part of the primaries white; toes connected at base by broad membranes. Adult with the head and neck brown, intermixed with greyish-white; breast and sides of the body spotted, and waved with brown on white ground; abdomen white; tail-coverts white, barred with brown; tail greyish-brown, barred with darker brown—the outer two feathers lighter; rump brown; fore part of the back and wing-coverts brown, largely spotted with dull white; primaries blackish-brown, broadly banded with white; secondaries white. Length fifteen inches and a half, wing eight."—*Giraud.*

Yelper.

Big Yellow-Legs—Greater Yellow-Shanks—Tell-tale Tatler.

Totanus Vociferus, Wils.

This is one of the most numerous of the bay-birds, and among the most highly prized for its sport-conferring properties. It stools well, although occasionally suspicious, and will often drop like a stone from the clouds, where it is fond of flying, upon receiving a response to its strong, clear, and easily imitated cry. It will also frequently come within shot in the open, when the sportsman is unaided by his decoys. Its flight is uneven, being often slow when approaching or pausing over the stools, and then exceedingly rapid and irregular when alarmed; and if there are no stools to make the Yelper hesitate, it has a bobbing motion, as if searching for the origin of the call, that makes it exceedingly difficult to kill. Moreover, it is vigorous, and will carry off much shot, as in fact is the habit with all the shore-birds, and is tough and sedgy on the table.

It does not associate in large flocks, but roams about in parties of three or four.

"*Specific Character.*—Bill along the ridge two and a quarter inches; tarsi two and a half; legs yellow. Adult with the bill black, at the base bluish; upper part of the head, loral space, cheeks, and neck, streaked with brownish-black and white; throat white; a white line from the bill to the eye; a white ring round the eye; breast and abdomen white, spotted and barred with brownish-black; sides and tail-coverts the same; lower surface of the primaries light grey—upper brownish-black, the inner spotted white; wing-coverts and back brown, spotted with white, and dusky; scapulars the same; tail brown, barred with white. Winter plumage, the upper parts lighter—larger portion of the breast and abdomen white; sides of the body barred with dusky. Length, fourteen inches; wing, seven and a quarter."—*Giraud.*

YELLOW-LEGS.

Little Yellow-Legs—Yellow-Shanks Tatler.

Totanus Flavipes, Lath.

Scolopax Flavipes, Wilson.

This bird in appearance is almost identical with the yelper, except that it is much smaller, not being more than half as large. It has several calls, consisting of one or more flute-like and shrill notes, which are rather difficult to imitate. It is probably the most plentiful of all the bay-snipe, making its summer visit in July, and continuing to arrive till late in September. It collects in immense flocks, and stools excellently, but its flight is irregular and rapid, and when frightened, it darts about in a confusing way that often baffles the sportsman. When wounded it will swim away, and, if possible, crawl into the grass to hide.

Although a pleasant bird to shoot, it is unattractive on the table, even when in best condition, unless killed along the fresh water, where it attains an agreeable and delicate flavor. Both it and the yelper are found in considerable numbers on the marshy shores of the western lakes, where it and the other smaller bay-birds are called, indiscriminately, plover.

Wonderful stories are told of the number of yellow-legs killed at one shot, and as it is a small bird, these are probably not exaggerated. By Wilson the yellow-legs, the yelper, and willet are classed among the *Scolopacidæ*, or snipe, but the other ornithologists have erected a separate genus for them.

"*Specific Character.*—Bill along the ridge one inch and three-eighths; length of tarsi one inch and seven-eighths; legs yellow. Adult with the bill black; throat white; upper part of the head, lores, cheeks, hind part and side parts of the neck, deep brownish-grey, streaked with greyish-white; eye encircled with white, a band of the same color from the bill to the eye; fore neck, sides of the body, and upper part of the breast, greyish-white, streaked with greyish-brown; lower part of the breast and abdomen white; lower tail-coverts white, the outer feathers barred with brown; scapulars and fore part of the back brown, the feathers barred and spotted with black and white; primaries blackish-brown, the shaft of the outer brownish-white, whiter towards the tip, the rest dark-brown; secondaries margined with white; hind part of the back brownish-grey; tail barred with greyish-brown, white at the tip; legs, feet, and toes, yellow; claws black. Length, ten inches and three-quarters; wing, six. Young with the legs greenish—and by those who have not recognised it as the young of the year, I have heard the propriety of its name questioned."—*Giraud*.

GODWIT.

Genus Limosa.

Generic Distinctions.—Bill very long, a little recurved from the middle, rather slender, and with the lower mandible the shorter. Wings long and very acute; tail short and even; legs long; toes four, and rather slender, the hind one being small and the middle toe the longest; anterior toes connected at the base by webs, the outer web being much the larger.

MARLIN.

Great Marbled Godwit.

Limosa Fedoa, Linn.

Scolopax Fedoa, Wils.

This is the gentlest and most abundant of the

large birds, approaching the decoys with great confidence and returning again and again, till frequently the entire flock is killed. In color it is a reddish-brown, lighter on the abdomen, and its flight is steady and rather slow. Although better eating than the willet, and very rich and juicy, its flesh cannot be called delicate. The ring-tailed marlin or Hudsonian Godwit, *Limosa Hudsonica, Lath.* is a finer but much scarcer bird, and resembles somewhat in color the willet, but has the marlin bill, which is longer than that of the last-named species.

"*Specific Character.*—Bill at base yellow, towards the end blackish-brown; upper parts spotted and barred with yellowish-grey and brownish-black; lower parts pale reddish-brown; tail darker, barred with black. Adult male with the bill at the base yellowish-brown, towards the end black; head and neck greyish-brown, tinged with pale reddish, streaked with dusky—darker on the upper part of the head and hind neck; throat whitish, lower parts pale reddish-brown; under tail-coverts barred with brown; tail reddish-brown, barred with dusky; upper tail-coverts the same; upper parts barred with brownish-black and pale reddish-brown, spotted with dusky; inner primaries tipped with yellowish-white; scapulars and wing-coverts barred with pale reddish-brown and greyish-white; shaft of the first primary white, dusky at the tip; inner shafts at the base white, rest part light brown, excepting the tips, which are dusky. Length, sixteen inches; wing, nine and a half. Female larger, exceeding the male from three to four inches."—*Giraud*.

Ring-Tailed Marlin.
Hudsonian Godwit.
Limosa Hudsonica, Lath.

"*Specific Character.*—Bill blackish-brown, at base of lower mandible yellow; upper parts light brown, marked with dull brown, and a few small white spots; neck all around brownish-grey; lower parts white, largely marked with ferruginous; basal part of tail-feathers and a band crossing the rump, white. Adult with the bill slender, blackish towards the tip, lighter at the base, particularly at the base of the lower mandible; a line of brownish-white from the bill to the eye; lower eyelid white; throat white, spotted with rust color; head and neck brownish-grey; lower parts white, marked with large spots of ferruginous; under tail-coverts barred with brownish-black, and ferruginous; tail brownish-black, with a white band at the base; a band over the rump; tips of primary coverts and bases of quills white; upper tail-coverts brownish-black—their base white; upper parts greyish-brown, scapulars marked with darker; feet bluish. Length, fifteen inches and a half; wing, eight and a half. Young with the lower parts brownish-grey, the ferruginous markings wanting."—*Giraud*.

Snipe.
Genus Scolopax, Linn.

Generic Distinctions.—Bill long, at least twice the

length of the head; straight, tapering, and flattened towards the end; eyes rather large, placed high in the head, and far back from the bill; neck of moderate length, and rather thick; body full; wings rather long and pointed; tail moderate and rounded; legs moderate; toes slender and rather long, except the hind one; middle toe longest, and connected at the base with the inner by a slight web, the outer one being free.

Dowitcher.

Dowitch—Brown Back—Quail-Snipe—Red-Breasted Snipe.

Scolopax Noveboracensis, Wils.

This is a beautiful, excellent, and plentiful bird; it abounds in the marshes during the entire summer, congregates in vast flocks, and although uttering a faint call itself, is attracted to the decoys by the cry of the yellow-legs, or almost any sharp whistle. It is remarkably gentle, individuals often alighting when their associates are slain, in spite of the unusual uproar; and it can be more readily approached than any of the bay-birds. Its flesh, moreover, is quite delicate, and when fat somewhat similar to that of the English snipe, which it greatly resembles in appearance. In general color it is brownish, with a light abdomen, but occasionally the breast is as red as that of a robin in full plumage. Its flight is steady, although when alarmed it "skivers," or darts about rapidly, and as it flies in close ranks, it suffers proportionally. Although it is rather looked down upon by persons who wish to make a show of large birds, I am always entirely satisfied with a good bag of well-conditioned dowitchers.

"*Specific Character.*—Spring plumage, upper parts brownish-black, variegated with light brownish-red; lower parts dull orange-red, abdomen paler, spotted and barred with black; rump white; the tail feathers and the upper and lower tail-coverts, alternately barred with white and black. In autumn the upper parts are brownish-grey; the lower parts greyish-white; the tail feathers and the upper and lower tail-coverts the same as in spring. Adult with the bill towards the end black, lighter at the base; top of the head, back of the neck, scapulars, tertials, and fore part of the back, blackish-brown, variegated with ferruginous; secondaries and wing-coverts clove-brown, the latter edged with white, the former tipped with the same; hind part of back white; the rump marked with roundish spots of blackish-brown; upper tail-coverts dull white, barred with black; tail feathers crossed with numerous black bands, their tips white; loral band dusky, the space between which and the medial band on the fore part of the head, greyish-white, tinged with ferruginous, and slightly touched with dusky; sides of the head spotted with dark-brown; lower parts dull orange-red, the abdomen lighter; the neck and fore part of breast spotted with dusky; the sides of the body with numerous bars of the same color; legs and feet dull yellowish-green. Young with the lower parts paler. Winter dress, the upper parts brownish-grey; neck ash-grey, streaked with dusky; lower parts greyish-white, with dusky bars on the sides of the body. Length, ten inches and a half; wing, six."—*Giraud.*

Curlew.

Genus *Numenius*, Briss.

Generic Distinctions.—Bill very long, slender, decurved or arched, with the upper mandible the longer, and obtuse at the end; head rounded and compressed above; neck long, body full, wings long, feet rather long; toes connected at the base; *tibia* bare a short space above the knee; legs rather long; tail short and rounded.

Jack Curlew.

Short-billed Curlew. Hudsonian Curlew.

Numenius Hudsonicus, Lath.

This is a graceful and elegant bird, but so shy and so well able to carry off shot, that it is regarded as the most difficult to kill of all the bay-birds. It has a long, rolling cry, and although it approaches the decoys, it rarely alights, or even pauses over them; but, detecting the deception, it turns off or passes on in its course. For this reason, the fortunate sportsman who kills a "Jack" is eminently satisfied, although its flesh is not remarkably fine.

"*Specific Character.*—Length of bill, three inches and three-quarters; tarsi, two inches; lower parts white. Adult with the upper part of the head deep brown, with a central and two lateral lines of whitish; a brown line from the bill to the eye, and another behind the eye; neck all round, pale yellowish-grey, longitudinally streaked with brown, excepting the upper part of the throat, which is greyish-white; upper parts in general blackish-brown, marked with numerous spots of brownish-white, there being several along the margins of each feather; wings and rump somewhat lighter; upper tail-coverts and tail barred with dark-brown and olivaceous grey; primaries and their coverts blackish-brown, all with transverse yellowish-grey markings on the inner web; the shaft of the first quill, white—of the rest, brown; breast and abdomen greyish-white, the sides tinged with cream color, and barred with greyish-brown; bill rather more than twice the length of the head, of a brownish-black color—at the base of the lower mandible, flesh colored. Length, eighteen inches; wing, nine and a half."—*Giraud.*

Sickle-bill Curlew.

Long-billed Curlew.

Numenius Longirostris, Wils.

The finest, largest, most graceful, and elegant of all the bay-birds is the magnificent sickle-bill; associating in large flocks, and with a spread of wings of little less than three feet, when it approaches the stand, the sportsman's heart palpitates with excitement, and the sky seems to have lost its natural blue and become of a rich brown tint. As these splendid birds, shrieking their hoarse call, set their wings for the stool, and crossing one another in their flight, pause in doubt; or, after alighting individually, rise again, and hesitate whether to remain or continue their course—the sportsman, cowering in his lair, and anxious to take advantage of this glorious opportunity, becomes wildly eager with excitement; and if, after having by a judicious selection brought several to the ground, he recalls the departing flock which again presents itself to his aim, his rapture knows no bounds, and with his reloaded breech-loader, he repeats, perhaps more than once, the exhilarating performance.

This lordly bird, the largest of the bay-snipe, is often extremely gentle, and may be lured by the imitation of its cry at an immense distance, and brought back to the decoys several times, where one or more of its companions may have fallen; but at other times it is wild and shy. Individuals differ considerably in size, the largest I ever saw having a bill eleven inches long, and some weighing nearly double as much as others; but all are of a beautiful reddish-brown or burnt sienna tint, with a yellowish shade on the abdomen. Their flight is steady, and their flesh tough, dark, and oily. Their eye is extremely bright, and their shape graceful.

"*Specific Character.*—Bill towards the end decurved; upper part of the throat, and a band from the bill to the eye, light buff; general plumage, pale reddish-brown; head and neck streaked with dusky; upper parts marked with blackish-brown; tail barred with the same; abdomen, plain reddish-brown; feet, bluish. Length, twenty-six inches; wing, eleven. The bill of the specimen from which this description is taken measures eight inches. The bills of individuals of this species vary, but the length is at all times sufficient to determine the species."—*Giraud.*

FUTE.

Doe-bird.—Esquimaux Curlew.

Numenius Borealis, Lath.

This is an upland bird, quite rare, but large, and rather delicate eating.

"*Specific Character.*—Bill, along the gap, about two inches and a quarter; tarsi, one inch and five-eighths; upper parts, dusky brown, with pale yellowish-white, marked all over with pale reddish-brown. Adult with a line of white from the bill to the eye; eyelids, white; upper part of the head dusky, spotted in front with greyish-white, a medial band of the same color; throat, white; neck and breast yellowish-grey, with longitudinal marks of dusky on the former, pointed spots of the same color on the latter; abdomen, dull yellowish-white; flanks, barred with brown; lower tail coverts the same as the abdomen; tail and upper tail coverts barred with pale reddish-brown and dusky, tipped with yellowish-white; upper parts brownish, the feathers tipped with pale reddish-brown, the scapulars margined and tipped with lighter; primaries, dark-brown, margined internally with lighter—the first shaft white, with the tip dusky—the rest brown. Length, fourteen inches and a half; wing, eight."—*Giraud*.

CHAPTER VI.

MONTAUK POINT.

THE eastern end of Long Island, that extremity which seems to stretch out like the hand of welcome towards the nations of the old world, beckoning their inhabitants to our hospitable shores, is divided into two long points like the tines of a fork. The upper point shuts in Long Island Sound, and protects our inland commerce from the violence of the "Great Deep;" while the lower prong, which is kissed on the one side by the blue waters of the Peconic Bay, and on the other is buffeted by the billows of the great Atlantic, is known as Montauk Point. The heaving ocean seems here to have solidified itself into a sandy soil, which rises and swells and rolls, much after the manner of its mighty prototype, except that a scanty garment of tawny grass clothes the outlines of the billowy waste. "Cattle on a thousand hills" here roam in a state of, at least, semi-independence, which they occasionally assert by charging upon the intruding sportsman in a manner which may be intended as playful, but which looks somewhat serious. For a dozen miles or so only a few houses break the monotony of the dreary expanse, and it is to one of these, distant some nine miles from the extreme point, that I am about to carry the reader, for here alone can plover-shooting be enjoyed in its fullest perfection.

There are numerous kinds of plover that make their migratory passages along our coasts; but the one to which I refer, while to the epicure it ranks almost, if not absolutely, the first upon the list, and affords, by the swiftness of its flight and the eccentricity of its habits, a prize not unworthy of the highest efforts of the sportsman, has been the victim of many a misnomer, but is correctly known by the appellation American Golden Plover, *Charadrius pluvialis* (P.). The Plover-family is large and of high respectability; but, when " upon his native heath," no one of its clans is entitled to wear a loftier crest than that which we now have under discussion. His near relative, the Bartramian Sandpiper or Grey Plover, is perhaps more aristocratically delicate in his figure, and is welcomed as heartily at the table of the epicure. But he is less social in his habits, and rarely affords any but single shots. He does not fraternize with wooden counterfeits, and his mellow whistle, as he rises at an impracticable distance, rarely responds to even the most seductive efforts of his pursuer. But our Golden friend, notwithstanding his auriferous title, his superior beauty of plumage, his swiftness and strength, and the savory reputation which he enjoys among the knowing-ones, is possessed of gregarious habits, of a singularly frank and unsuspicious nature, and is generally ready to stop and have a chat with anything which bears the faintest resemblance to a bird and a brother. It is well for his admirers that such is his nature; and although the wide appreciation of his merits certainly causes great destruction among his ranks, still the vast flocks which, sometimes for days together, fly past, within sight of the stands, unshot at, seem to warrant the hope that the hour of the final extinction of his race is very far distant.

Taking the Long Island railroad to Greenport in the early part of September, and having encountered and overcome the ordinary delay and difficulty of obtaining a sailboat to further prosecute our voyage, we find ourselves at last gliding on the waves of the beautiful bay, past Shelter and Gardiner's islands, and approaching the long low line of the Nepeague beach. With a favorable breeze we may expect to be landed on the smooth sand in a little cove, about one mile from our destination, in two hours from our time of departure; but if the wind is adverse and the fates unpropitious, we may have to follow the path from the shore in the dark, which will require our best instincts, aided by the guidance of the distant booming of the surf, and the assistance of our especial guardian angel.

Once there, however, and we will be repaid for our sufferings; we may find a table covered with "South-side" delicacies, and bearing in the centre a huge dish of beautiful, odorous, melting plover, cooked to a turn, and we will undoubtedly meet kindred spirits and generous sportsmen who are on the same errand as ourselves. As we dispose of the former, the latter will pour into our sympathetic ears wonderful accounts of their sport, and rival one another in recounting the long shots and the good shots they have made, the numbers of birds they have killed, and the pounds of bass they have caught.

Under the influences of a delicious supper and moderate "nightcap," we seek our couch with fond visions of the great flocks, and hopeful dreams that we will do as well on the morrow. At earliest dawn we spring from our bed, and rushing to the primitive little casement have only time to rejoice in the promise of a fine day, ere we note the welcome cry of our noble prey hurrying westward over the beach.

To don our shooting costume, to grasp our gun and ammunition, to load ourselves with the basket containing decoys and incidentals, and to emerge into the cool air of the September morning, require but a few minutes; we hasten across the sandy hillocks to our appointed spot, marked by a hollow scooped out for the concealment of former visitants, and by the quantity of feathers and cigar-stumps lying loosely around; and with hands trembling with impatience, we distribute the stools in what seems to us to be the most artistic and seductive manner,—for the birds are now beginning to fly just within a tantalizing yet impracticable range, and we long for action.

How wild, how glorious is the hour and the scene! The heavy boom of the ocean, which rolls almost at our feet, is relieved by the soft, mellow notes of the sea-birds which float through the air in varied yet harmonious cadence, and by the low of distant cattle, just shaking off their slothful dreams. Hardly have we disposed our body to the requisite flatness, when a chattering chorus of melody makes our heart leap with eagerness, and our eyes strain with impatience to discern its source. Aha, we have them now! that small, erratic cloud to the eastward, bearing directly before the wind towards our covert, sends a thrill through our being, which the whole "spacious firmament on high," even on the loveliest of nights, has, we honestly confess it, never succeeded in imparting. On they come, nearer, nearer, nearer. We pucker up our lips to greet their approach, but the saucy gale renders our rude efforts futile, and we commit our trust to Providence and our painted counterfeits. Now they are within easy range, but somewhat scattered; with a violent effort at self-command, worthy of a higher cause, we remain motionless, for there are evident indications of a social spirit in that joyous group. They pause, they swerve, they wheel upon their tracks, and with motionless wings and a sweet low-murmured greeting, they approach the fatal stools. How rash the confidence! How foul the treachery! But, we must also confess, how intense the excitement, as we pull the right trigger at the critical moment, and then, as the deluded victims scatter wildly, with an outburst of appeal against man's cruelty, give them the left barrel, and add three more to the list of feathered martyrs. With lightning speed, their thinned ranks vanish beyond the neighboring sand-hills, and reloading our gun, we hasten to gather up the slain.

Six with the right and three with the left barrel, are pretty well for a beginning; but we had better have remained at our post, for while we are chasing up one of the wounded birds, two more flocks pass within easy range of our hiding-place. Hurriedly twisting the neck of the fugitive, we resume our lonely watch, and before the breakfast-hour of eight, which our unwontedly early exertions have made a somewhat serious epoch, we have had two more double shots, and increased our score to twenty-one. Beautiful, "beautiful exceedingly" is the burden of game which we proudly carry back to our inn, leaving our stools as they stand.

A hearty breakfast makes us feel like *a new man*, and, after a fair discussion of its merits, lighting our pipe, we again wend our way to the scene of our triumph. The cry is still they come; flock after flock presents its compliments, and leaves mementoes of its presence; but towards noon the hot sun disposes the birds to listless inactivity, the flight diminishes, and finally stops. Returning to the house with a bag larger by only three birds than that of the morning, we kill the hours before dinner by a few casts into the breakers, and land a ten-pound bass.

With sharpened appetite, we welcome the savory dinner, and are quite contented to rest and let our prey rest till five o'clock, when fifteen more birds reward our post-prandial exertions, and make up a total for the day of sixty plover and one bass. We sink to sleep that night with the proud consciousness that our first day's plover-shooting has been a great success; our heart prays silently for a continuance of our good fortune, and we indulge in sweet thoughts of home, and the pleasure our return laden with spoils will cause, when our friends greet us and them at the social board.

The next day is as delightful; the sweet, thrilling music again fills the air at short intervals; again our trusty breech-loader sends its charge into the thickest of the "brown," or cuts down the straggler looking for "former companions all vanished and gone." Again we call the swift-travelling flock from the very zenith, or whistle our lips into a blister, endeavoring to attract the wary knowing ones that pause to look, only to flee the faster; and the night finds us with a still larger bag, but without a bass. So eager have we become, so fearful that we should lose a shot, and judging by the accumulating clouds in the east that on the morrow it may storm, that we stay out all day, except the necessary moments for our meals, and give no thought to the monsters of the deep.

Nor were we mistaken; the morrow comes, the gathering storm has broken, and no creature of mortal mould can face its fury—at least no bird, with any pretensions to common sense or respectability, would imperil his plumes by an unnecessary exposure to such an ordeal. So with forced patience, we get through the live-long day as best we can;

and on the following day, hail a sky as cloudless as the most ardent sportsman could desire. But alas! the flight has gone by, scared away perhaps by the storm, or retreating before the advancing fall; and when we take our seat at the breakfast-table, we are obliged to admit that only nine birds have fallen to our gun.

But the irrepressible and inextinguishable host rises triumphant in this emergency. He boldly suggests that there *must be* some sluggards, who have tarried, spell-bound by the attractions of such a terrestrial, or, rather ornithological, paradise; and accordingly, he *hitches up* a venerable specimen of the genus "*Equus*," and we start for an excursion "over the hills and far away." Before we have advanced a couple of miles we have bagged a half dozen solitary specimens of Bartram's Sandpiper or Grey Plover, so dear to the sportsman and the gourmand, but have seen no trace of the object of our pursuit. When, suddenly, as we surmount one of the swelling eminences which are the prevailing feature of this district of country, we come upon a sight such as, perhaps, but few sportsmen have ever beheld. A gentle hollow spreads before us, for several acres, literally covered with the ranks of the much-desired, the matchless Golden Plover.

As they stand in serried legions, the white mark on their heads gives a strange chequered weirdness to the phalanx; and we involuntarily pause, spell-bound by the novelty of the spectacle. Our host himself, though an old hand, owns that he has never before gazed on such a sight. There they stand with heads erect, and bodies motionless, just out of gunshot. Their number is computed by our companion to be not less than three thousand, closely packed, and apparently awaiting our onset. What is to be done? Delay may be fatal, but precipitancy would be equally so: and our pulses stop beating under the stress of the emergency. Our horse also stops, obedient to an involuntary pull of the reins. We accept the omen, and cautiously descend from our vehicle; warily crawling to within seventy yards, we halt as we see unmistakable evidences of uneasiness and suspicion among the crowded ranks. They stoop, they run, they rise with "a sounding roar," to which the united report of our four barrels savagely responds. Away, away with headlong speed, scatters and dissolves that multitudinous host, and we hasten to secure our spoils.

But, seventy yards make a long range for plover-shooting, and we are somewhat chagrined to find that only six dead and seven wounded birds remain as proofs of the accuracy of our aim, and the efficiency of our weapons. Hurriedly we plant our stools, hoping for the return of at least a considerable portion of the vanished forces; but they have apparently had enough of our society, and, after two hours spent in ambush, with only an occasional shot at single stragglers or small flocks, we wend our way back to the house.

On the morrow we kill a dozen birds over the

stools, before breakfast, among which are two specimens of the beautiful Esquimaux Curlew or Fute, as he is commonly called, and which seems to be on terms of the closest intimacy with our Golden friend. We find him to be a heavier bird, equally inclined to obesity, and, as future experiments satisfy us, nearly as perfect in delicate richness of flavor.

At nine o'clock Dobbin is again harnessed, and we start for the scene of yesterday's exploit. But the sighing wind now sweeps over only a deserted moor, and we direct our course in a direction to make an inspection of Great Pond. Here, by good luck and management, we bag five teal and a black duck, as well as three passing plover. A few large flocks of the latter are seen, but they are wary and unapproachable; and after several fruitless efforts, we abandon their pursuit and start for dinner.

Having rendered full justice to the merits of a bountiful repast, which, if it is made prominent in this account, was still more prominent in our hungry thoughts, we stroll to the ocean-side and make a dozen casts for bass, but our luck seems to be on the turn and we decide to leave on the morrow for Greenport. About an hour before sunset, a few birds are on the wing, and we again seek the field of our first success. Here we make our final effort, and are rewarded with five noble victims, killed singly at long shots, and we restore our breech-loader to its case. We have no reason to be dissatisfied with our four-days' sport, and it is with a certain reluctance, and a sincere resolve to renew our visit at an early date, that we pack our valise in anticipation of a start on the morrow.

Our team is at the door; we bid adieu to some ladies of the household (of whom while writing these lines we have thought much, though we have, until now, said nothing), and, mounting by our host's side, we trot merrily over the hills, till we reach the deep sandy desert of the Nepeague beach. "A long pull, and a strong pull" for an hour, brings us to "terra firma" again, and rattling through the quaint old town of Easthampton, after a charming drive, we reach Sag Harbor, where a most absurdly diminutive steamer, of just *seven-horse* power, awaits to convey us to Greenport. We part from our host with sincere gratitude for the genial kindness which he has shown to us during our visit, and step on the narrow deck of the tiny craft. A voyage of thirteen miles, made under a full head of steam in just two hours and a quarter, brings us once more to the beautiful village of Greenport, where the cars are awaiting us.

We return with a bag full of game, and the following general conclusions and precepts impressed upon our mind: In plover shooting use No. 6 shot in the left barrel, for the birds are of wonderful strength and require to be hit hard, or they will fly an immense distance even if "sick unto death," and if crippled, will sneak, and hide, and run, and cause much loss of time that is precious indeed. Do not fire too soon; as the flock will generally "double" if allowed sufficient time, and then is the chance to "rake 'em down." Be patient, keep cool, aim ahead of the birds, and keep wide awake.

On almost any day, from the 25th of August to the 10th of September, there are sport and pleasure to be had among the wild sand-hills of Montauk; and if there has been a north-easterly storm, with pitchforks full of rain and caps full of wind, there will be such an abundance of birds as only experience can conceive of or appreciate. That is an event that most of us have yet to wait for. Reader, I wish I were sufficiently unselfish to say honestly—may you enjoy it first.

Since I first went to Montauk, when large and jolly parties of sportsmen congregated every fall at Lester's and Stratton's, some changes have taken place. The plover have diminished until the chance of sport is uncertain, although occasional good days are had; and there is a probability that the railroad will intrude on its "everlasting hills," and that fashionable watering places will replace the old-time sporting hotels. Then bid farewell, a long farewell, to all the shooting.

CHAPTER VII.

RAIL SHOOTING.

Success in this delightful sport depends as much upon the proper accessories, together with experience in minor matters, as in the great art of properly handling the gun. The best shot, badly equipped, will be surpassed by an inferior marksman accustomed to the business, and thoroughly fitted out for it. The shooting is done among high reeds, and from small, light, and unstable skiffs, which are poled over muddy shallows with an unsteady motion that puts an end to skill which is not founded on long practice. The sport lasts only during the few hours of high water, when the entire day's bag must be made, and requires, after the bird has been killed, a sharp eye to retrieve him amid the weeds and floating grass.

The number bagged, however, is sometimes prodigious; and although we rarely now hear of hundreds killed "in a tide," as was formerly not unusual, the shots are still frequently rapid, and the result satisfactory. The bird rises heavily, its long legs hanging down behind; flying slowly, it presents an easy mark to any one upon *terra firma*, and if not shot at, will alight after proceeding thirty or forty yards.

It comes on from the north during the early part

of September, and disappears so instantaneously with the first heavy frost, that our superstitions baymen imagine it retires into the mud. It can, however, fly strongly, as I have occasionally had unpleasant evidence under peculiar circumstances, and in wild, windy weather. During low water, when it can run upon the muddy bottom among the thick stalks, which it does rapidly, it can hardly be flushed by any but the strongest and toughest dog, and is not frequently pursued; although many persons enjoy the hard walking and exposure of this plan, preferring to tramp over the quaking surface of our broad salt meadows, and flushing the rail from amid some tuft of reeds, kill him with the aid of their loved fellow-playmate, a high-strung setter or untiring water spaniel.

As the tide rises, however, and covers the bottom with a few inches of water, the rail, caught feeding among its favorite wild oats, or on the grains of the high reeds, and alarmed at the advancing boat, is forced to take wing and present an easy mark to its destroyer. But if missed, although marked down to an inch, it rarely rises a second time, having probably escaped by swimming—a thorough knowledge of which is among its numerous accomplishments. The rail has a long, thin, and soft body, which it appears to have the faculty of compressing; as it can glide amid the thick stems of reeds and grass with wonderful rapidity; and if wounded, it will dive and swim under water, leaving its bill only projecting, so as to bid defiance to pursuit.

The first necessity of equipment for this sport is a breech-loading gun, which not only enables the sportsman to kill double the number of birds, but will occasionally give him the benefit, by a rapid change in the charge, of a favorable presentation of a chance flock of ducks. But as many persons, out of a want of knowledge or of funds, still cling to the old muzzle-loader, it may be well briefly to mention the articles that tend to modify its inferiority.

Of course, as the shooting occupies but a few hours, and in good days the birds are perpetually on the wing, it is essential to load rapidly; and to do this the sportsman places on a thwart before him a tin box divided into compartments for powder, shot, caps, and wads, or, as I prefer, two boxes, one filled with powder and the other with the other materials. For many reasons there should be a lid over the powder—to prevent its being ignited by a chance spark or blown away by a strong wind—and the ordinary flask is frequently used in spite of the consequent delay. A double scoop, made of tin or brass, and regulated to the precise load, is placed among the powder and the shot, and a solid loading stick lies near at hand.

By these means the rapidity of loading is more than doubled; the powder is dropped into both barrels at once by means of the double scoop, wads are driven home by a single blow of the rod, both barrels are charged with shot at once in the same manner, the caps are within easy reach, and the gun is loaded in less than half the time consumed in the ordinary process. The shot may be made into cartridges of paper with a wad at the upper end, and thus a few additional of the precious seconds saved. Both barrels are discharged before either is reloaded, and the birds are retrieved immediately.

The sportsman stands erect, without any support to modify the unsteadiness consequent upon the irregular motion of the boat, and requires practice, not merely to enable him to take aim, but even to retain his footing. Where the water is low and the reeds strong, this difficulty is augmented, as the boat entirely loses its way after every push, and advances by jerks that utterly confound a novice. Experience, however, being acquired in loading rapidly and in retaining his balance, the sportsman's labors are easy; but the punter requires many different qualities, and upon his excellence mainly depends the final result.

He must possess judgment to select the best ground, strength to urge on the boat unflaggingly, and an inordinate development of the bump of locality to mark the dead birds. The bird once killed and the sportsman part ended, then the punter displays his ability; and if thoroughly versed in his craft will push the boat through tall reeds, and matted weeds, and fallen oat-stalks, and drifted grass, with wonderful accuracy to the very spot, and peering down amid the roots, will distinguish the brown feathers almost covered with water and hidden by the vegetable growth.

In order to retrieve quickly, a wide-meshed scap-net is a great convenience; but to mark well, a man must be endowed by nature with that peculiar gift. Among the vast mass of undistinguishable marine plants that spring from the muddy bottom and rise a few inches or many feet above the surface, it would seem impossible to determine, within an approach to accuracy, where some bird, visible only for a moment and cut down when just topping the reeds, has fallen; and when another bird rises to meet the same fate, and perhaps a dozen are down before the first is retrieved, successful marking becomes a miracle. With some punters on the Delaware, where their names are famous, so wonderful is the precision that every bird, if killed outright, will be recovered, and even a poor marksman will make a respectable return; but when the gentleman shoots badly and the man marks worse, rail-shooting is unprofitable.

For this sport, thus followed, it will be seen that a punter is indispensable, and it is made the business of a large class of men along the salt marshes where the rail most do congregate; and wherever a punter cannot be obtained, as in the wilder portions of our country, rail-shooting cannot be had.

From the necessity for rapid firing, the immense advantage of a breech-loader must be apparent; the tide rarely serves for over two or three hours, and to kill more than a hundred birds in that time with a muzzle-loader is a remarkable feat, as it requires almost the entire time for the mere loading and firing of the gun; but the breech-loader may be charged in an instant, and enables the sportsman to improve the lucky chance of coming upon a goodly collection of birds, and make the most of the scanty time permitted to him.

None of those vexatious mistakes that occasionally happen to the best sportsmen can befall him; the shot cannot get into the wrong barrel, nor the cap be forgotten; the powder is not exposed to ashes from a careless man's cigar; and there being no hurry, there is more probability of steady nerves and a true aim.

The charge should be light—three-quarters of an ounce of shot and two drachms of powder being abundant to kill the soft and gentle rail—and pellets at least as fine as No. 9 are preferable to coarser sizes. Old cartridges, that have been split and mended by gumming a piece of paper over the crack, may be used in the breech-loader, provided the sportsman desires to indulge in praiseworthy economy, or is deficient in a supply.

The sport is extremely exciting: the boat is forced along with considerable rustling and breaking of stems and stalks; the bright sun streams down upon the yellow reeds and lights up the variegated foliage of the distant shore; the waves of the bay or river, rising apparently to a level with the eye, sparkle in the gentle breeze that bends the sedge grass in successive waves; neighboring boats come and go, approach and recede; the rapid reports are heard in all directions, like fireworks on the Fourth of July; the sportsman stands erect, and eager with delirious excitement, near the bow; the punter balances himself, and wields his long pole dexterously on a small platform at the stern.

Silently a bird, rising close to the boat, wings its way, with pendent legs and feeble strokes, towards some one of its numerous hiding-places; instantly the punter plants his pole firmly in the bottom, holding the skiff stationary, the sportsman brings up his piece, and, with deliberate aim, sends the charge straight after the doomed rail, which pitches headlong out of sight. The punter has marked him by that single wild rice-stalk with the broken top, and heads the boat at once towards the place; but ere he has advanced a dozen feet, another bird starts and offers to the expectant sportsman, who has his gun still "at a ready," another favorable chance, and, meeting the same fate, falls into that low bunch of matted wild oats. The breech-loader opens, the charges are extracted and others inserted, just in time to make sure of two rail that rise simultaneously, still ere the first has been reached, and which are both tumbled over and marked down — one, however, wing-tipped, and never to be seen by mortal eye again.

Thus have I experienced it on the Delaware, at Hackensack, and, in former days, among the tributaries of Jamaica Bay, and at many other places where more or less success has attended me. Although never having enjoyed great luck, never having advanced beyond the first hundred, and claiming to be no such marksman as several of my friends, I have had wondrous sport. Of a good day, when the tide is favorable and the game plenty, the excitement is continuous, and increased by a sense of competition.

Other sportsmen are on the same ground, stopping probably at the same hotel and shooting in close proximity—occasionally too close, if they are thoughtless or careless. Not only will a charge of mustard seed sometimes rattle against the boat, but is apt, now and then, to pierce the clothes and penetrate the skin, followed by an irritation of mind and body; but when the tide has fallen, and the sport is over, a comparison of the bag made by each sportsman is inevitable, and no general assertions of round numbers will answer, but the birds must be produced. It is vain to claim what cannot be exhibited, and more than useless to talk of the immense quantities that were killed but not retrieved; such excuses are answered by ridicule, and if the poor shot would avoid being a butt, he must be modest and submissive.

There is danger too, at times, although an upset in the weeds can result in nothing worse than a wetting of oneself and one's ammunition, and the ruin of the day's enjoyment; but I was once on the Delaware, opposite Chester, when a fierce north-wester was blowing, which had driven much of the water out of the bay and river. The tide, of course, was poor, having difficulty to rise at all against the gale, which kept on increasing every moment, and the birds were scarce and difficult to flush. The work of poling was laborious; the boats stopped after every push, and the heavy swell from the broad river, rolling in a long distance among the reeds, added a new motion to their natural unsteadiness.

Of course the sport was not encouraging, and the accidents were numerous; several sportsmen fell overboard, one upset his boat, and my man came so near it—his pole slipping at the moment he was exerting his utmost strength upon it—that his efforts to recover his balance reminded me of dancing the hornpipe in a state of frenzy. He kicked up more capers, and indulged in more contortions on the little platform, scarcely a foot square, which he occupied, than I supposed possible without dislocation of a limb; but he managed, however, to regain his equilibrium, and neither fell overboard nor upset the skiff.

These little incidents, and the shooting, such as it was, kept the party, which was numerous, interested until the time came for recrossing the river to our hotel. There was no stopping-place on our present side of the river, which presented one apparently endless view of waving reeds; and the alternative was simply to cross the open river, or pass the night in our boats. The swell had increased into high waves capped with snowy foam, and threatened destruction to our low-sided, short, and narrow boats. Many were the consultations between the various punters, and grave were the doubts expressed of a safe crossing; but as there was no help for it, the trial had to be made.

Selections were chosen of favorable starting-points, and most of the party put out at about the same time—the sportsman lying on the bottom at full length in the stern, and the oarsman timing his strokes to the violence of the sea. The waves broke over us continually; it was necessary to bail every few minutes, and several had to put back when they met with some more than usually heavy wave, and take a fresh start, after emptying the superfluous water. Of course we were drenched to the skin, but found a species of consolation in knowing that no one had the advantage of another. Had any of our boats upset, although we might have clung to them and drifted back among the reeds, we could have effected a landing nowhere, and would probably have terminated our career then and there; had this happened to a certain little skiff that held two men and very few rail, this account would probably never have been written. However, fate ordained otherwise, and we reached our destination in safety.

The best locality for rail-shooting is along the marshy shores of the Delaware River, above and below Philadelphia; many birds are also killed on the Hackensack and the Connecticut; they are abundant on the James River, and doubtless further south, but are not shot there; and they are found scattered over the fresh as well as the salt marshes throughout the entire country. I have killed them in the corn-fields of Illinois while in pursuit of the prairie chicken, and have bagged several and heard many among the wild rice of the drowned shores of Lake Erie. They are a migratory bird, and pass to the southward in the early fall rather in advance of the English snipe, and alight at any damp spots for a temporary rest wherever the growth of plants promises nutriment.

They are often flushed by the snipe-shooter, together with the larger fresh-water rail, *rallus elegans*, and their curious cry resounds along the reedy marshes where the wild-fowler pursues the early ducks. Nevertheless, they are difficult to flush and kill where there is no tide to drive them from their muddy retreats, and where the ground is too heavy for a dog; and, comparatively speaking, on fresh water, unless the wind shall have caused a temporary rise, they are safe from injury.

Their voices reply with the guttural "krek-krek-krek" to the noise of the boat, and tauntingly boast of their abundance and their security. Moreover, in a new country, where larger game is still plentiful, the excellences of the tender but diminutive rail are lost sight of by comparison with his more profitable compeers; and except along the Atlantic coast, he is known as a game-bird neither to the sportsman nor the cook.

From the fact that he is rarely seen in the spring, and does not at that season give his enemies a chance to prevent his reaching his nesting-places at the far north—but only visits us during a few short weeks in the fall, and then is not much exposed, except in certain localities—his race will be preserved in undiminished numbers for many generations; the light skiffs will carry the eager city sportsman along the shores of the Delaware, the Hackensack, and the cove on the Connecticut, and the rapid reports will continue to reverberate over the reedy marshes.

There are two varieties, the short-billed or sora-rail, *rallus Carolinus*; and the long-billed, or Virginia rail, *rallus Virginianus*, which are easily distinguished by this peculiarity, and differ, also, slightly in plumage. The sora-rail are by far the most numerous, especially along the sea-coast, and are usually referred to as "the rail," but both are shot and eaten indiscriminately. Their habits, mode of flight, and gastronomic qualities, appear to be identical, but I think the Virginia rail are proportionally more numerous at the West, having a slight preference, perhaps, for the fresh water. Their food must be, however, essentially different; for while the sora, on account of its short bill, must be confined to the seeds of its favorite reed, zimosa, or the grains of the wild oats, the Virginia rail, with its longer bill, also draws much of its nourishment from snails and aquatic insects, and is considered by some less delicate in flavor than the former variety.

About the fifth of September, before the English snipe are numerous, although their taunting "scaip" may be occasionally heard on their broad, open feeding-grounds; ere the ducks have marshalled their legions in retreat from the chilly blasts of the north, after the bay-birds, with the exception of the "short-neck," shall have mainly passed to the southward, and before the quail are large enough to kill— the sportsman arms himself with his breech-loader, and driving to Hackensack or taking steamboat from

Philadelphia, embarks in the slight skiff usually called a "rail-boat," and practises his hand—possibly out of exercise since the woodcock days of early July—upon the tame and languid rail.

His cartridges are prepared for the occasion; as he does not intend to devote more than a day or two to the amusement, he takes with him a light suit, appropriate to the boat and the weather, gaiter shoes, flannel pants and shirt, and his waterproof, to meet a temporary shower, and he lays in sufficient liquid for himself and his man, knowing that salt air produces thirst, and country inns bad spirits. Thus armed and equipped, if he is fortunate enough to have high tides, he is almost sure to enjoy fine sport, and bring home a bag of game that will furnish forth his table right handsomely to a goodly company, or go far and spread much satisfaction among his friends who may be the fortunate recipients. The heats of the summer solstice are over, the birds will keep several days with care, and the sportsman has not to dread either the burning sun of August or the freezing blasts of winter.

Many double shots present themselves in rail-shooting; and upon the manner in which these are turned to account, and the brilliancy with which a bird that rises while the sportsman is in the act of loading, is covered with the hastily charged barrel and cut down, depends the superiority of one marksman over another. In the days of the muzzle-loader, I have killed many a bird with one barrel while the ramrod was still in the other, and have shot several with the barrels resting on my arm, when they had slipped from my hand in bringing the gun up hurriedly to my shoulder. Every single rise should be secured as matter-of-course, and most of the double ones, care being taken in the latter to obey that great rule, of always killing the more difficult shot first; if you shoot right-handed, as the majority of persons do, and one bird flies to the right and the other to the left, shoot first at the former, and you will have less difficulty in bringing back the gun towards the latter

Never relax your vigilance, as the birds rise silently, without the warning whistle of the woodcock or whirr of the quail, at the least expected moment; and if the punter attempts to direct your attention, the chances are ten to one that you look in the wrong quarter.

The rail, while being a pleasant bird to shoot, is also a pleasant bird to eat. There is no variety of our wild game, large or small, that is more delicious; its flavor is excellent, and its tenderness beyond comparison; it may not have the rich full flavor of that noblest of them all, the big-eyed woodcock, nor the savory raciness of the full-breasted quail, nor the strong game taste of the stylish ruffed grouse, nor the unequalled richness of the kingly canvas-back—but in tender, melting delicacy it is hardly surpassed. If cooked in perfection, it drops to pieces in the mouth, leaving only a delightful residuum of enjoyment. It should be floated in rosy wine, and washed down with the ruby claret, and accompanied by fried potatoes, thin and crisp as a new bank note. It may be preceded by the *pièce de resistance*, and should be followed only by salad, which may in fact be eaten with it, if dressed with sufficient purity.

Kill your rail handsomely in the field, missing not more than one in twenty, present him properly and with due appreciation on the table, and eat him with the gratitude that he deserves.

It is only of late years that many rail were killed at the South. The old-time battue of the negroes at night-time, with paddles and torches, did not amount to much, but now hundreds are killed daily through the season in the rivers below Washington, although the weather is usually so hot that half of them spoil. In those extensive marshes, two hundred to a gun is a moderate day's bag. Still the numbers of this excellent little bird have not sensibly diminished, and good sport is had every year on the Connecticut and the Delaware.

CHAPTER VIII.

WILD-FOWL SHOOTING.

It is not proposed to give any extended account of wild-fowl shooting as practised on the waters of Long Island, or in the neighborhood of the great Northern cities; the unsportsmanlike modes of proceeding which are there in vogue, and which, while contravening all true ideas of sport, insult common sense by the ruthless injury they inflict, have been fully set forth by other writers.

In stationing a battery—that imitation coffin, which should be a veritable one, if justice had its way, to every man who enters it—and in lying prone in it through the cold days of winter, the marketman may find his pecuniary profit, but the gentleman can receive no pleasure; while the permanent injury inflicted by driving away the ducks from their feeding-grounds, and making them timorous of stopping at all in waters from any and all portions of which unseen foes may arise, is ten times as great as the temporary advantage gained; and as for calling that sport, which is merely the wearisome endurance of cold and tedium to obtain game that might be killed more handsomely, and in the long run more abundantly, by other methods, is an entire misapplication of the word.

So long as the shooter confines himself to points of land or sedge, whether he uses decoys or awaits the accidental passage of the birds, he not only permits himself a change of position and sufficient motion to keep his blood in circulation, but he allows the frightened flocks that have already lost several of their number in running the gauntlet, a secure retreat in the open waters, and undisturbed rest at meal time. And so long as this is granted them they will tarry, and trust to their sharp eyes and quick ears to save their lives; but when they cannot feed in peace, and when they can find no haven of safety in the broad expanse of water, they will inevitably continue their migration, and seek more hospitable quarters.

Wild-fowl shooting, as pursued at the West, or even at the South, is glorious and exhilarating; there the sportsman has exercise, or the assistance of his faithful and intelligent retriever, and is required to bring into play the higher powers of his nature. He manages his own boat, or he stands securely upon the firm ground, and if he has not a canine companion, chases his crippled birds and retrieves the dead ones by his own unaided efforts.

At the West, although the vast numbers do not collect that congregate in the Chesapeake Bay and Currituck Inlet, there is an independence in the mode of pursuit that has a peculiar charm; and from the facilities afforded by the nature of the ground, the excellent cover furnished by the high reeds, and the immense number of single shots, the average success is as great as in the more open waters of the Southern coast.

The employment of retrievers is not general in our country, which is, by the character of its marshes and growth of plants, better suited for the full display of their capacities than any other. There are certain objections to the use of a dog in wild-fowl shooting, which, although entirely overbalanced in the writer's opinion by the corresponding advantages, are unquestionably serious. The season for duck-shooting is mainly late and cold, when it is essential to the shooter's comfort that his boat should be dry; but the dog, with every retrieved bird, comes back dripping with wet, and if he does not let it drain into the bottom of the skiff, where it "swashes" about over clothes and boots, shakes himself in a way to deluge with a mimic cataract every person and thing within yards of him.

It is unreasonable to ask of the intelligent and devoted but shivering creature, that he should remain standing in the freezing water or upon the damp sedge; and if the master is as little of a brute as his companion, and has a spare coat, the dog will have it for a bed, regardless of the consequences.

Nor is this the only difficulty; for unless the animal has instinctive judgment as well as careful training, he may in open water upset the frail skiff, by either jumping out of it, or clambering into it injudiciously. A thoughtful creature may be taught to make his entry and exit over the stern, but unfortunately, some of the most enthusiastic and serviceable dogs have little discretion or forethought; and unless he is trained to perfect quiet, and broken to entire immobility at the most exciting moments, he is apt to interfere sadly with the sport.

In spite of these inconveniences, however, the loss of many of his birds—amounting, amid the dense reeds of the western lakes, to nearly one-half of the whole number—will satisfy the sportsman that the retriever, with his devoted and wonderful sagacity, to say nothing of his delightful companionship, is a most desirable acquisition. Where the sportsman is forced to pursue his calling solitary and alone, so far as human associates are concerned, he will find the presence of his four-footed friend a great satisfaction, and, amid the solitary and unemployed midday hours, a pleasant resource.

The dog is the natural companion of the sportsman—the partaker of his pleasures, the coadjutor of his triumphs; and whenever his peculiar gifts can be used to advantage, it is a gratification to both to call upon him. The knowledge that he will acquire in time is truly marvellous. Not only does he possess the power of smell, but his eyesight and hearing far surpass those of man; he will often discern a flock long before it is visible to human eyes, and his motions will warn his master of its approach.

His training can be carried on beyond limit; his knowledge increases daily, and his devotion is unbounded. Of all the race, the retriever is probably the most intelligent; as, in fact, intelligence is one of his necessary qualifications. For this work no breed has the slightest value unless the individuals possess rare sagacity and almost human judgment. Some of the most valuable English dogs have been from an accidental cross; and a pure cur with a heavy coat is often as good as any other.

There is in England a strain of dogs known as retrievers; they are mostly used in connexion with upland shooting, as English pointers and setters are not broken to fetch; but the favorite animals for wild-fowl shooting, which have made their name notorious in connexion with this specialty, have generally come from parents neither of which possesses the true retriever blood.

In this country the best breed will have some of the Newfoundland strain; the animal must be clothed with a dense coat of thick hair to endure the severe exposure to which he is subjected, and must be endowed with a natural aptitude and passion for swimming. The usual color is dark, which, in the writer's judgment, is a great mistake; and the only really distinct breed of retrievers is known as that of Baltimore.

In the Southern States the dog, as an assistant in wild-fowl shooting, has always been in far greater repute than at the North; although the inland lakes of the latter, the extensive marshes closely grown up with tall *zimosas*, matted wild oats, and thick weeds, make his services far more desirable. At the South alone has any intelligent attention been given to raising a superior strain of retrievers; and

SHRIMP FISHING.

whether we seek an animal that by his curious motions will toll ducks up to the stand, or by his natural intelligence will aid the punt-shooter in recovering his game, it is at the South alone that we can find any admitted pedigree.

In the Northern States, however, the "native," as he is called at the West—probably from the fact that he is invariably a foreigner—selects any promising pup, and by means of much flogging and steady work trains him to a faint knowledge of his duties. A young dog loves to fetch, and will take pleasure in chasing a ball thrown for him round the room, and if he is a water-dog, naturally brings from the water a stick cast into it, so that the routine part is easily impressed upon him; but an animal with this proficiency alone is scarcely worth keeping.

A good dog must have intuitive quickness of thought and judgment; he must know enough to lie perfectly motionless when a flock is approaching; he must understand how to retrieve his birds judiciously, bringing the cripples first; he must have perseverance, endurance, and great personal vigor. A duck is cunning, and to outwit its many artifices and evasions the retriever must have greater shrewdness; it can skulk, and hide, and swim, and sneak, and he must have the patience to follow it, and the strength to capture it. Wonderful stories are told of the many exhibitions of what seems much like human reason, evinced by some of the celebrated retrievers.

But probably the rarest quality for a dog or man to possess, and the most necessary to both, if they would excel in field sports, is the power of self-restraint. To ask an animal, trembling all over with delirious excitement, to lie down and remain perfectly motionless during those most trying moments when the ducks are approaching and being killed, is to demand of him a self-control greater than would be often found in his master. Yet upon this quality in the dog depends the entire question of his value or worthlessness; if he makes the slightest motion, the quick eyes of the birds are sure to discern it; and if he bounces up at the first discharge, he will certainly destroy his master's chance of using his second barrel, and perhaps upset him over the side of the boat.

It is to avoid the sharp eyes of the ducks that a black color for the dog has been condemned. Amid the yellow and brown reeds of the marshes, or upon the reflective surface of the open water, black, from its capacity for absorbing the rays of light, is visible at an immense distance. Yellow, brown, or grey are the best shades; and any color is preferable to black. Red is selected by the Southerners for their tolling dogs, but this is with the purpose of making them attractive.

Many persons conceive that a dark coat is warmer for an animal than white, an idea that is carried into practice in the ordinary winter dress of human beings; but it is refuted not only by the simplest principles of science, but by the natural covering of the animals that inhabit the cold climes of the north. The polar bear is clothed in white, while the southern bear is of a deep black; and many of the animals and some birds that pass the winter in the arctic regions, change their dress in winter from dark to grey or pure white.

Undoubtedly with a retriever the first point is to consider his protection against cold; plunging as he does at short intervals into water at a low temperature, and exposed when emerging to the still colder blasts of Æolus, he must be rendered comfortable as far as possible at the sacrifice of every other consideration. This is attained by the thickness more than the color of his coat; and the writer has always fancied, whether correctly or not, that curly hair is warmer than straight hair.

The matted coat of the Newfoundland dogs—the smaller breed being preferable by reason of size—is extremely warm, and where its color is modified by judicious crossing, is all that can be desired; while the instinctive intelligence, the devotion, faithfulness, docility, and interest in the sport, of these admirable animals, fit them in an extraordinary degree for wild-fowl shooting. Coming from the north and accustomed to playing in the water, they can, without danger, face the element in its coldest state; and whether it be to chase a stick thrown into the waves by their youthful human playmates, or to recover ducks shot by their sporting owner, they take naturally to all aquatic amusements.

Nevertheless, as has been heretofore remarked, although it is well to have a slight strain of the Newfoundland, no distinct breed is necessary to make a good retriever. Our ordinary setters are sometimes unsurpassable for the purpose; and any tractable dog, if well trained, will answer in a measure.

How different it is to stand in the narrow skiff among the tall reeds at early dawn, with the eager and expectant, though humble, associate, crouched in the bottom upon his especial mat, and there in the increasing light that paints the east with many changing hues, to single out the best chances from the passing flocks, and have your skill doubly enhanced by the intelligent coöperation of your companion; than to lie, cramped, cold, and suffering, all through the weary hours, stretched at full length upon your back with eyes staring up to Heaven and straining to catch a glimpse of the horizon over your beard or forehead; and occasionally to rise to an equally constrained posture that is neither sitting nor lying, and do your best to discharge your gun with some judgment at a passing flock of fowl! Who can hesitate in selecting the mode in which he will pursue the sport of wild-fowl shooting? Most of the favorite varieties of ducks, including many that are known among ornithologists as sea-ducks, *fuligulæ*, are found in the many scattered ponds, the shallow marshes, or the extensive inland seas of the great west; while the swans and geese are shot, the former along the larger rivers and lakes, and the latter in the corn-fields. It is true that the enormous flocks that collect in the lagoons and bays of the South are rarely seen; but the flight of small bodies or single birds is more continuous, and probably the total number even larger.

It is impossible to particularize localities as pre-eminent for this sport where so many are good; and the swamps, rivers, lakes, cultivated fields, and even open prairies of Ohio, Illinois, Indiana, Michigan, Iowa, Nebraska, Dakota, Colorado, Minnesota, and Wyoming, and the Western country generally, abound in their seasons with various descriptions of wild-fowl. An English sportsman, who had spent many years in the West, gave it as his opinion that the best place for all varieties of sport in the world was Southern Minnesota.

Although the use of a light skiff is always desirable and adds enormously to the comfort of the shooter, circumstances will often arise that will deprive him of its use; and in such case he has no better resource than to don his long wading boots, and tramp through the shallow water until he comes to a favorable spot, perhaps the deserted house of a family of beavers; and there, perched upon its summit and concealed by the surrounding reeds, to resign himself to the inevitable inconveniences of his position. When his feet grow cold in spite of their india-rubber casing, and his muscles weary for want of rest, he will long for the dry skiff; and when he comes to "back" his load of game—consisting, if he is successful, of geese, canvas-backs, red-heads, mallards, blue-bills, widgeons, and perhaps a swan—across the muddy flats a mile or two to dry land, he will long for it still more intensely.

For shooting ducks the best weather is dark, or even rainy, as at such times the birds fly closer to the earth, being unable to follow their course, and do not perceive the sportsman so readily. But as a natural consequence, the sportsman's ammunition becomes damp and his clothes wet, while the old-fogy owner of the muzzle-loader will unjustly anathematize Eley's water-proof caps when his gun misses fire, instead of blaming his own stupidity. The insides of barrels will foul and the outsides rust; the loading-stick will become dirty and the sportsman's hands and face grimy; and then the happy possessor of the breech-loader, when he handles his clean cartridges, although one occasionally may stick, will thank his good fortune and bless Lefaucheaux.

A strong wind forces the birds out of their safe course, up and down the open "leads," upon the various points where the fowler, selecting the most favorable by watching the flight, takes his stand; and, when they are heading against it, reduces their speed from the lightning rate of ninety miles an hour to reasonable deliberation; but when they are travelling with it, renders the art of killing them one of no easy acquisition.

In shooting wild-fowl, or in fact any rapid flying birds, it is necessary to aim ahead of them — not that the gun is actually fired ahead of them, but to allow for the time, hardly perceptible to man, but noticeable in the changed position of the birds, necessary to discharge the piece; and the distance allowed must depend not only on the rapidity of their flight, but on the customary quickness of the marksman. The great fault of sportsmen is, that they shoot below and behind their birds; and this is particularly apt to be the case where the game, as with wild-fowl, appears to move more slowly than it really does.

To the novice in this peculiar sport, the second difficulty to overcome will be the inability to judge distances. Not only do objects appear over the water nearer than they really are, but there is no neighboring object that will aid the judgment in coming to a correct conclusion; and by changes in the weather birds in the air will seem to be nearer or further off, and their plumage will be more or less distinctly visible, according to circumstances. After several days' experience in dark, cloudy weather, the greatest proficient will, on the first ensuing day of bright sunshine, throw away many useless shots at impracticable distances.

There is no criterion to determine the distance of any bird high above the horizon, and any recommendation to wait till the eyes can be seen—the book-maker's rule—is worse than useless; it is a matter of experience and judgment.

There is no better time to kill ducks than when they are coming head on, the commonly promulgated idea that their feathers will turn the heavy shot being simply absurd; and all the marksman has to do is to cover his bird, pitch his gun a trifle upwards, and pull the trigger.

In the matter of ammunition, the high numbers of shot and the light charges of powder of old times have changed by general consent; and for ducks, one ounce and a quarter of No. 4 or 5, and perhaps No. 3 late in the season, and of No. 1 or 2 for geese, driven out of the ordinary field-gun by three and a half drachms of powder, will be found preferable. I say a field-gun, because, although the heavy duck-gun, with its enormous charge of six drachms of powder and three ounces of shot, is undoubtedly more killing when discharged into large flocks, the waste of ammunition would be immense were it used at the scattering flight of the western country.

Many kinds of wild-fowl will, like bay-snipe, be attracted by an imitation of their cry; and, when decoys are used, the mastery of these calls is necessary to the proficiency of the bayman. But at the West, where the use of decoys is not customary, and where the nature of the ground prevents full advantage being obtained from these devices, a knowledge of the art is not so necessary. Nevertheless, there is something thrilling in the "honk" of the wild goose; when it is heard, the sportsman is earnest in his efforts to imitate it, and if successful—which he often is, for the bird responds readily—is not only proud of the result, but amply rewarded for his skill.

In shooting from any species of cover, when ducks are approaching, it is more important not to move than to be well hid; the slightest motion startles and alarms the birds, that would possibly have approached the sportsman in full view if he had remained motionless. If they are suddenly perceived near at hand while the sportsman is standing erect, let him remain so without stirring a muscle, and not attempt to dodge down into the blind. The ducks may not notice him—especially if his dress is of a suitable color—among the reeds, but will inevitably catch sight of the least movement.

So much for general suggestions and advice, which will be regarded or disregarded by the gentlemen for whom this work is written, much according to their previously conceived ideas; and which may or may not be correct according to the opportunities of judging, and the skill of turning them to account, of the writer; and now we will record a few personal experiences, in the hope, if not of further elucidating and supporting the views herein expressed, of furnishing the reader with more interesting matter.

CHAPTER IX.

DUCK-SHOOTING ON THE INLAND LAKES.

Out West—'way out West—a very long distance from our eastern cities in miles, but, thanks to steam and iron, a very short one in hours, upon an island lying in a bay that debouches into one of the great chain of lakes, is situated a large, neat, white-painted and comfortable house, where a club of sportsmen meet to celebrate the advent and presence of the wild ducks. The mansion—for it deserves that name from its extent and many conveniences—peeps out from amid the elms and hickories that cover the point upon which it stands, almost concealed in summer by their foliage, but in winter protected, as it were, by their bare, gaunt limbs. From the piazza that extends along the front a plank pathway leads to the wharf, which shelves into the water, like the levees on the Mississippi, and down or up which each sportsman can, unaided, run his light boat at his own sweet will. Adjoining the wharf is the out-house, where the boats are stored in tiers, one above another, and are protected summer and winter from the weather. Not far off stands that most important building, a commodious ice-house, suggestive of the luxuries and comforts that a better acquaintance with the ways of the place will realize.

The island is not large, but wherever it is tillable, a garden, orchard, and grapery have been planted, and furnish the household with delicious fruit and vegetables. Quail have been introduced, and, being protected by the regulations of the establishment, have increased and multiplied; and wild turkeys occasionally commit upon the vines depredations which are condignly punished. It is a lovely spot, far from other habitations, and affords shelter during the fall months to as pleasant a set of sportsmen as can be found the world over.

The President, with his short figure and grey hair, but sharp, clear eye, was selected for his superior success as a marksman, and rarely returns from a day's excursion without a boat-load of game. The Vice-President and Secretary are the only other officers, and upon their fiat it depends whether any outsider shall trespass upon their inland Paradise. Promiscuous invitations were once extended to the brethren of the gun and rod, but so many spurious counterfeits presented themselves, that a stringent rule had to be adopted to exclude all but the genuine article.

The shooting lasts from the 1st of September till the chill breath of winter closes the bay and drives the birds to more hospitable localities. It is pursued in a small, light, flat-bottomed boat, similar, on a larger pattern, to the rail-boats used on the Delaware. Each boat is provided with a pair of oars working on pins that fit into outriggers; and also with a long setting-pole, which has a bent wire, like a tiny two-pronged pitchfork, on the end, to catch against the reeds in poling. A place is made to rest the gun on upon one of the thwarts; an ammunition-box, containing separate compartments for shot of several sizes, wads, and caps, is stowed away in the bottom, and a heavy loading-stick, in addition to the ramrod, is carried. Two guns are an absolute necessity, unless the sportsman has a breech-loader; for many birds are crippled and require a second shot before they escape into the thick weeds, where they are hopelessly lost; and when the flight is rapid, he requires, at least, four barrels, and would be thankful if he could manage more.

The bay, which stretches in vast extent, is filled with high reeds and wild rice, and rarely exceeds a few feet in depth except where open passages mark the deeper channels. It is a matter of no little intricacy for a stranger to find his way, and after nightfall the oldest *habitué* will often become bewildered, as the various bunches of weeds, tufts of rice, or stretches of pond lilies look alike, and when a southerly wind is blowing the water falls and leaves all but the deep channels nearly or quite bare. If a man under such circumstances once loses his course he may as well make up his mind to pass the night in his boat; though he work himself almost to death trying to pole over bare spots, he will but travel in a circle and grow momentarily more bewildered.

I landed at the wharf in the middle of October, of a year ever famous for the immense numbers of birds that were killed during it, and met with a hearty greeting from a goodly company collected round the groaning board of mine host of the white-flowing locks. There was our worthy President, and our Secretary and Treasurer gracefully combined in one; there our lucky man and the unlucky man, and there a famous black-bass fisherman, and there my special friend, and others of lesser note.

We sat down to tea with roasted canvas-backs at one end of the table, broiled steaks at the other, and beautiful potatoes flanking each that had been raised on our own premises and were tumbling to white particles, as though they were trying to be flour; jolly, round, baked apples sitting complacently in their own juice, vegetables of all sorts, grapes from our grapery, and so many other inward comforts that one hardly knew where to begin and never knew where to leave off. Our comely hostess, who had prepared these good things, poured out the tea for us, and put in sly remarks to her favorites; and, altogether, it was truly pleasant.

After tea and adjournment to the sitting-room, while enjoying the practical cigar or comfortable pipe, we discussed the varied fortunes of the day and the probabilities of the morrow; compared views on the habits of fish, flesh, or fowl, and related experiences of former expeditions. But eager for the morning sun, we retired early and dreamed of victory.

As soon as the lazy dawn streaked the east, dressing being done by candle-light, we hastily disposed of our breakfast and prepared for the start. Having selected our boats and arranged them on the wharf, we stowed our guns, ammunition-boxes, over-clothes, a few decoys, and such other articles as fancy suggested; and then taking two little tin pails, we put a nice lunch of cold duck, steak, bread, pickles, cake, and fruit in one, and into the other water with a large lump of ice bobbing around in the centre; and thus equipped, each man slid his boat down the inclined wharf, and shipping his oars, pulled for his favorite location.

My friend and myself joined forces, and made our first pause at a little bunch of wild rice not far from the house, called Fort Ossawatomie. Decoys are not generally used in this region, as they cannot be seen from any considerable distance by the birds on account of the reeds; but my friend had left his at this place over night, and they were still "bobbing around"—pretending to swim and looking deceitfully innocent—when we ensconced ourselves among the reeds near by, crowding down into the bottom of our boats well out of view.

Several flocks were seen hovering over the horizon, or moving along in the distance, scarcely discernible against the morning clouds; and although occasionally they bade fair to approach, our hopes were destined to disappointment, till a single bird turned and headed directly towards us. When a bird is approaching head on, it is almost impossible to tell whether he is not going directly from you; and at times, except for his growing plainer every moment, we should have doubted which way this bird was flying. Once he turned, from a change of fancy or fearing danger, but perceiving some other cause of alarm he again straightened his course towards us.

We were bent down, peering eagerly through the high reeds, as at last he came by, within a long gun-shot, on the side of my companion. The latter, rising at the exact moment, wheeled round, brought up his gun, and fired in an instant. It was just within range, but the bird turned over, killed dead, and fell with a great splash into the water, sending the spray six feet into the air. Seizing the pole, I pushed out to him, and found that he was a blue-bill, one of the best birds of the Western waters, and at this time in perfection.

We again concealed ourselves; but noticing that the birds shunned the spot, I determined to leave it, and pushed out alone to one of the principal land-marks, where the landscape presents so great a uniformity—a large umbrella-like elm upon the distant shore. I did not follow the regular channel; and at first the way was a difficult one, being directly through a fringe of wild rice, where the water was shallow and the stalks reached high above my head, but beyond, an open patch of water-lilies stretched for half a mile.

The broad, smooth leaves of this remarkable plant, far larger than those of the pond-lilies of the Eastern States, lay in numbers upon, or half buried in, the water; while standing up a few feet above its surface with their straight stems, and gracefully waving in the wind, were the cup-like pods that contain the seeds.

When the pods first form the seeds are entirely hidden from view, but as they increase in size, holes form in the covering, through which they peep as through a window. The seeds and pod are originally green, but darken and turn blue, and then brown, as the season advances; and the holes, which begin by being small, become larger till they open sufficiently for the seeds to fall out. The seeds or berries are elliptical in shape and of almost the size of a chestnut; in the green state they are soft, and can be readily cut with a knife; but when ripe and black, they are as hard as stone, and will turn the edge of a knife like agate.

When about half ripe, or bluish in color, they are good to eat, and after the removal of a little green sprout hidden in the centre, are sweet, tasting much the same as a chestnut. As they ripen and their covering recedes, their stems hold them upright; but the first heavy frost breaks down the stems, and lets the seed fall out into the water, where they lie till next year.

The working of nature is wonderful, as no one observes more frequently than the sportsman; all this care is taken to preserve the seeds for their appointed work. If they were permitted to fall out when green or even half ripe, the action of the water would soften and destroy them; extreme hardness is necessary to resist its action for so long a time; while, on the other hand, if they were retained longer and exposed to excessive cold, their germinating principle would be annihilated.

Wood-ducks are fond of them in their unripe state, and frequent the marshes, especially in the early fall, to procure a supply. With a view to nuts and grapes for dessert, I paused to gather a number of pods, and was carelessly pushing along, when from out a bunch of weeds, with a great clatter, sprang a couple of those birds. Dropping the setting-pole, I threw myself forward to seize the gun; but for this shooting, infinite practice and great aptitude are required; and although well accustomed to kill rail from the floating cockleshells on the Delaware river, and able to take one end of a birch canoe with any man, I was bunglingly in my own way, and, when at last one barrel was discharged, a shameful miss was the only result. Anathematizing my awkwardness, I was dropping the butt to reload, when, roused by the report, another bird sprang not more than twenty yards off. In an instant the gun was at my shoulder, and, when the fire streamed forth, the bird doubled up, riddled with shot, and pitched forward into the weeds. It was a drake, and, although young, the plumage was resplendent with the green, brown, and mottle of the most beautiful denizen of our waters—the elegant woodduck.

Several more rose, far out of range, before the lilies were passed and my destination in the open channel reached. Stopping on the brink of the latter, to watch the flight of the birds, I noticed that they frequently crossed a reedy island in the middle of the channel, and consequently proceeded to conceal myself in what among our association is called the Little Bunker. It was an admirable location; the channel on each side did not exceed one hundred yards in width, and the weather having become thick, with an easterly wind blowing and a slight rain driving, the promise of sport was excellent.

Once fairly hidden, and my work commenced; bird after bird and flock after flock approached, and although the boat, even while pressed in among and steadied by the stiff reeds, was far from firm, a goodly number was soon collected. How much more exhilarating is this noble sport as it is pursued in the West than upon our Atlantic coast, where, stretched upon his back in a coffin-like battery, the sportsman has to lie for hours cooling his heels and exhausting his patience! There he is not confined to one position; but, after shooting down a bird, has the excitement of pushing after it, and, if it is only wounded, of following it, perhaps in a long chase before it is retrieved; and then he must make all haste to return to the hiding-place, over which the birds are flying finely in his absence, and thus he keeps up a glow and fire of activity and exercise.

It is a glorious sight to see a noble flock of ducks approach; to watch them with trembling alternations of fear and hope as they waver in their course, as they crowd together or separate, as they swing first one flank of their array forward, then the other; as they draw nearer and nearer, breathlessly to wait the proper time, and, with quick eye and sure aim, select a pair, or perhaps more, with each barrel. It is still more glorious to see them fall— doubled up if killed dead, turning over and over if shot in the head, and slanting down if only wounded, driving up the spray in mimic fountains as they strike; and glorious, too, the chase after the wounded—with straining muscles to follow his rapid wake, and, when he dives, catching the first glimpse of his reappearance to plant the shot from an extra gun in a vital spot. Glorious to survey the prizes, glorious to think over and relate the successful event, and glorious to listen to the tales of others.

Sad, however, is it when the flock turns off and pushes far out to the open water; sadder still when the aim is not true and the bird goes by uninjured; sad when the chase is unsuccessful and the weeds hide the prey, or he dives to grasp a root and never reappears; and saddest of all to fall overboard out of your frail bark—a fate that sooner or later awaits every one that shoots ducks from little boats.

I had had all these experiences except the last, and almost that—when pushing through the weeds, my friend appeared, attracted by my rapid firing, and after comparing our respective counts, ensconced himself in one of the points opposite me on the channel. By this plan all birds that came between us gave one or the other a shot, and each could mark birds approaching the other from behind.

The morning passed rapidly away amid splendid shooting, and noon found us united in my hiding-place to eat a sociable meal together. During the middle of the day the birds repose, and the sportsman employs the time in satisfying the cravings of hunger or even in a nap, interrupted though he may be in either by an occasional whirr of wings, that, when it is too late, informs him of lost opportunities.

We talked over matters. As the day had cleared off and become warm, the prospect of sport for some hours at least was over, and my friend suggested we should visit the snipe ground. To approve the suggestion, to push out and to ship our oars, was the work of a moment, and we were soon at Mud Creek bridge, a pull of about two miles through an open lead, from which the ducks were continuously springing on our approach. Having anchored our boats a short distance from shore, to prevent the wild hogs paying us a visit, we waded to land, and substituting small shot for the heavy charges in our guns, walked a few yards up the road and crossed the fence.

I had brought my setter with me, and he had proved himself a model of quietness in the boat, from the bottom of which he had raised his head only once all day; when my first duck dropped he rose on his haunches, and watching where it fell, sniffed at it as I pushed up, and then, satisfied he had no part in such sport, lay down to sleep.

The moment he touched land his vigor returned; at a motion, he darted out into the meadow of alternating broad slanks and high field grass that lay before us, and ere he had traversed fifty yards, as he approached an open spot, hesitated, drew cautiously, and finally paused on a firm point. Stepping to him as fast as the impressible nature of the ground permitted, we flushed three birds, rising as they are apt to do one after the other, and killed two, one springing wide and escaping unshot at.

While going to retrieve the dead birds we flushed two more, both of which were bagged, one a long shot, wing-tipped, and not recovered till some time afterwards; for, ere we reached him, we had sprung a dozen, most of which were duly accounted for. The missed birds, after circling round high in the air, returned to the neighborhood of their original locality, and pitching down head-foremost, concealed themselves among the high grass near enough to lure us to their pursuit.

The walking was terribly hard; the clayey mud uncommonly tenacious; the day was already well advanced, and splendid as was the sport, we resolved, after having pretty well exhausted ourselves and bagged twenty-six birds, that we must hasten back to the rice swamp, or we should lose the evening's shooting.

We returned to our boats, and stowing the game, pulled with the utmost vigor down the channel of Mud Creek, and in a short time were again hidden among the high reeds, awaiting the ducks. This time my friend selected a spot near a sort of semi-island, that was submerged or not, according to the state of the water, and near which was a favorite roosting-place.

The sun was leisurely dropping down the western sky, throwing his slanting rays across the broad bay, and lighting up the distant club-house as by a fire. The fringe of land, trees, and bushes, that shut out the horizon and rose but little above the water level, was growing dim and hazy of outline. The wind had died away; and stillness, but for the quacking of the ducks, the splashing of the coots, or so-called mud-hens, and the occasional report of a gun, reigned supreme. A lethargy seemed to have fallen upon the birds; a distant flock alone would at long intervals greet our eyes, and for some time our evening's sport bade fair to prove a failure.

However, as the sun was about to sink, the birds began to arrive, at first one or two at a time, then more rapidly and in larger flocks, till at last it was one steady stream and whirr of wings. Faster than we could load, faster than we could shoot, or could have shot had we had fifty guns, from all quarters and of all kinds they streamed past; now the sharp whistle of the teal, then the rush of the mallard, sometimes high over our heads, at others darting close beside us; by ones, by twos, by dozens, by hundreds, crowded together in masses or stretched in open lines, in all variety of ways, but in one uninterrupted flight.

Such shooting rarely blesses the fortunate sportsman; we drove down our charges as best we could, sometimes having one barrel loaded or half loaded, sometimes the other, oftener neither, when we were interrupted with such glorious chances; our nerves, eyes, and muscles were on the strain, and to this day we have only to regret that we did not then possess a breech-loader.

The air was alive with birds; the rustle of their wings made one continuous hum; the heavy flocks approached and passed us with a sound like the gusty breeze of an autumn night rattling through the dying leaves. When the sun fled and darkness seemed to spring up around us, they appeared in the most unexpected and bewildering manner; at one time from out of the glorious brilliancy of the western sky, then from the deep gloom of the opposite quarter, darting across us or plunging down into the weeds near by.

Our birds lay where they fell, and when the approaching night bade us depart, we retrieved sixty-seven—the result of about one hour's shooting—doubtless losing numbers that were not noticed, or which, being wounded, escaped. Had we not been awkward from a year's idleness, or had we shot as the professionals of Long Island and each used a breech-loader, I could hardly say how many we might not have killed. As it was, the sport was wonderful, and the result sufficient to satisfy our ambition.

We lost no time in escaping from the weeds into the channel-ways, whither the open-water ducks—

the red-heads and canvas-backs—had preceded us, and were still directing their flight; and then started for the few dim trees that we knew surrounded the club-house, rousing in our course immense flocks of the worthless American coot, *Fulica Americana*, the mud-hen of the natives.

The wharf reached, the boats landed, supper over, the birds counted and registered, the social pipe illumined, and we gathered in a circle round the fire of our parlor for improving conversation.

"How many birds have we killed this year?" inquired a member.

"The record shows a goodly total of 2,351," replied the Secretary, turning to the register; "almost as many already as the entire return of last season, during which we only killed 2,908."

"And the better varieties seem this year to be more numerous."

"In that particular there is surprising uniformity from year to year. Last season the return is made up as follows: canvas-backs, 246; red-heads, 122; blue-bills, 395; mallards, 540; dusky-ducks, 108; wood-ducks, 601; blue-winged teal, 474; green-winged teal, 39; widgeons, 204; pin-tails, 50; gadwalls, 67; spoonbills, 11; ruddy-ducks, 2; butter-balls, 7; geese, 2; quail, 14; cormorants, 2; turkeys, 3; great hell-diver, 1; and this year the average is about the same."

"But I think," said the President, "the canvas-backs and red-heads are earlier and better than usual."

"They are rather earlier in making their appearance abundantly. The variation is never great, however, and the birds appear in the following order: the wood-ducks first, being plentiful early in September; the blue-winged teal begin to surpass them about the 20th of that month, and soon afterward the mallards arrive; widgeons are abundant by the middle of October, and canvas-backs and red-heads are the latest."

"Ah," burst forth the unlucky man, enthusiastically, "the wood-duck shooting is my favorite; when they rise from the lilies they are easier to kill than when flying past at full speed; and you have a punter to pole the boat and help mark the wounded birds."

"October has my preference," responded the President, with glowing eye; "the large ducks— the mallards, canvas-backs, and red-heads—have then arrived; the blue-bills and teal are numerous; and, when a single teal flies past, a man has to know how to handle his gun to keel him over handsomely."

"But mallards dodge, when you rise to shoot, at the report of the first barrel; and red-heads and canvas-backs, if not killed stone dead, dive and swim off under water, or, catching the weeds in their bills, hold on after death and never reappear. Have you noticed the large teeth, or nicks, in the bills, especially of red-heads?"

"Yes. Those long, recurved teeth aid them in tearing up the wild celery, on which they feed. I have had them serve me the trick you complain of when they were at the last gasp—so nearly dead, that I have pushed out and been on the point of picking them up. When not so badly hurt, they will swim off with their bill only projecting above the surface, and if there is the least wind this is entirely invisible. The trick is known to others of the duck family; even the ingenuous wood-duck will have recourse to the same mean subterfuge occasionally, as one that was but slightly wounded proved to me to-day."

"Is it true," inquired the fisherman, "that other ducks steal from the canvas-backs the wild celery that they have exhausted themselves in procuring?"

"The widgeons have the credit of doing so; but I have never seen, and somewhat doubt it. The canvas-back is too large and strong a duck to be readily trifled with, and is by no means exhausted by diving to the depth of a few feet after celery. This celery, as we call it—which has a long, delicate leaf, resembling broad-grass, and bears the name of *Zostera valisneria* among the botanists— grows in water about five feet deep, and its roots furnish the favorite and most fattening food of the canvas-backs, red-heads, and, strange to say, mud-hens. The widgeon is not a large nor powerful duck; can dive no further than to put its head under water, while its tail stands perpendicularly above the surface; and, although a terrible torment to the weak and gentle mud-hen, would think twice before incensing the fierce and powerful canvas-back. Of a calm day it is amusing to watch the flocks of noisy mud-hens, collected in front of the clubhouse, diving for their food, and being robbed of it by the widgeons. The latter swims rapidly among them, and no sooner does he espy one coming to the surface, with his bill full of celery, than he pounces upon and carries it off. He is watchful and voracious, and quickly devours the food; while the injured mud-hen, with a resigned look, takes a long breath and dives for another morsel."

"Do they not combine to drive the robber away?"

"Occasionally; but he minds their blows as little as their scoldings, and generally swims off with his prize. The canvas-back, however, would soon teach him better manners."

"Are the western canvas-backs as delicate and high-flavored as those of the Chesapeake?"

"Fully so, as my friends in New York, who have been fortunate enough to share my luck, have often testified. Of course, when they first come they are thin and poor, but having the same food as is found in the Chesapeake, and being less disturbed, they soon attain excellent condition, and are entirely free from the slightest sedgy flavor."

"That sedgy or fishy taste is confined mainly to birds shot on the salt water, and is rarely found in any birds killed upon the inland lakes, so that many —for instance the bay-snipe—that are barely passable when shot along the coast, are excellent in the interior."

"And yet the naturalists class the canvas-back among *fuligulæ*, or sea ducks."

"That arises from some scientific peculiarity, and is not universal. He is certainly a fresh-water duck, and thousands are shot here yearly."

"I lose a great many crippled birds," said the unlucky man, meditatively; "I wonder what becomes of them all?"

"Many die, a few recover, some are frozen in when the bay freezes over; after the first hard frost large numbers can be picked up, but they are so poor as only to be fit to send to the New York market. Most sportsmen lose many ducks that they should recover; considerable practice is required to mark well, but the search after a bird should be thorough, and not lightly abandoned. The boat, when pushed into the reeds, must be so placed that it can be easily shoved off, and the pole kept ready for instant use. If, however, a mallard is only wounded, and falls into the weeds, it is useless to go after him.

"On the other hand, if a canvas-back, but slightly touched, falls in open water, he will be rarely recovered; the one hides in the weeds, the other dives and swims under water prodigiously. The mallard and canvas-back are the types of two classes—the former is a marsh duck, the latter an open-water duck. The mallard lives on the pond-lily seeds, and affects the shallow, muddy pond-holes; the canvas-back seeks the broad channels, and devours the roots of plants; the one dodges at the flash of the gun or sight of the sportsman, the other moves majestically onward, regardless of the havoc that the heavy discharges make in his ranks. Of nearly the same size, of unsurpassable delicacy on the table, of equal vigor, they differ utterly in their habits."

"Speaking of types," said the unlucky man, recalling unpleasant reminiscences of numerous misses, "you might call blue-bills types of the fast-flying and dodging ducks. When they come down before a stiff wind, and are making their best time, lightning is slow by comparison, and shot does not seem to me to go quite fast enough."

"They are the scaup or broad-bill of the East, *Fuligula Marila*, and are aptly termed the bullet-winged duck. They are undoubtedly the most difficult duck to kill that flies. I have known a thorough sportsman and excellent shot on quail, shoot all day at them without killing one. You must make great allowance for their speed."

"And, moreover," added the President, "you must load properly; there must be powder enough behind the shot to send it clear through the bird; one pellet driven in that way will kill a bird that would carry off a dozen lodged beneath the skin or in the flesh."

"Perhaps so, but I doubt its feasibility," was the response; "no small shot was ever, in my opinion, driven through the body of a duck with any charge of powder at over thirty yards. I use light powder and plenty of shot."

This announcement was received with unanimous dissent, and the President expressed the general feeling when he continued—

"Heavy shot will make a gun recoil painfully; but if the shot is light the charge of powder may be large without producing unpleasant effects; the shot will be driven quick and strong, and the bird deprived of life instantaneously. Perhaps the pellets are not driven through the body, but the blow is severer and the shock is more stunning. I use one ounce of shot and three drachms of powder, and would prefer to increase rather than diminish the powder. It is a mistake to suppose powder does not burn because black particles fall to the ground if it is fired over snow or white paper; these, I take it, are flakes of charcoal and not powder, and some will fall, no matter how light may be the load."

"For my part," persisted the unlucky man, "I think the crippling of birds arises from our inability to judge distances, and from our firing at birds out of reasonable range. The patent breech was meant to remedy the necessity for such heavy charges of powder as are used in the old-fashioned flint-locks. Johnston, the author of an admirable treatise on shooting, which is now out of print, is my authority, and he says that an over-charge of powder makes a gun scatter prodigiously without adding proportionately to the force."

"That depends upon the character of the bore," answered the Secretary; "if it is relieved at the breech, and after narrowing above, made a perfect cylinder towards the muzzle, the more the powder the better it will shoot."

Seeing that an interminable discussion was about

to open, branching off, in all likelihood, into the comparative qualities of powder and manufactures of guns, the President interposed.

I slipped off and went to bed. Being a comparative stranger at the club house, for this was the first year of my membership, I had made it a rule to follow the advice and direction of the older habitues, but I wanted to get a chance to try some experiments of my own. This would require a little preparation for which I needed the early hours before the others should be up.

As I have said, the members were not at the time of which I am writing in the habit of using decoys. There was a prejudice against them, their weight in the boat was an admitted disadvantage, which it was claimed was not compensated by any corresponding benefit. My experience in a country where birds were not so plenty, assured me that this was a mistake, but having come to the club house unexpectedly, I had not brought my decoys with me, and had to rely upon such substitutes as could be got up on the spur of the moment. It was with the intention of preparing these that I retired so early.

In those ancient days of Western civilization, it was the habit not only to put several beds in one room, but often to devote one bed to the accommodation of two men, but by being content with a very small apartment, I had succeeded in getting a room all to myself. The bedstead was nothing more than a cot, none too long and by no means too wide. There was a feather bed on it, a couch we Eastern people do not always approve, but which has its compensations of a cold night in a loosely framed house. When I had once felt the insidious wind creeping down my back where the clothes left an open place for it, I learned the superiority of experience to theory. I slept, however, as only the just and the sportsman sleep, my head dropping into unconsciousness as it touched the pillow, and never returning to it until the daylight penetrated the open window with its welcome rays—sleep without a dream, such as youth and health and tired nature only know.

Next morning I borrowed a saw and a hatchet, all the tools that the place boasted, and fashioned as best I could some floats. These I carefully concealed in my boat, and said nothing about them. After breakfast, when we pushed off, I took my course alone. I went pretty well up into the marsh, in fact as far as in my ignorance of the intricacies of the swamp I dared. I chose a point between two creeks, and going carefully into my blind from behind, so as not to break it down in front, a precaution which I observed most of the sportsmen neglected, I concealed myself, and waited the course of events. Mere waiting never suited my views, but on this occasion there was nothing else to do. It was some time before I killed a duck, and I was wondering whether I should have any opportunity to try my floats, when a solitary mallard came within long range, and I was so fortunate as to bag him.

It was a beginning, I set him on one of the blocks of wood I had roughly trimmed into shape that morning. I had noticed the day before that the water was too deep to set up a dead duck in the ordinary way. Neither had I been able to find weights of half bricks, which are the main reliance of the Long Island gunner, or stones, which were an unknown quantity in that muddy country. So the best I could do, was, to thrust down a long reed with a string tied to it at the proper distance from the bottom. My decoy was not as natural as I could have made it with better appliances, but it was the best I could manufacture, and it did some service. In less than five minutes it was joined by another mallard, which first came to look, and was then persuaded to stay by the gentle influence of an ounce and a half of shot.

In a short time all my floats were occupied, and although they bothered me, and wasted my time by breaking away in consequence of not being properly arranged, they brought me, I do not doubt, twice as many birds as I should have got without them. I have much faith in being well hidden. For black ducks, which are the most wary, it is absolutely necessary not to disturb a leaf that their sharp eyes will notice. If the reeds are thick enough of themselves to conceal the shooter, do not either add to them or break them down. I have seen blinds built up, till they looked like straw mattresses set on end, of which the birds would be more shy than of the man himself. I was killing shoal-water ducks, not of course getting canvas-backs, red-heads, or broad-bills so far back in the marsh, and it was not desirable to have many stools for the same reason that it is not right to have too large a blind, they are apt to awaken suspicion.

One great improvement noticeable after the decoys were set out was, that the birds came in closer, and gave me better shots. Without them there is nothing to attract the ducks out of their line of flight, they drive straight along, perhaps in a direction to bring them to the gunner, more likely not, but if there are a few decoys, they will at least make a dash toward the stand. Situated as I was, surrounded almost entirely with marsh, only a little open water on front and on either side of me, I felt the want of a dog sadly. My setter, which I had brought from the East solely for snipe shooting, had shown himself on the day before so utterly worthless as a retriever, that I had not taken him with me again. Many of my ducks fell into the reeds, and if they were killed dead, they were hard to find, and if they had the least life in them, they would crawl away, and sneak so effectually that if I got them at all it would be after I had wasted much valuable time. Had my retriever been with me, I am sure that I should have doubled my bag.

Of all the retrievers which have ever been used in this country, none equal those which are called the Chesapeake Bay dogs. Their hair is so thick and matted that they can stand any amount of cold without suffering, they are capital swimmers, and I have seen them dive for a wounded duck, and they seem to have an adaptation for this shooting, developed perhaps by generations of training, which no other dogs possess. On one occasion I remember taking out a pup for the second time that he had ever been shot over. He was so eager that I had to tie him in the blind, and only let him loose after a bird had been shot down. Yet on that day I saw him recover a wounded duck after following him half a mile, twice drop a dead one which he had in his mouth, to bring a live one, and jump on another and hold him with his paws till he could reach him by putting his head entirely under water. The wonderful instances of intelligence reported of this breed would be incredible, if something only a little less astonishing were not known to every man who has owned one.

On this occasion I did not have my dog, and much was the time and many the duck I lost in consequence. It seemed as though most of those which were killed dead, fell into the marsh where I could not find the half of them, and that the wounded fell into the open water, whence they made their way to cover, before I could run the boat out and pick them up. The sun was shining brightly from a cloudless heaven, and although the air was cold, I was so sheltered by the reeds that I was as warm as I desired to be. That is one of the points of superiority of inland over battery shooting; had I been lying in the battery with the same wind, no amount of sun would have kept me warm.

I had to pick up early, as it would be no joke to be lost in those monotonous marshes during the night. To get out after dark would have been impossible, and almost equally impossible for any assistance to reach me. I was fain to be satisfied with a moderate bag, and lose the evening's flight rather than lose myself. When I arrived at the club house, I found that with the aid of my improvised stools I had made the second-best bag of the day. Comparative stranger as I was to the marshes, this result was more than satisfactory. My supper tasted all the better in consequence, but I did not say anything about the means which I had taken to bring about the result.

That evening, when we had collected around the social fire and lighted our still more social pipes, the president referred to the fact that the night before, after I had gone to my welcome couch, the rest of the members had been repeating stories and called upon the unlucky man to fulfill a promise he had made to give some personal experience of trout fishing.

UNLUCKY MAN.—" But my adventure occurred on Long Island, whither I had gone to learn trout-fishing. I had a new rod of Conroy's best and most expensive pattern, a book full of flies, a basket, a bait-box, a net, a gaff, and all things appurtenant, and was especially proud of my fishing suit, which a brother of the angle had kindly selected for me. My boots came above my knees, and were of yellow Russian leather, with which my brown pants matched admirably, while a blue vest, a white flannel coat, red neck-tie and crimson cap, combined all the colors that were least likely to alarm the fish.

"The other anglers collected at the hotel kindly aided me with their advice, for which I was truly grateful. They rigged out my leader with flies, and convincingly proving that the more flies used the more fish must be taken, fastened on thirteen. Conroy had hardly served me fairly in selecting my assortment, for they were pronounced by all not to be half large or bright enough. It was clear that the larger the fly the easier the fish could see it, and the more surely it would catch; so they loaned me a number, principally yellow, green, and blue, which was the more generous of them, as they had but few of the same sort themselves.

"They impressed upon me to be up early, because trout will not bite after sunrise—besides, I knew from the proverb that worms were more easily obtained early; and it was still dark when, having passed a restless few hours, I awoke and dressed. The house was silent, not a person to interfere with me, and having set up my rod the night before, I crept cautiously down stairs. The tip would slash about and knock at the doors and on the walls as I passed, and gave me great trouble in turning the corners of the stairs, but I reached the hall door safely and stepped out upon the piazza.

"I had hardly congratulated myself, when, hearing a suspicious growl, and recollecting that the tavern-keeper had a cross mastiff, I turned, and saw him in the dim light making straight for me. Running was never my forte, but, gentlemen, my speed round that house with that mastiff after me has rarely been equalled; he kept it up well, however, and if he could have turned a corner readily, would have caught me. Recovering my presence of mind in the third round, I darted through the hall door, and slamming it to behind me, heard my enemy bounce against it, and after a growl and a sniff or two, turn away in disgust.

"Upon regaining my breath, I ascended to my room, and loading the revolver which I always carry on dangerous journeys, returned to the attack, determined on revenge. Strange to say, however, the cowardly beast, the moment the pistol was presented at him, uttered a low whine and shrank away. Disgusted with his cowardice, I seized up my rod, which had been dropped in my first flight, and pursuing him howling piteously three times round the house, laid it on him soundly.

"It must have been poor stuff, for the tip broke. Conroy mended it afterwards, without charge, when I told him the circumstances. But I put in a spare one, and having dug my box full of worms, went to the shed where my horse was left standing, ready harnessed, from the night before. There is nothing like attention to these little matters in time; for, if the hostler had had to harness him, he might have detained me many precious minutes.

"A half-hour's drive soon brought me to the pond, and, after hitching the animal to the fence—

for it was necessary to turn into the field from the main road—I walked down to the bank and jumped into a boat. Unfortunately, it was chained to a staple and padlocked; the inn-keeper had forgotten to give me the key. They were all the same but one, lying on the shore and turned bottom up, that did not seem to be sound. No time, however, was to be lost; the streaks in the east were beginning to turn red—an indication that the sun was rising—and the hour for fishing would soon be over. I launched the boat, such as it was, and pushed off.

"Casting the fly is difficult, but casting thirteen flies is almost impossible. The boat was leaky; the fish did not rise, and the water did. I bailed as well as I could with one hand, and fished with the other, till at last, almost exhausted, I saw the sun rise. As a desperate resource, however, the bait-box came into play. I removed the flies and substituted a hook and worm; but while thus employed, and unable to bail, the water gained on me rapidly. Hardly had the bait touched the water before a fine fish seized it. I tried my best to pull him out, but he would not come—the rod was such a miserable, weak affair that it bent like a switch. The trout swam about in every direction, and tried to get under stumps and weeds and to break my line; but I held him fast and reeled in—for my friends had explained to me what the reel was for—and was about to lay down my rod and fish him out with the landing-net, when—the boat sank."

Chorus—"Could you swim?"

"No; but the water was only up to my arm-pits, and I was about to wade ashore, when a colored gentleman, who had arrived and been sitting on the bank for the last few minutes, shouted to me that it was his boat and I must bring it with me. I answered, savagely, that I would do nothing of the sort, when he began to abuse me and call me thief, and say I had stolen his boat, and he would have me arrested. So I thought I had better comply, and waded along, dragging it after me. The bottom was muddy, and I slipped once or twice and went all under. It was probably then that the fish got off; but my colored friend took pity on me, and pointed out to me the best places to walk.

"I was nearly ashore, and had clambered upon a bog, as the gentleman advised, and, by his direction, I jumped to a piece of nice-looking green grass. I have always thought he deceived me in this, for it turned out to be a quagmire, and I sank at once above my waist in solid, sticky mud. The matter now became serious; my weight is no trifle, and every motion sank me deeper and deeper. I implored the colored man to help me out; to wade in to me, and let me climb on his back; I offered him money profusely; and—would you believe it?—he laughed, he roared, he shouted, he rolled over in an agony of mirth. He asked me whether I was afraid to die—that only cowards were afraid to die. I did not dare to say no, lest he should take me at my word, and was ashamed to say yes; but, as I kept on sinking, I had to own up that I was afraid, and then he only laughed louder than ever.

"My feelings were beyond description—fury does not adequately describe my rage; but fear so tempered it, that I seemed to change suddenly from the extreme of heat to the extreme of cold. I would begin by swearing at him, and end by imploring; I begged, cursed, prayed, and raved. Overcome by his unrestrained delight, at last I threatened—pouring out upon him the vilest abuse, and dire menaces of what I would do when I did get out. The prospect of that, however, rapidly diminished—the nasty, slimy mud rose by perceptible degrees—and then he made me take back all my threats and apologize to him. In the agony of my returning terror, he actually made me beg his pardon.

"When, however, hope was nearly over with me, he slowly, with maddening deliberation, took a rail from the nearest fence, and, interspersing the operation with much improving advice, began to pry me out. As I rose towards the upper world my courage returned, and my revenge was merely waiting till my body touched *terra firma* to take ample amends. Even that satisfaction was destined to disappointment; for when I was so far out, that with the aid of the rail I could help myself, he dropped it, and, suspecting my intention, he scuttled off as fast as his black legs would carry him.

"What an object I presented after effecting my escape—from head to foot one mass of mud; my handsome clothes, my hands and face, all blacker than my ebony friend, and stiff and heavy with the noisome conglomeration. After resting for a few minutes, I gathered up my rod and started for the wagon, when what should I see in the other end of the lot but a bull. A single glance showed me what I had to expect; no bull could stand such an object as I was. I ran and he ran. I made for the wagon and he after me. Such a picture as I must have presented, flying from an infuriate bull, may seem funny to you, gentlemen, but was not to me. We both reached the wagon and both went into it together—I into the seat, he into the body; the result being that I went flying out again, on the other side, over the fence. The horse, which at that moment must have been dreaming, or sleeping the sleep he did not have the night before, aroused by the crash, cast one look behind and burst his bonds and fled.

"It was a long walk home; people looked strangely at me on the way, and some unfeeling ones laughed. My wagon was broken, my horse was ruined, my clothes were spoiled; and the only consolation I had, was that my brother anglers at the hotel felt and expressed such intense sympathy for my sufferings."

The resigned tones and manner of the speaker were inimitable, and his story was received with great satisfaction and closed the evening's amusements. All parties having resolved upon an early start, retired early, and enjoyed a rest such as the sportsman only knows.

One of the attachés of our club-house, without whom it would be deprived of many pleasant features, and who is a remarkable and eccentric character, is called Henry—a Canadian Frenchman. He possesses the lightheartedness, the honesty and trustworthiness of that peculiar class, with the strongest prejudices against mean and underhanded actions and those who are guilty of them; he is, in his own obstinate way, devoted to the service of those who enjoy his esteem. Animated with strong dislikes, he is barely polite to those who have excited his distrust, while he will do anything for his favorites. He is a good shot, and thoroughly acquainted with the marsh and the habits of the birds, but on no terms will he make any suggestions as to the most promising localities. To the question, no matter how casually or confidingly uttered:

"Well, Henry, where had I better go, to-day?"
He will respond, looking you calmly in the face, and in a slightly admonitory tone:

"You know I never give advice, sir."

His greatest favorites can obtain no more satisfactory answer, and in fact not much information of any kind, from him in relation to the flight or haunts of the birds. He appears to have discovered that knowledge worth having is worth working for, and is resolved that every man shall be his own schoolmaster. He has quite an insight into character, and appreciates the members of the club and their peculiarities.

One day a party, including a number who were not members, had been snipe-shooting, and some of the latter indulged the habit of pushing on before their neighbor to shoot any bird they may have seen alight, or had reason to believe was upon his beat. Afterwards Henry remarked, as a sort of soliloquy, "He was a poor man—did not have much education, and supposed he did not know; but he did not think it right for one sportsman to run in ahead of another in order to shoot a bird before him. Probably he was wrong; but that was the way he felt, and could not help it."

It was this curious individual who waked us the next morning at an hour before daylight, and enjoyed heartily the satisfaction of rousing us up at that unseemly time. We were no way loth, however, and hastily swallowing our breakfasts and launching our boats, pushed out under cover of the darkness for our respective points. As yet the water and land were scarcely distinguishable, and localities could only be determined by intuition. Night was still brooding with outstretched wings on the earth; the sky seemed to be close overhead, and the clouds could not be distinguished from the open heavens. Slowly, however, the outlines of the horizon became apparent; then the heavy masses of lowering cloud that hung in the eastern sky, and left a narrow, transparent strip of light between themselves and the horizon, came out in strong relief; the stars faded and turned dim; trees, bushes, and distant elevations—the minutiæ of the landscape—appeared; long lines of sedge-grass and reeds sprang up from the water; the eastern sky, and especially the bright strip beneath the cloud, became lighter; a roseate tinge spread itself over the meadows, deepening to intensity in the east, and at last the sun peeped over the horizon.

Occasionally ducks will move at the first break of dawn; but frequently, as in the present instance, they do not fly till about sunrise; then the canvas-backs commenced coming in from the open water; the red-heads accompanied them; and the mallards, aroused from safe beds among the reeds, flew with loud quackings overhead. Later, the rapid blue-bills and teal darted past, the pin-tails moved majestically in stately lines, and the diminutive butter-balls hurried by. The rising sun dissipated the clouds, and the increasing wind announced a glorious ducking-day.

To enjoy this sport thoroughly, or to make the most of the chances offered, requires long practice and peculiar skill; but, when this skill has been acquired, no specialty in sportmanship can be carried to higher perfection, or confer more intense delight. To observe quickly and note the direction of flight of the distant flock; to catch sight of the single bird just topping the reeds; to hide well from the sharp eyes of the approaching ducks; to keep a steady footing, yielding to the treacherous motions of the unsteady boat without losing self-command; to measure the distance accurately from birds passing high in air; to select the proper moment to fire, and to determine correctly the speed of the moving object; to do all these things at once, without hesitation or failure in any particular, requires in a man the highest qualities of a sportsman. The wonder is that success is so often attained; for there are many men who will kill almost every bird that comes fairly within range, and who will tell you before they shoot whether they are sure of killing or not.

Unfortunately our party, although tolerably proficient, were far from perfect. Many were the fair shots missed, or only half hit, and more still were the impossible shots that were wasted. The wind drove the birds upon the long neck of reeds called Grassy Point, where several of us had located ourselves, and the river-scows, or small boats, occasionally passing kept them in motion.

During the morning several flocks of swans were seen, looking, when they passed in front of a dark cloud, like flying snow-flakes. Although somewhat resembling the appearance of geese, at a distance, the beat of their wings and their trumpet-voiced cry are altogether different. They were very shy, keeping far out of range; but excited our nerves at the mere thought of what glory would be conferred if they should happen to come within the proper distance.

One of our party, however, acquired but little credit by a shot which he made at a flock of geese that passed within twenty yards of him. He was of Milesian descent, and explained the occurrence afterwards as follows:

"You see, I was watching them come closer and closer, and making my calculation to pick out two fine ones. I knew the fellow at the head was an old gander, and tough; but right behind him came two tender, juicy youngsters—altogether the fattest and best in the whole flock. Well, it took me some time to make this selection, and, letting the old one go by, I was just about preparing to knock over the two others right and left—and done it I should have, because I intended to, you know. Well, I put up my gun, and was about taking aim, and was waiting for them to get just in the right position—for I was as cool as I am this moment; an old hunter like me is not easily flurried. Well, they were almost ready, and I was on the point of cutting them down, when somebody else—bad luck to him—about a hundred yards off, fired into the flock. Of course they flirted in every direction, and darted about so, that I lost sight of those I selected; and how could you expect me to kill any others when I had made up my mind to have those? You need not laugh because I missed with both barrels; I wouldn't have missed if the birds had been in their proper places, where I was pointing my gun."

So it was that we obtained no geese. But the canvas-backs and mallards, in the early morning, made up for the deficiency; and when, towards midday, they ceased flying, some of our party resolved to pole for wood-ducks.

To do this, as has been heretofore intimated, requires more practice than even shooting from "points"—exacting from the sportsman not merely readiness in handling the gun, but activity of motion and accuracy of balance. The gun, at full cock, is laid in its rack across the thwart; or, as I prefer, from one thwart to another, with the triggers up; the sportsman, standing erect on the stern, wields his pole with care, avoiding noise, and never by any chance touching the side of the boat with it, for nothing alarms the birds so much as rapping on the side of the boat, although it is not easy to avoid doing so. He faces forward, raises the pole carefully, and replacing it without a splash or a blow on the crackling stems or leaves of the lilies, uses his body as a fulcrum as often as he wishes to alter the direction of the boat. He works his way against the wind as much as possible, and, casting his eyes in every direction, is always on the alert. Suddenly, with a roar like distant thunder, a wood-duck, generally the male, starts from the weeds, and with a curious cry, like that of a wailing infant, makes the best of his way from the approaching danger; instantly the sportsman drops the pole, wherever it may be—in mid air or deep in the mud, just planted or at its full reach—and springing to his gun, raises it with rapidity but deliberation, and, if the bird has not already gained a safe distance, discharges it with the best effect he is able to command. Frequently, at the report, another bird will start, and offer a fair and generally successful shot.

To one accustomed to kill quail, this shooting,

after the awkwardness arising from the motion of the boat is overcome, is not difficult; but the knack of dropping the pole at once is almost unattainable. Most persons, at first, frantically endeavor to deposit the pole in the boat, and cannot drop it instantly; others give it an energetic push. The former allow the birds time to escape, while the latter increase the unsteadiness of the boat.

The birds usually rise well, attaining the height of twenty feet before they move directly away, and hence present a good shot. If they are missed, they may be marked down, pursued, and started again; and as they are frequently very numerous, and rise at unexpected moments, they keep the sportsman excited, until, worn out with the excessive and unaccustomed labor, he has to stop and rest. If the water is low the poling is hard work, and at the most favorable times will be found sufficiently exhausting. The birds principally frequent the lily beds, which stretch out in broad patches where the water is moderately deep; but they are also found in open spots among the high reeds, and occasionally among the deer-tongue.

There are several kinds of weeds growing in the shallows of the bay, and restricted in their extent by its depth. The reeds, which in the fall resemble a ripe field of grain, have crimson stems, and narrow yellow leaves, almost inclosing the stems at their base and streaming gracefully in the wind at the top; they thrive in shallow water, and, attaining a height of twelve feet, form the hiding-places of the sportsman. The wild rice has a greenish-yellow stem, with longer joints and without leaves; it branches at the end into the seed-receptacles, and is not found in such large patches. The deer-tongue grows in deeper water, and retains its green hue till the weather intimates that winter is present. It has a leaf like a dull spear-head, that projects but a few inches above the surface; and its stout stems, springing up close together, constitute a serious obstacle to the advancing boat. There are also scattered patches of weeds, usually called grass because they are green, but with a round, hollow, tapering stem, or leaf, that has no resemblance whatever to grass.

Early in the season, when there are few birds flying over the points, and the young, tender, and gentle wood-ducks crowd the marshes and will permit an easy approach, it is customary to employ a punter, who poles the boat while the sportsman sits on the forward thwart, gun in hand, ready in a moment to cut down the feeble birds. But if any of the shooting is to be done from the points, the punter will be found in the way, increasing the unsteadiness of the boat and augmenting the danger, already sufficiently great. Although by no means proficient, I always prefer poling myself, and will never permit any guns in the boat but my own.

On the day more particularly referred to in this chapter, we found the birds plentiful, although rather wild, and had grand sport, starting the crying wood-ducks and the quacking mallards from their hiding-places, and killing a goodly number in spite of their sharp ears and strong wings.

Of the particular shots, the numerous misses, the various mishaps, it were vain to tell. A baptism in the shallow bay-water is regarded as a necessary initiation, and not being dangerous, the ceremony is frequently repeated. Good shots are rarer than bad ones, even with the best marksmen, and perhaps the author would have to vindicate truth by telling some awkward blunders of his own, and thus forfeit the reader's respect for ever. It is sufficient for the reader to recall the best day's sport at ducks he ever had, to imagine his own shooting considerably improved, his strength and activity augmented, and his promptest deliberation surpassed; and he will have a faint idea of our performance. It is enough to say the birds were there, and we were there.

Towards night we occupied a series of points above the Gap, as it is called—an opening between the island where the house is situated and the land beyond—and waited for the evening flight. The wind had died away, and as the sun was setting, the mallards came in from the lake to pass the night. Innumerable flocks, one after another, appeared from behind the trees, and passing overhead, settled down into the reeds. By twos, threes, or hundreds in a flock, in straight, even lines of battle, or bent like the two sides of a triangle, or in long single file, their wings whistling in the still air, or producing reports like pop-guns as they flirted or touched one another —immense numbers moved over us.

Having ascertained by several ineffectual shots that they were far out of range, we watched them with delight and curiosity, wondering whence they could all come, and whither they were going. There was no abatement or pause till the increasing darkness shut them out from our sight. Had we been prepared with Ely's wire cartridge we could have rained destruction among them, but as it was we only killed a few chance birds; and then reassembling our party where the open lead joined the bay, we returned to the club-house together.

The next day being clear and still, it was devoted to fishing and exploring. A Kentuckian who was among our numbers, having no fishing in his own State, and knowing nothing of salmon or striped-bass, and little of trout, was devoted to black-bass fishing. Persuading the writer to go in the boat with him, while two friends accompanied us in another, we crossed the bay, and having fastened large Buel's spoons to the end of stout hand-lines, proceeded to troll in the most primitive manner.

The bass were plentiful, and rushing from their lairs in the weeds close to the shore, darted out after the boat had passed, and devoured our baits. Although quite large, they gave feeble play, turning over and over in the water, and rarely jumping with the vigor of fish brought up in cooler latitudes; in fact, the river and lake bass differ so greatly as to seem almost to belong to different species. The river fish, which lie in the discolored water where long weeds grow from a bottom of deep mud, are yellow in color, have a large head, and a yellow iris to the eye. The lake fish, which prefer the clearer element near rocky shoals, have a small head and reddish eye, are dark-sided and vigorous, have a large forked tail, and are infinitely preferable on the table.

One of our friends in the other boat was a practical joker, and of a lively turn of mind. He at first amused himself by jerking the line of his companion who sat nearer the bow, to induce him to think it was a bite; then he landed all the fish that were taken on either hook; and finally, having accidentally caught his hook into his companion's and drawn it in without the latter's knowledge, he hung it on the gunwale and had the fishing to himself. As the portion of the line, or bight as sailors call it, which still towed overboard kept up the ordinary strain, his associate was in great wonderment at his bad luck, and did not discover the reason till the fishing was over.

Having absolutely filled our boats with bass that weighed from two to four pounds, and having ordered a good dinner at the club-house to entertain some strangers, we returned, rather disgusted with such tame sport.

We caught, besides the bass, a few pickerel and a small pike-perch, *lucioperca Americana;* and found the most successful bait was a red and tin spoon, with a white feather on the hook. The natives call the pickerel a grass-pike, and the pike-perch a pickerel. Those curious nondescripts—half fish, half reptile—bill or gar-fish, *lepidosteus*, relics of antediluvian ages, were seen in the water, but are only taken in the net.

The weather had been clear, mild, and still; it continued so for several days, and as storm and wind are necessary to duck-shooting, our sport, although pleasant, was greatly diminished. Consequently we rose at reasonable hours, ate comfortable breakfasts, and smoked our pipes before we left the house. One morning, as I was about departing, the Kentucky fisherman, who had found the weather admirable for his sport, offered to bet ten of the largest fish he would catch against the largest bird I should shoot, that I would not kill a dozen ducks. Of course I accepted the wager.

It was unpromising weather, still and warm, and there was absolutely no flight either during the morning or evening; but by chance two cormorants came close to my stand. Without waiting to distinguish what they were I fired, killing one dead, and dropping the other some distance off in the open water. My disgust on picking up the one nearest, and observing the thick legs, ugly shape, and crooked yellow bill, was only diminished by the recollection of my bet. I lost, failing in the end to bring home the dozen birds—although I shot more than that number, but was unable to recover several that fell in the weeds—and on my return, using that fact as an excuse, endeavored to beg off. The Kentuckian was delighted; imagining from my conversation that I had shot a canvas-back, and anticipating an amusing triumph, he insisted upon the letter of the law.

Our discussion, as was intended on my part, attracted the attention and interest of all the members, and my opponent waited with a victorious air till I should bring him my largest bird. At last, after much procrastination, it was produced amid such shouts as rarely rang through the old clubhouse. In vain did my Kentucky friend attempt to disclaim his acquisition or propose to waive his rights; "he would have the bird, and he must take him; it was a remarkably fine one of the kind, and a good specimen." At last he burst forth:

"Oh, get out with your cormorant; take him away; do, and I'll never make another bet with you as long as I live."

To this day, in that section of the West, a man who is too exacting occasionally wins a cormorant.

The time that circumstances permitted me to devote to pleasure was drawing to a close, and the last morning that was to be appropriated to the ducks had arrived, when, as I was about loading my boat, Henry stood before me, and with great earnestness remarked:

"I am going to shoot with you to-day, sir."

If he had said, "I am going to shoot you," he could not have spoken with more firmness and solemnity; or, if he had anticipated the most violent contradiction, he could not have assumed a more convincing manner. The proposal, as it suggested an augmented bag for my last day, was, however, cordially welcome; and, as soon as he was ready, I inquired in an unconcerned manner:

"Well, which way shall we go?"

The effrontery of the question fairly took him aback, and, pausing in apparent irresolution as to whether he was not in danger of being caught at last, he seemed for a moment half inclined to run for it. Incoherently he commenced his usual response about not giving advice; paused, and then, in a sadly reproachful tone, remonstrated as follows:

"You know if I were to give advice to gentlemen, and they were to have bad luck, they would blame me; and how can I know all the time where the ducks are flying?"

"But, Henry, as we are going together, I must certainly be told where the place is to be."

This appeared to surprise him; for, after a moment's deliberation, he jumped into his boat, and, seizing his paddle, said, "I am going to Grassy Point," and made off as fast as he could.

"Well, Henry, I suppose I shall have to go with you, instead of you with me; but the difference is not very great."

He seemed confused, and in doubt whether he had not compromised himself, and paddled with such speed that I could scarcely keep up with him. Seated with his face towards the bow of the boat, his guns lying ready for instant use in front of him, he plied his double paddle—that is to say, a long paddle with a blade at both ends, which are dipped alternately—with a vigor that would have distanced, for a short stretch, the most expert rower. Like the other natives, he preferred the double paddle to the oars. While using it he could make an accurate course—an important consideration in the intricate channels; could watch for a chance shot ahead of him, or chase a wounded duck advantageously; at a moderate speed, could travel a long journey; and, for a spurt, could surpass the same boat propelled by oars; and was not annoyed by catching the blades in the innumerable weeds. So great was the respect that I acquired for the double paddle, from his manner of wielding it, that I thereupon resolved to have one and learn to use it, even if I did suffer somewhat in the attempt.

We proceeded in unbroken silence, and, reaching the point, located ourselves well upon it, not far apart, and awaited the ducks. Henry was an excellent shot, and set me an example that I did my best to follow; but as the birds did not fly well, we left at the expiration of a couple of hours, and crossed Mud Creek into the main swamp, called Lattimer Marsh. On the way, happening to pass an old muskrat house, my curiosity was excited, and I inquired:

"Are there any animals in that house now?"

"I don't know whether there are any animals, sir; there might be some sort of animals, but there are not any rats."

"Where are the rats, then?"

"They all disappear in summer; they leave their houses, and in the fall build new ones. I can't tell what becomes of them; but they have queer ways.

They build a big house—a sort of family house, as I call it—where a number of them dwell; and around it, about fifty rods off, smaller ones, where each rat appears to feed or go when he wants to be alone. There are generally two entrances, one above and the other under water, so that when the bay is frozen over they can get in."

"How do you catch them?"

"We set spring-traps of iron, but without teeth, so as not to hurt the skin, near their houses, and where we think they will be apt to step into them. The time to catch them is from the 1st of March till the 10th of April."

"Can anybody trap them?"

"Oh no, sir; that wouldn't do at all; a person has to own the land, or have the right to trap. The land isn't worth much, though—only about a dollar an acre."

"The Indian name of muskrat is said to be musksquash?"

"I don't know how that is; but I have heard people call them so. There are a good many in the marsh, and we sometimes make three or four hundred dollars a year from them."

"But, as the swamp fills up and the land makes, won't they disappear?"

"No, sir; the swamp isn't filling up; but the land is sinking, or the water rising—either one or the other; for the swamp is growing larger. The trees on the island are being killed by the water—some are dead already; and every year more high land becomes meadow, and the meadow turns into swamp."

"I thought the Western lakes were growing shallow, and receding yearly."

"Not here, sir. Why, that long spit of reeds beyond Grassy Point was dry land once, so that you could drive a team clear over to Squaw Island; there were large trees on it, but they are all dead, and the channel between it and the island is six feet deep."

"All the better for us sportsmen. Have you any other valuable animals besides the rats?"

"A few otter; but not many. No, sir; the ducks are the most valuable things we have."

"They will soon be killed off."

"No, sir; as there is no shooting allowed in the spring they are becoming more plentiful. They are tamer, too; and some stay here all summer and breed. It was the spring shooting, when they were poor and thin, that killed them off or drove them away."

"How many birds can a good shot average daily the season through?"

"I think I can kill forty a day, but perhaps there are some men who can shoot better. But now, sir, if you will choose your stand, I will go a little way below."

I ensconced myself in a bunch of high weeds surrounded by a pond of open water, and killed a few mallards. The birds did not fly well, however, and we moved from place to place in the hope of better luck, and with a restlessness that showed increasing dissatisfaction on the part of Henry; so that I was not surprised when, early in the afternoon, he told me that he must return to the club-house. I remained for some hours where he left me; but hearing rapid shooting near the Gap, I poled my way there through a broad field of lilies, known as the Pond Lily Channel, and there, to my surprise, found Henry.

Whether it was the desire to be alone, for his peculiarity of preferring to shoot by himself has been mentioned, or whether he was tempted by a favorable flight of birds, I never knew; when I appeared, he paddled hastily away as though ashamed, and made no answer to my inquiries as to what detained him, or how they could manage without him at the house. Unceremoniously occupying his place, I completed the evening, and the allotted hours of my stay, with some excellent shooting at flocks of mallards, widgeons, and blue-bills, that poured through the Gap in endless flights, till after dark.

Then, for the last time, I rowed through the darkness towards the well-known point; for the last time sat down at the groaning board which our kindhearted landlady had furnished so liberally; played my last game with the euchre-loving son of Kentucky; smoked a farewell pipe of Killikinnick in the sociable circle around the air-tight; slept for the last time in the comfortable bed under the hospitable roof of the club-house; and next morning, having seen my associates depart, each in his little boat, and bid them all farewell, I set out, with my birds packed in ice, for the City of New York. My friends welcomed me and my birds gladly. Reader, had you been my friend, you would also have welcomed us both.

It is surprising how well the duck-shooting in the confluents of the great lakes has held out in spite of time and breech-loaders. Wild ducks, like tame ones, lay fifteen to twenty eggs, not like the English snipe, which rarely lays more than four. They go to inaccessible places to breed, and are so tough, strong, and active, that they can put their natural enemies almost at defiance. Spring shooting has been forbidden, and the result is that as many are now killed every fall as were killed twenty years ago.

CHAPTER X.

SUGGESTIONS TO SPORTSMEN.

The word "sport" has been more abused, ill-treated, and misapplied than any other in our language; of a high, pure, and noble signification, it has been debased to unworthy objects; of a restricted and refined significance, it has been extended to a mass of improper matters; from its natural elegant appropriateness, it has been degraded to vulgar and dishonest associations.

The miserable wretch who lives on the most contemptible passion in human nature, and with practised skill cheats those who would cheat him—winning by the unfair rules of games, so-called, of chance—or, with less conscience, converting that chance into a certainty, calls himself a sporting man. The individual who, having trained a horse up to the finest condition of activity and endurance, drives or rides him under lash and spur round a course to win a sum of money, although he may call himself a sportsman, is really a business man. The daring backwoodsman of the Far West, who follows the fleet elk or timid deer, and who attacks the formidable buffalo or grizzly bear, is less a sportsman than a mighty hunter; the man who shoots with a view of selling his game is a market-gunner; and he who kills that he may eat is a pot-hunter.

The sportsman pursues his game for pleasure; he does not aspire to follow the grander animals of the chase, makes no profit of his success, giving to his friends more than he retains, shoots invariably upon the wing, and never takes a mean advantage of bird or man. It is his pride to kill what he does kill elegantly, scientifically, and mercifully. Quantity is not his ambition; he never slays more than he can use; he never inflicts an unnecessary pang or fires an unfair shot.

The man who, happening to find birds plentiful in warm weather, and, after murdering all that he can, leaves them to spoil, is no more a sportsman than he who fires into a huddled bevy of quail, or who considers every bird as representing so much money value, and to be converted into it as soon as possible.

The sportsman is generous to his associate, not seeking to obtain the most shots, but giving away the advantage in that particular, and recovering it if possible by superiority of aim; for although to be a sportsman a person must naturally be an enthusiast, he should never forget what he owes to his friend, and above all what he owes to himself.

Boys and Germans need not imagine that killing robins or blackbirds on trees, no matter how numerously, is sport. Robins and blackbirds, the latter especially, if the old song is to be believed, make dainty pies, but do not constitute an object of pursuit to the sportsman. Diminutive birds shot sitting are as far beneath sport as gigantic wild animals shot standing or running are above it. The only objects of the sportsman's pursuit are the game birds; not in the confined sense used in old times by the English, when the very prince of all—the woodcock—was excluded from the list, but embracing every bird, fit for the table, that is habitually shot on the wing. Many of these, perhaps the finest, gamest, and bravest, are shot over dogs, where the wonderful instinct of the animal aids the intelligence of the human; but whether followed by the faithful setter, or lured to bobbing decoy; killed from points where, prone in the reeds, the eager sportsman, insensible to cold or wet, at the grey of dawn or dusk of night, awaits his prey; or from the convenient blind which the deluded birds approach without suspicion, or pursued with horse and wagon on the open plain—these all are game birds, and he who follows them legitimately is a sportsman.

Wild birds, like the tame ones, are given for man's use, and the best use that can be made of them is the one that will confer most health, nourishment, and happiness on mankind. Fanatics imagine that although birds may be killed, it must be done only to furnish food; as if there was nothing beyond eating in this world, and as if contribution to health were not as essential as supplies to the stomach. The two may and should be combined; a man who is hungry may kill that he may be satisfied, the man who is sickly may kill that he may recover—neither may kill in excess; and a third may kill lest he become sick, provided nothing is injured that is not used.

Death before the muzzle of a gun, in the hands of an experienced marksman, when the body of the charge striking the object terminates life instantly—and even when, in the hands of a bungler, the wounded bird is not put out of his pain till he is retrieved—is far more merciful than after capture in a trap, accompanied with agonies of apprehension and perhaps days of starvation, till the thoughtless boy shall remember his snare and awkwardly end life. The birds of the air and beasts of the field are given for man's use and advantage, whether domesticated, or wild as they once all were; and if they serve to supply him with food or healthful exercise, and especially if they do both, they have answered their purpose. It is certainly no more brutalizing to shoot them on the wing or in the open field, when they have a reasonable chance to escape, than to wring their necks in the barn-yard, or knock them on the head with an axe.

To become a sportsman, the first thing to acquire —provided nature has kindly furnished the proper groundwork of heart and body, without which little can be done—is the art of shooting. A few, very few men become, through fortuitous circumstances of nature and practice, splendid shots; many shoot well, and some cannot shoot at all. The author of this work has handled a gun from his twelfth year, and been out with thousands of sportsmen, but he never yet saw a dead shot—one who can kill every time.

Crack shots, however, are numerous; and include,

according to Frank Forester, those who, in covert and out of covert, the season through, will kill three out of five of the birds that rise fairly within range; but in the opinion of the author, the application should be extended to any man who can kill two out of five on an average. This calculation, however, has no reference to fair shots; every bird that rises within twenty-five yards and is seen, though it be but for an instant, and many that rise at thirty-five yards, are to be counted.

In our country there is so much covert, that the man who picks his birds and only fires at open chances, is a potterer, unworthy even of the common-place name of gunner; he has nothing of the sportsman and little of the man about him. Afraid to miss, anxious to boast of his skill, desirous of surpassing his friends, he unites the qualities of braggart and sneak.

Be liberal in your shots; do not grudge ammunition, nor dread the disgrace of a miss—the disgrace of eluding the trial is far greater; and no man who waits for open shots, and acquires a hesitating manner, will ever effect anything brilliant. If you miss, there are always plenty of excellent excuses at hand—your foot slipped, the bird dodged, a tree intervened; or, you hit him hard, cut out his feathers, or even killed him stone dead, but he did not fall at once. If you doubt the validity of these excuses, go out with the best shot you know, and observe whether he does not furnish you with ten times the number in a week.

Now, the author cannot shoot, and never could; but he manages to bring home as many quail, woodcock, snipe, rail, ruffed grouse, and ducks, on the average, as any of his friends. He observes that most of them miss as often as he does, with no better excuses, and some far oftener; but still he never, to the best of his belief, saw the season during which he killed—that is, bagged—one-half of the birds he shot at. Some professionals, of course, shoot at one kind of game wonderfully; the gunners of Long Island Bay are astoundingly accurate on wild-fowl, but would not kill one quail in a week; while some men who could scarcely touch a duck, handle their guns splendidly in the thickest cover. Professionals, however, usually yield the best chances to their employers, and may be more skilful than they seem; but among amateurs the author claims a rank that will at least entitle him to judge of others.

The majority of persons rarely consider how many birds escape, without the fault of the marksman; at over thirty yards the best gun, especially when a little dirty, will leave openings in the charge where a bird may be hit with only one shot, if at all. Ducks, the larger bay-snipe, ruffed grouse, and, above all, quail late in the season, will carry off several shots — flying away apparently unhurt, although in the end they may fall dead. If the gun was held perfectly straight this would happen less frequently; but to so hold it is almost impossible, for no living man could kill, once in a dozen times, a flying bird with a single ball; and even then the probabilities are, that a yellow-leg snipe shot at more than thirty-five yards off, would once in five times carry away the few pellets that may strike him; and at forty yards escape entirely untouched. If the reader will select the best target his gun can make with an ounce of No. 8 shot at forty yards, and see how many spaces there are entirely vacant large enough to contain a snipe, he will be convinced that the above statement is correct; and at fifty yards, the chances are three to one against the marksman. Sir Francis Francis, who is a good authority in England, says, that to kill one bird in two shots is good shooting; and there the grounds are almost always open, while the reverse is the case with us.

Do not be discouraged, therefore, if the sun gets in your eyes, your foot slips, the bird dodges, a few floating feathers are the only result of your effort, or you make a clean miss; others do the same. Neither lose your temper nor curse your luck, as by so doing you may excite your nerves and injure your shooting, and cannot improve it. Be cool, never shoot without an attempt at aim, if it is only where the bird disappeared; take your disappointments pleasantly, strive to do your best, and you will improve.

Many ducks fly at least ninety miles an hour; that is, twenty-six hundred yards a minute, or forty-four yards a second; if, therefore, a duck starts at your feet with that velocity, and you require a second to cover him, he will be out of range; or if he is flying across, and you dwell one forty-fourth part of a second on your aim, you will miss him. A quail, late in the season, flies as fast as this, and rises with a rapidity equal to his flight. He is often found in coverts, dodges and twists with remarkable skill and judgment, frequently flies off in a direct line behind the thickest bush, and requires the perfection of training to bring down with certainty. These are difficulties that patience alone can overcome; for if shooting were simple, there would be no art or pleasure in it.

All books on sporting tell you to fire ahead of cross shots, and in this they are right; but the reason they give is, that time is necessary for the shot to reach the object—in this they are wrong; shot moves infinitely faster than the bird, and for practical purposes, reaches its mark instantaneously. Human nerves and muscles, however, are imperfect, and it requires an instant, an important one, to discharge the gun after the aim is taken. The result, therefore, is the same, and you must endeavor to shoot ahead of the bird; and if he is flying fast, far ahead of him. If the motion of the object is followed and the gun kept moving before the discharge, some writers allege no allowance need be made, but it is so difficult not to pause slightly, that it is better in all cases to allow some inches.

To follow the motion of a very fast-flying bird, is almost, if not quite impossible, and the attempt to do so at all, is apt to create a popping habit. When a broad-bill, driving before a strong northwester, darts past, the best plan is to try and fire many feet, even ten or fifteen, ahead of him; and then you will rarely succeed in discharging your piece before he is abreast of the muzzle, and frequently will lag behind him. The aim must be taken on the line of flight, and a little attention will convince you that the bird is up with the sight ere the trigger is fairly pulled. A knowledge of this principle, and an ability to practise it, may be said to be the art of duck-shooting; as in that there are a vast majority of cross shots, and the birds fly rapidly.

There is an erroneous idea that the eye must be lowered close down to the breech, in order to have a correct aim; but, while it is apparent if the neck is not bent at all there can be no aim, a slight inaccuracy will not only make no difference, but will give an advantage by throwing the shot high. It will be perceived, on fastening the gun in an immovable position, that the eye may be moved from near one hammer to the other, and the aim altered but a few inches, on an object thirty yards distant—an inaccuracy, considering the spread of shot, which is utterly unimportant.

So also, although by the attraction of gravitation the charge falls somewhat, the deflection is too inconsiderable to merit attention.

After watching himself carefully, reading what the best authors have written, and comparing experiences with his friends, the author has concluded that experienced sportsmen miss from hesitation in pulling the trigger, dwelling on the aim, and nervously shrinking from the recoil. The first fault arises from some temporary or permanent condition of mind or body, the second from anxiety to make assurance doubly sure, and the last from habit.

If a man is naturally slow he can never shoot fast-flying birds, but if his fingers are stiff from cold he can warm them. A resolution to fire boldly, and not to dread missing, will cure the over-anxiety that destroys its own intent, but to meet the recoil without giving to it, or pushing against it, which is the more common mistake, is often extremely difficult. This unfortunate habit, occurring at the moment of highest excitement amid the noise and smoke, is rarely noticed by the guilty party, and some will at first stoutly deny its existence.

To mind the recoil of a gun seems pusillanimous, and few can believe, till assured by actual experiment, that it equals sixty or seventy pounds, and will crush the bones of the body if immovably fixed. Let the reader observe the next time that his gun is unwittingly left at half-cock, how far he will pull it out of aim, and how he will push against it, when attempting to discharge it at game. An acquaintance of the writer, who would scout the idea of being affected by the recoil of his gun, and indeed would have sworn "it did not kick a bit," was once chasing a diver on a placid, sluggish stream, in a dug-out. When the bird rose close to the boat, the sportsman was standing erect, poising himself with care in the unsteady craft, but as he pulled the trigger he instinctively pushed so hard, that, as the cap snapped, he lost his balance, upset the canoe, and pitched forward head-foremost overboard!

Probably one half of the fair shots that are missed escape on account of this unfortunate nervousness; and it is a habit that can only be cured by incessant care and unrelaxed watchfulness. Anything that affects the nerves, as smoking or drinking, increases the difficulty, and the sudden flushing of a bird will cause it. Unhappily it is apt to be most prevalent when the shooting is good and the sportsman excited, thus ruining many of his best days. With heavy loads, or what is known as a kicking gun, the error will be aggravated; and most persons have no idea of the proper proportions of powder and shot, putting in immense quantities of the latter and sparing the former.

The true load for a gun not exceeding eight pounds in weight, regardless of its size or bore, is one ounce and a quarter of shot and three drachms of the strongest powder, or three and a half drachms of common powder. The same proportion should be retained if the gun is heavier or the charge increased. Where more shot is used power is lost and recoil aggravated; and if the powder is not augmented one ounce of shot will do better execution than two.

Many persons who have ascertained this fact and practise upon it, will inform you that they drive their shot through the birds, and consequently kill them instantly. This is a mistake; small shot are rarely, if ever, driven through a bird; but where the force is increased the blow is much harder, and stuns. It is the velocity rather than the size or number of the shot that tells. A soldier in battle was struck on the belt-plate by a spent minié bullet not a half inch in diameter, and he described himself as feeling that he had been torn to pieces, and that a cannon-ball had gone directly through his body.

The size of the shot is to be proportioned to the size of the bird—weight, of course, being an element of power and telling on each individual pellet —but the more the aggregate amount can be reduced the less the recoil. Six drachms of powder and one ounce of shot, will not occasion as much recoil as three drachms of powder and an ounce and a half of shot.

The gun should always be held firmly to the shoulder, and the shoulder never rested against a solid substance; indeed, the collar-bone may be broken by simply firing directly upwards. Therefore, never fire in the air while lying on your back upon the ground, and be careful when shooting at ducks from a boat not to support yourself upon the latter.

If the reader still doubts the universally disastrous effects of cringing at the moment of discharge, let him have an assistant to load the gun out of sight, who without his knowledge shall vary the load, and occasionally put in none at all. Then let the reader fire at a mark, and in spite of the efforts which he will naturally make, he will find when there is no load, and consequently nothing to distract his attention, that he does shrink, and pull the muzzle somewhat off the object.

This book is not written for beginners; there are plenty of works with every variety of instruction in them, and the reader is supposed to have read them, digested their contents, acquired a knowledge of the gun, and some skill in its use, and to have been frequently in the field, but to be perfect neither in the use of the gun, nor the practice of the sportsman's art. There are, however, a few simple suggestions that may prove valuable, not only in acquiring the ability to shoot, but in restoring it where, from want of practice, it has diminished.

The sportsman must be as quick and ready in handling his gun as the juggler in handling his tools; he must be able to bring it to his shoulder and point the muzzle at a stationary mark simultaneously, to aim in every direction with equal facility, and to follow a moving object accurately. This is merely mechanical, and is acquired, like every other mechanical art, by dint of practice.

Some writers recommend firing at turnips tossed through the air by an assistant, and this is well; but an equally advantageous plan is to throw a soft ball about a room and take aim at it, pulling the trigger every time, with an unloaded and uncocked gun. The sole, but important, recommendation of this idea is, that it may be carried out anywhere and at all seasons, and if the reader will try it daily for a week before going into the field, he will perceive the effects.

So also, to acquire quickness: if the reader will throw two small objects—pennies, or the like—into the air, and endeavor to aim at or hit them both before they reach the ground, he will in a short time obtain such facility that he will be able to lay down his gun, and after throwing the pennies, to pick it up and hit them both twice out of three times.

To shoot at pigeons from a trap, robins from trees, and even swallows on the wing, although the practice differs greatly from shooting at game, is useful to a certain extent; but steady and long-continued practice of this nature is injurious rather than beneficial. It is somewhat notorious that the celebrated pigeon-shots are generally poor marksmen in the field, and entirely at a loss in thick covert.

After all, however, the best place to learn the use of the gun, while it is by all odds the pleasantest, is in the field; where, amid the thousand beauties of nature, and under the excitement of the presence of game, the sportsman by slow degrees overcomes the innumerable difficulties that surround the art of shooting flying.

Closely allied to skill in killing the right object is the ability to avoid killing the wrong one. A gun is extremely dangerous—how much so is known only to those who have handled it long; in spite of the best care it will occasionally go off at unexpected times, and in careless hands is sure, sooner or later, to do terrible damage. Every possible precaution must be taken, vigilance must never be relaxed, the muzzle must under no circumstances point towards the owner or his companions; if two men are crawling through thick brush, the gun of the first must point forwards, and of the last, backwards; the caps of muzzle-loaders should be removed on getting into a wagon, and when the loaded weapon is left in a house the hammers ought never to be left down on the caps; but, above all, no man who is not in search of an early grave should pull a gun towards him by the barrels.

These rules are simple, and the reasons for them apparent; if the hammer is on the cap, a blow on it, or its catching on a twig, will discharge the load; if a horse runs away, as horses have an unpleasant habit of doing, even if the lock is at half-cock, the tumbler may be broken down; if a gun is capped in a house, every one but an idiot knows it is loaded; and if it is drawn towards a person—as will be often done by thoughtless people in taking it from a wagon or lifting it from a boat or from the ground —it is almost sure to go off.

In the field it should be carried either at whole or half-cock; authorities differ as to which of these two modes is the safer. If the hammer is at full cock, a touch on the trigger will set it loose; if it is at half-cock, in the excitement of cocking it when a bird rises unexpectedly, it will often slip unintentionally. I prefer the former method, believing that the sense of danger makes the person more careful, and that the risk of a twig's touching the trigger in spite of the trigger-guard is very slight, while the weapon is ready for instant use, and only has to be pointed at the object and discharged. Moreover, I have twice seen a gun that was at half-cock discharged when the sportsman was in the act of cocking it hastily, and twice when putting it back to half-cock; but the piece should never for a moment be trusted out of the sportsman's hands without his first putting it at half-cock; nor should he ever cross a fence without the same precaution. In changing from whole to half-cock, pass the hammer below the first notch, so as to hear a distinct click when it is drawn back.

Countrymen when about to walk a log over a rapid stream, will usually carefully put the hammers down on the caps, and placing the butt on the log, steady themselves by it, thus insuring their destruction if they should happen to slip; and if they stand on a fence they do the same thing, and rest the stock on the upper rail. Not only should such follies be avoided, but the gun should never be leaned against a tree, as thoughtless people are apt to do when they stop at a spring to drink, and never placed where it can slip or roll.

When you desire to reload a muzzle-loader, put the hammer of the loaded barrel at half-cock, and if the right barrel has been discharged, set down the butt so that the hammers are towards you, and the contrary way if the left barrel is to be loaded; in this manner you will avoid bringing your hand over the loaded barrel, and in case the other charge should go off you would lose the end of your thumb, perhaps, but save most of your fingers.

From the foregoing rules, which apply mainly to muzzle-loaders, it will be seen how much safer are breech-loaders; with them the entire charge can be withdrawn on entering a house or getting into a wagon, and there is absolutely no danger to fingers or thumb in the process of loading. And in carrying the weapon on long tramps in the woods, where it is frequently removed from boat to shoulder, from shoulder to boat, and from wagon to case, and when it has to be ready at any instant, with the muzzle-loader the only possible precaution is to leave the nipples without caps, which are to be carried in the vest pocket, and must be removed after every vain alarm; while with the breech-loader, the charge itself is not inserted till needed.

With these few suggestions, which are applicable not merely to the kinds of sport treated of in this volume, but to every species of shooting, we leave the young sportsman to his own resources and to the knowledge that he will acquire in the field, hoping that he may find something in them that will aid him to kill reasonably often the game he points at, and to avoid the dreadful misfortune of injuring a friend or companion.

CHAPTER XI.

DIRECTIONS FOR BUILDING A BATTERY.

A battery, or sink-boat as it is called in some parts of the country, is a narrow box with a platform around it, so arranged that the weight of the shooter will sink it so nearly level with the water that the ducks will not notice it when it is hidden among the stand of stools that are always anchored around it. The box is almost square, narrowed a little on the bottom and at the foot, twenty-two inches across at the head, eighteen at the foot on the top, and four less on the bottom; the two end pieces are of one and a half inch oak, the sides of three-quarter inch white pine. It is fifteen inches deep, except at the head, which shoals up to six inches, beginning about two feet abaft the end. This is done in order to enable the sportsman to look over the edge of the box without getting a cramp in his neck, and besides to reduce the flotation of the battery as much as possible, which is a most important thing to effect. The narrowing of the bottom is for the same purpose of diminishing the buoyancy, for as it has to be sunk to the level of the water if the weight of the sportsman will not bring it down sufficiently, iron weights, or what is far preferable, iron decoys, have to be placed in it or on it, and weights in the box are always in the way.

Two oak carlings are cut out six feet long, one and a quarter inch thick, and two and a half wide in the middle, tapering off to one and a quarter at the ends, with a bow or spring of an inch from the center to the extremities. Nail these firmly on each end an inch below the top of the box, and to them fasten the platform, which is made of planed stuff ten feet long, and to each end of which a batten is nailed as well as a short additional carling in the middle, projecting from the side of the box. Fill in the head and foot of the platform with short pieces, so as to make it compact, and take especial care to have it fit tightly around the box. As it is made of three-quarter inch stuff, there will be left a quarter of an inch all around the box to which, when the other work is done, a narrow piece of lead is nailed that can be raised to keep out the water in rough weather. Two boards, or what is better, two frames covered with duck, are hinged together by leather hinges. These are one foot wide each, and as long as the platform, and are hinged to it on both sides. A foot-piece made of two boards is hinged to the foot in the same way. To the head it is customary, on Long Island, to fasten a fender of the width of the battery and wings, and eighteen or twenty feet long. It is made of duck nailed to thin wooden slats, is tied on to the battery when in use, and taken off at other times. In other parts of the country it is customary to dispense with the fender and substitute a head wing of three boards hinged on like the foot and side wings. A single board, fourteen to sixteen inches wide, can be used at the foot in place of the double foot wing. Sometimes an additional row of lead is put on about the middle of the platform as an additional breakwater.

The battery is anchored at both ends. From the head of the fender a sort of bridle, a short rope tied into the two corners, is fastened at the center or bight to the anchor rope. A small grapnel or light anchor is used at the head, as it is important that it should not drag, while at the stern, to a rope led through a hole in the foot board, a stone is fastened. This is arranged in this way as it is occasionally necessary to haul it in and throw it out again on a change of wind. The entire surface of the battery, wings and all, is to be painted a dull blue, as near the color of the water as possible. The necessary iron decoys, to bring the whole structure down to a level with the water, are set upon the platform, and the stand of stools, not less than a hundred and fifty, and double that number is better, are placed around the battery, mostly at the foot and towards the left side if the shooter is right-handed. A bottom board of half-inch stuff, with half-inch cleats under it, is put in the bottom of the box for the gunner to lie on, and all is ready for the exercises to begin. A sink-box made on this plan will stand quite a heavy sea, but care must be exercised in taking it up that the wind does not get under the fender when it is being hauled aboard the sailing vessel, that is ordinarily used in this kind of shooting, for if it does, and it is blowing at all hard, the fender, box, platform and all will be lifted out of the water and tossed skyward. Wear dull-colored clothes, never a red shirt, and a cap in battery shooting. And first and last, remember never to rise to shoot before the birds are well into the lower portion of the stools. More birds are lost by getting up too soon to shoot than from any other cause.

APPENDIX.

The following technical descriptions are taken mainly from "Giraud's Birds of Long Island," a work that is now almost out of print, but which is more valuable to the student of nature than some of its more pretentious rivals; and I have interpolated such suggestions and made such alterations as my experience dictated and the purposes of this work demanded. A discourse on the wild-fowl of the Northern States hardly seemed complete without such a description of them as would enable the sportsman to distinguish one from another; and yet it was not within the purview of a work intended for sportsmen, to devote much attention or many of its pages to ornithology. This is therefore condensed into an Appendix, where it will not trouble the general reader, but will be easy of reference when the information it contains is wanted.

The Goose.

Genus Anser, Briss.

Generic Distinctions.—In this class of birds, the bill is shorter than the head, rather higher than broad at the base; head small, compressed; neck long and slender; body full; feet short, stout, and central, which enables them to walk with ease; wings long; tail short, rounded.

The Wild Goose.

Canada Goose.

Anas Canadensis, Wils.

Specific Character.—Length of bill from the corner of the mouth to the end, two inches and three-sixteenths; length of tarsi, two inches and seven-eighths; length from the point of the bill to the end of the tail, about forty inches; wing, eighteen; the head and greater portion of the neck black; cheeks and throat white. Adult with the head, greater part of the neck, primaries, rump, and tail, black; back and wings brown, margined with paler brown; lower part of the neck and under plumage, whitish-grey; flanks, darker grey; cheeks and throat white, as are the upper and under tail-coverts. The plumage of the female rather duller.

This bird is nowhere very abundant, but migrates across the Northern States in their entire breadth from ocean to ocean; it obeys the call well, and stools readily if the gunner is carefully concealed. It is the latest in its migrations of the wild-fowl.

The Brant.

Barnacle Goose—Brent Goose.

Anus Bernicla, Wils.

Specific Character.—Bill black; head and neck all round black; a patch on the sides of the neck white;

upper parts brownish-grey, the feathers margined with light greyish-brown; quills and primary coverts greyish-black; fore part of breast light brownish-grey, the feathers terminally margined with greyish-white; abdomen and lower tail-coverts white; sides grey; feathers rather broadly tipped with white. Length two feet; wing fourteen inches and a half. Female rather smaller.

The brant is not fond of the fresh lakes and streams, but prefers the ocean and its contiguous bays and lagoons; it is far more abundant along the sea-coast than upon the western waters, and in fact I am not aware that I have ever killed one in the inland States. It responds to its peculiar note, stools well, and is often killed in great numbers on the South Bay of Long Island.

The Swan.

Genus Cygnus, Meyer.

Generic Distinctions.—Bill longer than the head, higher than broad at the base, depressed and a little widened towards the end; upper mandible, rounded, with the dorsal line sloping; lower mandible flattened, with the angle very long, and rather narrow; nostrils placed near the ridge; head of moderate size, oblong, compressed; neck extremely long and slender; body very large, compact, depressed; feet short, stout, placed a little behind the centre of the body; tarsi short; wings long, broad; tail very short, graduated.

The White Swan.

American Swan.

Cygnus Americanus, Aud.

Specific Character.—Plumage, pure white; bill and feet black; length of the specimen before us, four feet; wing twenty-one and a half inches.

These magnificent birds, the most majestic of the game-birds of our continent, are rarely shot to the northward and eastward of Chesapeake bay, but are much more abundant in the far West—even to and beyond the Rocky Mountains.

Fresh-Water Ducks.

Genus Anas, Linn.

Generic Distinctions.—Bill higher than broad at the base, widening towards the end, and about the same length as the head; the upper mandible with a slight nail at the end; neck rather long; body full; wings moderate, pointed; feet short, stout, and placed behind the centre of the body; walks with a waddling gait; hind toe furnished with a narrow membrane.

Mallard.

Green Head, English Duck, Grey Duck (female), the Duck, the Wild Duck.

Anas Boschas, Wils.

Specific Character.—Speculum bright purple, reflecting green, bordered with black; secondaries broadly tipped with black; secondary coverts towards their ends white, broadly tipped with black; adult male with the entire head and upper part of the neck bright green, with a few touches of reddish-brown passing from the forehead, on the occiput; middle of the neck with a white ring; the lower part of the neck and breast reddish-brown, approaching to chocolate; fore part of the back light brown, rest of the back darker; rump black; upper tail coverts greenish-black; upper parts of the wings brown, intermixed with grey; breast, sides, flanks, and abdomen, grey, transversely barred with dusky; bill greenish-yellow; feet reddish-orange; tail rounded, consisting of sixteen pointed feathers, nearly white; speculum violet; length two feet, wing eleven inches.

Female smaller than the male; speculum less brilliant; general plumage brown; head and neck streaked with dusky; the feathers on the back and flanks margined with white, with a central spot of brown on the outer webs; bill black, changing to orange at the extremity.

This bird is abundant both at the West and along the coast, but on the fresh water it frequents the mud-holes and shallow marshes, in contradistinction to the open water-ducks that affect the broad unbroken stretches of water.

Black Duck.

Dusky Duck.

Anas Obscura, Wils.

Specific Character. — General plumage dusky; speculum green, reflecting purple, bordered with black; secondaries tipped with white. Adult with the forehead, crown, occiput, and middle space on the hind neck brownish-black, the feathers slightly margined with greyish-brown; cheeks, loral space, and sides of the neck dusky grey, streaked with black; throat reddish-brown; general plumage dusky, lighter beneath; under wing-coverts white; speculum brilliant green; bill yellowish; feet reddish-orange. Female rather smaller, plumage lighter, speculum less brilliant. Length of male about two feet; wing eleven inches.

These ducks are killed equally in the fresh and salt waters; they come to the decoys warily.

Gadwall.

Welsh Drake, German Duck.

Anas Strepera, Wils.

Specific Character.—Speculum white; secondary coverts black; upper wing-coverts chestnut red; general plumage dusky grey, waved with white; abdomen white. Adult with the bill bluish-black; head and upper part of the neck grey, streaked with dusky—darkest on the upper part of the head, as well as the middle space on the hind neck; lower neck, upper part of the breast and fore part of the back blackish-brown, the feathers marked with semi-circular bands of white, more distinctly on the fore part of the neck and upper part of the breast; sides of the body pencilled with greyish-white and dusky; lower part of the breast and abdomen white, the latter barred with dusky towards the vent; lower and upper tail-coverts and sides of the rump greenish-black; tail greyish-brown, margined with white; hind part of the back dark brown, faintly barred with white; primaries brown; secondaries greyish-brown, tipped with white; middle coverts reddish-brown; a few of the outer secondaries broadly margined with greenish-black; inner scapulars brown, broadly margined with dull yellowish-brown; outer undulated with dark brown and yellowish-white; feet dull orange. Female two inches shorter; about four inches less in extent. Length twenty-one inches and a half; wing eleven.

This is an ugly duck, and not much esteemed by epicure or sportsman.

Widgeon.

Bald-pate.

Anas Americana, Wils.

Specific Character.—Bill short, the color light greyish-blue; speculum green, banded with black; under wing-coverts white. Adult male with the loral space, sides of the head below the eye, upper part of the neck and throat, brownish-white, spotted with black; a broad band of white, commencing at the base of the upper mandible, passing over the crown; behind the eye, a broad band of light green, extending backwards on the hind neck about three inches; the feathers on the nape rather long; lower neck and sides of the breast, with a portion of the upper part of the breast, reddish-brown; rest of the lower parts white, excepting a patch of black at the base of the tail; under tail-coverts same color; flanks brown, barred with dusky; tail greyish-brown, tipped with white; two middle feathers darker and longest; upper tail-coverts white, barred with dusky; lower part of the hind-neck and fore part of the back undulated with brownish and light brownish-red, hind part undulated with greyish-white; primaries brown; outer webs of inner secondaries black, margined with white—inner webs greyish-brown; secondary coverts white tipped with black; speculum brilliant green, formed by the middle secondaries. Length twenty-one inches, wing ten and a half. Female smaller, plumage duller, without the green markings.

This duck is much prized along the sea-coast, but at the West he holds an inferior rank.

PINTAIL.

Sprig-tail—Pigeon-tail—Grey-Duck.

Anas Acuta, Wils.

Specific Character.—Bill long and narrow, lead color; at the tip a spot of black, at the corner of the mouth a spot of similar color; neck long and slender; speculum bright purple, with reflecting deep green bordered with black; the feathers broadly tipped with white; tail long and pointed. Adult male with head, cheeks, throat, upper parts of the neck in front and sides, dark brown; a band of light purple behind the eye, extending about three inches on the sides of the neck; on the hind neck a band of black, with green reflections, fading as it extends on the back—a band of white commencing between the two former, passing down the neck on the lower part of the fore neck; breast and fore part of the abdomen white, tinged with pale yellow—hind part of the abdomen and vent greyish-white tinged with yellow, and marked with undulated lines of brown or dusky; at the base of the tail a patch of black; under tail-coverts black, margined with whitish; two middle feathers black, with green reflections, narrow, and about three inches longer than the rest, which are rather long and tapering; upper tail-coverts ash-grey, margined with yellowish-white, with a central streak of dusky. Rump greyish-brown, marked with undulating lines of white; sides of the rump cream color; sides of the body, back, and sides of the breast, marked with undulating lines of black and white. Primaries brown; shafts brownish-white, darker at their tips; secondaries and scapulars black, with green reflections, the former margined with grey, which is the color of the greater part of the outer web, the latter margined with white; speculum bright purple, with splendid green reflections edged with black, the feathers broadly tipped with white. Length twenty-nine inches, wing eleven. Female with the upper part of the head and hind neck dark brown, streaked with dusky; sides of the throat and fore neck lighter; a few touches of rust color on the chin and on the base of the bill. Upper plumage brown, the feathers margined and tipped with brownish-white; lower plumage brownish-white, mottled with brown; speculum less extensive, and without the lengthened tail feathers so conspicuous in the male.

This duck is more abundant in the neighborhood of the great lakes than along the margin of the ocean; in epicurean qualities it ranks with the black duck.

Wood-Duck.

Summer-Duck.

Anas Sponsa, Aud.

Specific Character.—The pendant crest, the throat, upper portion of the fore neck, and bands on the sides of the neck white, with the speculum blue, glossed with green and tipped with white. Adult male with the bill bright red at the base, the sides yellow; between the nostrils a black spot reaching nearly to the black, hooked nail; the head is furnished with long silken feathers, which fall gracefully over the hind neck, in certain lights exhibiting all the colors of the rainbow; a narrow white line from the base of the upper mandible, passing over the eye; a broader band of the same color behind the eye, both bands mingling with the long feathers on the occiput; throat and upper portion of the fore neck pure white, a band of the same color inclining towards the eye; a similar band on the sides of the neck, nearly meeting on the nape; lower portion of the neck reddish-purple, the fore part marked with triangular spots of white; breast and abdomen dull white; sides of the body yellowish-grey, undulated with black; the feathers towards the ends marked with a broad band of black, succeeded by a band of white; tips black; tail and upper tail-coverts greenish-black; lower tail-coverts brown; sides of the rump dull reddish-purple; rump, back, and middle portions of the hind neck, dark reddish-brown, tinged with green; a broad white band before the wings, terminating with black; lesser wing-coverts and primaries brown, most of the latter with a portion of their outer webs silvery white; the inner webs glossed with green towards the ends; secondaries tipped with white; their webs blue, glossed with green; the inner webs brown, their crowns violet-blue; secondaries black.

Female, upper part of the head dusky, glossed with green; sides of the head, upper portion of the sides of the neck, with the nape, greyish-brown; a white patch behind the eye; throat white, the bands on the sides of the neck faintly developed; fore part and sides of the neck, with the sides of the body, yellowish-brown, marked with greyish-brown; breast and abdomen white, the former spotted with brown; lower tail-coverts greyish-white, mottled with brown; tail and upper tail-coverts dark brown, glossed with green; rump, back, and hind neck, dark brown, glossed with green and purple; bill dusky, feet dull green. The crest less than that of the male, and plain dull brown. Length twenty inches; wing eight inches and a half.

This is an extremely beautiful duck, but of moderate size; it is rare on the sea-coast, but absolutely swarms during the month of September among the lily-pads of the Western swamps. Fed upon the berry of this plant, called at the South chincapin, it becomes fat and deliciously tender. It does not pay much attention to decoys.

GREEN-WINGED TEAL.

Anas.

Anas Crecca, Wils.

Specific Character.—Bill black, short, and narrow; the outer webs of the first five secondaries black, tipped with white; the next five plain rich green, forming the speculum; secondary coverts tipped with pale reddish-buff. Adult male with a dusky band at the base of the bill, of which color is the throat; a faint white band under the eye; upper part of the neck, sides of the head, and the crown, chestnut brown; a broad band of bright green commencing behind the eye, passing down on the nape, where it is separated by the terminal portion of the crest, which is dark blue; lower part of the hind neck, a small space on the fore neck, and the sides of the body, undulated with lines of black and white; lower portion of the fore neck and upper part of the breast reddish-brown, distinctly marked with round spots of brownish-black; abdomen yellowish-white, faintly undulated with dusky; a patch of black under the tail; outer tail-feathers buff, inner white, with a large spot of black on the inner webs; tail brown, margined with whitish, the outer feathers greenish-black; upper parts brown, faintly undulated with black and white, on the fore part of the back; outer scapulars similar, with a portion of their outer webs black; lesser wing-coverts brownash; greater coverts tipped with reddish-cream; the first five secondaries velvety-black; the next five bright green, forming the speculum, which is bounded above by pale reddish-buff, and on each side by deep black; before the wing a transverse, broad white band.

Female smaller; head and neck streaked with brownish-white and dusky, darker on the upper part of the head; lower parts reddish-brown, the feathers margined with dusky, upper parts duskybrown, the feathers margined and spotted with pale reddish-white, without the chestnut red and the green on the head; the black patch is wanting, as is the white band before the wings, the conspicuous spot on the wings is less extensive. Its short and narrow bill is at all times a strong specific character;

length fifteen inches; wing seven inches and a half.

This is an excellent little duck, too confiding for its own security, but capable of saving itself by great rapidity of flight. It is greatly attracted by decoys, and will generally alight among them if permitted.

Blue-Winged Teal.

Anas Discors, Wils.

Specific Character.—Bill bluish-black and long in proportion with the other dimensions of this species; smaller wing-coverts light-blue; speculum purplish-green. Adult male with the upper part of the head black; a broad band of white on the sides of the head, before the eye margined with black; rest part of the head, and upper part of the neck greyish-brown, with purple reflections on the hind neck; chin black; lower parts reddish-brown; lower part of the fore neck and sides of the body spotted with blackish-brown; breast and abdomen barred with the same color; lower tail-coverts blackish-brown; tail brown, margined with paler, the feathers pointed, a patch of white on the sides of the rump; back brownish-black, glossed with green; the feathers on the fore part of the back and lower portion of the hind neck margined with yellowish-white; primaries brown; inner webs of the secondaries same color; outer vanes dark green, which form the speculum; secondary coverts brown, the outer broadly tipped with white, the inner tipped with blue; tertials dark-green, with central markings of deep buff; feet dull yellow.

Female without the white patch on the sides of the head; throat white; lower parts greyish-brown, the feathers spotted with darker; upper parts blackish-brown, the feathers margined with bluish-white and pale buff; smaller wing-coverts blue; speculum green; secondary coverts the same as those of the male; length fourteen inches, wing seven inches and a half.

This species greatly resembles the last.

Spoonbill.

Shoveller.

Anas Clypeata, Wils.

Specific Character.—Bill brownish-black, about three inches in length, near the end it is more than twice as broad as it is at the base; much rounded and closely pectinated, the size of the upper mandible at the base having the appearance of a fine-toothed comb. Adult male with the head and the neck for about half its length glossy green, with purple reflections; lower part of the neck and upper part of the breast white; rest of the lower plumage deep chestnut-brown, excepting the lower tail-coverts and a band across the vent, which is black, some of the feathers partly green; flanks brownish-yellow pencilled with black and blackish-brown; inner secondaries dark green with terminal spot of white; outer secondaries lighter green; primaries dark brown, their shafts white, with dusky tips; lesser wing-coverts light blue; speculum golden-green; rump and upper tail-coverts greenish-black, a patch of white at the sides of the rump; tail dark brown, the feathers pointed, broadly edged with white, of which color are the inner webs of the three outer feathers.

Female with the crown dusky; upper plumage blackish-brown, the feathers edged with reddish-brown; breast yellowish-white, marked with semicircular spots of white. Young male with similar markings on the breast; length twenty inches and a half, wing ten.

Sea-Duck.

Genus Fuligula.

Generic Distinctions.—In this class the head is rather larger, neck rather shorter and thicker, than in the preceding genus (Anas), plumage more dense, feet stronger, and the hind toe with a broad appendage, which is the principal distinction.

Canvas-Back.

Fuligula Valisneria, Wils.

Specific Character.—Bill black, the length about three inches, and very high at the base; fore part of the head and the throat dusky; irides deep red; breast brownish-black. Adult male with the forehead, loral space, throat, and upper part of the head dusky; sides of the head, neck all round for nearly the entire length, reddish-chestnut; lower neck, fore part of the breast and back black; rest of the back white, closely marked with undulating lines of black; rump and upper tail-coverts blackish; wing-coverts grey, speckled with blackish; primaries and secondaries light slate color; tail short, the feathers pointed; lower part of the breast and abdomen white; flanks same color, finely pencilled with dusky; lower tail-coverts blackish-brown, intermixed with white; length twenty-two inches, wing nine and a quarter.

Female, upper parts greyish-brown; neck, sides, and abdomen the same; upper part of the breast brown; belly white, pencilled with blackish; rather smaller than the male, with the crown blackish-brown.

This is without question the finest duck that flies, as it is the largest and gamest; it is abundant late in the season, but wary.

Red-Head.

Fuligula Ferina, Wils.

Specific Character.—Bill bluish, towards the end black, and about two inches and a quarter long; irides yellowish-red. Adult male with head, which is rather large, and the upper part of the neck all round, dark reddish chestnut, brightest on the hind neck; lower part of the neck, extending on the back and upper part of the breast, black; abdomen white, darker towards the vent, where it is barred with undulating lines of dusky; flanks grey, closely barred with black; scapulars the same; primaries brownish-grey; secondaries lighter; back greyish-brown, barred with fine lines of white; rump and upper tail coverts blackish-brown; tail feathers greyish-brown, lighter at the base; lower tail-coverts brownish-black, rather lighter than the upper; length twenty inches; wing nine and a half. Female about two inches smaller, with the head, neck, breast, and general color of the upper parts brown; darker on the upper part of the head, lighter on the back; bill, legs, and feet, similar to those of the male.

This duck, as it is scarcely distinguishable from the canvas-back, and has mainly the same habits, is but little inferior to that incomparable bird.

Broad-Bill.

Blue Bill, Scaup, Black Head, Raft Duck.

Fuligula Marila, Linn.

Specific Character.—The head and neck all round, with the fore part of the breast and fore part of back, black; the sides of the head and the sides and hind part of the neck dark green, reflecting purple; length of bill, when measured along the gap, two inches and five-sixteenths; length of tarsi one inch and three-eighths; length from the point of the bill to the end of the tail nineteen inches; wing eight inches and five-eighths; a broad white band crossing the secondaries and continues on the inner primaries. Adult male with the forehead, crown, throat, and upper part of the fore neck brownish-black; sides of the head, neck, and hind neck, dark green; lower portion of the neck all round, with the upper part of the breast, purplish-black; rest of the lower parts white, undulated with black towards the vent; under tail-coverts blackish-brown; tail short, dark brown, margined and tipped with lighter brown; upper tail-coverts and rump blackish-brown; middle of the back undulated with black and white; fore part black; wings brown, darker at the base and tips; speculum white, formed by the band crossing the secondaries and inner primaries; scapulars and inner secondaries undulated with black and white; secondary coverts blackish-brown, undulated with white. Female with a broad patch of white on the forehead; head, neck, and fore part of the breast umber brown; upper parts blackish-brown; abdomen and lower portions of breast white; scapulars faintly marked with white.

Whistler.

Golden Eye, Great Head.

Fuligula Clangula, Linn.

Specific Character.—Bill black, high at the base, where there is quite a large spot of white; head ornamented with a beautiful crest, and feathers more than an inch long and loose; insides yellow; the entire head and upper part of the neck rich glossy-green, with purple reflections, more particularly so on the throat and forehead; rest of the neck, with the entire plumage, white; sides of the rump and vent dusky grey; tail greyish-brown; back and wings brownish-black—a large patch of white on the latter, formed by the larger portion of the secondaries and the tips of its coverts; legs reddish-orange. Length twenty inches; wing nine inches. Female head and upper part of the neck dull brown; wings dusky; lower parts white, as are six of the secondaries and their coverts; the tips of the latter dusky. About three inches smaller than the male.

Dipper.

Butter Ball, Buffel-Headed Duck, Spirit Duck.

Fuligula Albeola, Linn.

Specific Character.—Bill blue, from the corner of the mouth to the end about one inch and a half, the sides rounded, narrowed towards the point; head thickly crested, a patch behind the eye and a band on the wings white. Adult male with the plumage of the head and neck thick, and long forehead; loral space and hind neck rich glossy green, changing into purple on the crown and sides of the head; from the eye backwards over the head a triangular patch of white; the entire breast and sides of the body pure white; abdomen dusky white; tail rounded, greyish-brown; upper tail-coverts lighter; under tail-coverts soiled white; back and wings black, with a patch of white on the latter. Female upper plumage sooty-brown, with a band of white on the sides of the head; outer webs of a few of the secondaries same color; lower part of the fore neck ash-color; breast and abdomen soiled white; tail feathers rather darker than those of the male. Male fourteen and a half inches long; wing six inches and three-fourths. Female rather smaller.

The dipper is quite plentiful everywhere in the Northern States, but not much valued.

Old Wife.

South Southerly, Old Squaw, Long-Tailed Duck.

Fuligula Glacialis, Linn.

Specific Character.—Length of bill, from the termination of the frontlet feathers to the point, one inch and one-sixteenth—the upper mandible rounded; the sides very thin; the bill rather deeply serrated, and furnished with a long nail; tail feathers acute. In the male the middle pair of tail feathers are extended about four inches beyond the next longest, which character is wanting with the female. Adult male with the bill black at the base; anterior to the nostril reddish-orange, with a dusky line margining the nail; fore part of the head white, the same color passing over the head down the hind neck on the back; eyes dark red; cheeks and loral space dusky-white, with a few touches of yellowish-brown; a black patch on the sides of the neck terminating in reddish-brown; fore neck white; breast brownish-black, terminating in an oval form on the abdomen—the latter white; flanks bluish-white; primaries dark brown; secondaries lighter brown, their coverts black; a semicircular band of black on the fore part of the back; the outer two tail feathers white—the rest marked with brown, excepting the four acuminated feathers, which are blackish-brown, the middle pair extending several inches beyond the others. Female without the long scapulars or elongated tail feathers; bill dusky-green; head dark, greyish-brown—a patch of greyish-white on the sides of the neck; crown blackish; upper parts dark greyish-brown; lower parts white. Length of male from the point of the bill to the end of the elongated tail feathers twenty-three inches; wing eight inches and five-eighths. Female about six inches less in length.

This bird is abundant along the coast, but is generally tough and fishy.

Merganser.

Genus Mergus, Linn.

Generic Distinctions.—Bill straight, higher than broad at base; much smaller towards the end; upper mandible hooked; teeth sharp; head rather large, compressed; body rather long, depressed; plumage very thick; feet placed far behind; wings moderate, acute; tail short, rounded.

SHELDRAKE.

Shell-Drake.

Goosander Weaser.

Mergus Merganser, Wils.

Specific Character.—Forehead low; head rounded, crested; bill bright red, the ridge black, high at base; upper mandible much hooked. Adult male with the head and upper part of the neck greenish-black; lower portion of the neck white; under plumage light buff, delicately tinged with rose-color, which fades after death; sides of the rump greyish-white, marked with undulating lines of dusky; fore part of the back and inner scapulars glossy black; hind part of the back ash-grey; the feathers margined and tipped with greyish-white, lighter on the rump; upper tail-coverts grey, the feathers marked with central streaks of dusky; tail feathers darker; primaries dark brown; wing coverts and secondaries white, the outer webs of the latter edged with black; the basal part of the greater coverts black, forming a conspicuous band on the wings; under tail-coverts white, outer webs marked with dusky grey, which is the color of the greater part of the web; bill and feet bright red. Female with the head and upper part of the neck reddish-brown; throat and lower neck in front white; breast and abdomen deeply tinged with buff; upper parts and sides of the body ash-grey; speculum white. Length of male, twenty-seven inches; wing, ten and a half. Female about three inches smaller. Young like the female.

www.ingramcontent.com/pod-product-compliance
Lightning Source LLC
Chambersburg PA
CBHW032137010526
44111CB00035B/599